SHAMANISM

The angakkoq *Ajukutok from Ammassalik, east Greenland. Born about 1864, he was later baptised. Photographed by Th. N. Krabbe, 13 September 1908. National Museum of Denmark, Department of Ethnography.*

SHAMANISM

Traditional and Contemporary Approaches to the Mastery of Spirits and Healing

Merete Demant Jakobsen

Berghahn Books
New York • Oxford

First published in 1999 by

Berghahn Books

© 1999 Merete Demant Jakobsen

Library of Congress Cataloging-in-Publication Data
Jakobsen, Merete Demant.
    Shamanism : traditional and contemporary approaches to the
mastery of spirits and healing / Merete Demant Jakobsen.
        p.   cm. --
    Includes bibliographical references and index.
    ISBN 1-57181-994-0 (hardback: alk. paper).
    ISBN 1-57181-195-8 (paperback: alk. paper).
    1. Shamanism--Greenland.   2. New Age movement--
Greenland.   3. Greenland--Religion.   I. Title.
BL2370.S5J35   1999
299'.7812--dc21   98-4193
                                                       CIP

British Library Cataloguing in Publication Data
A catalogue record for this book is available from
the British Library.

Printed in the United States on acid-free paper

CONTENTS

List of Illustrations   vi

Acknowledgements   vii

Preface   viii

Introduction   x

Chapter 1 Shamanism: Definition and Description   1

Introduction   1

The Origin of the Term   2

Definitions of Shamanism   3

Definitions of Shamanism by Two Organisers of Shamanic
Courses   8

Trance/Ecstasy   9

**Chapter 2 Early Encounters Between Explorers,
Missionaries and Shamans**   18

The Work of Poul and Niels Egede in Greenland   26

Chapter 3 The Greenlandic Angakkoq   45

Apprenticeship and Initiation   52

The Pantheon   65

Paraphernalia   73

The Séance   75

Travels   85

Healing   89

The Concept of the 'Witch'   94

Burial Customs   100

Myths and Legends   103

Angakkut in Oral Tradition on the East Coast   114

Chapter 4 Neo-shamanism and the New Age 147

Old Traditions Moulded to the Needs of Westerners
   in Search of Spirituality 158

Courses in Neo-shamanism 165
   A Description of the People Participating in Courses 167

The Basic Course in Shamanism 182
   The Paraphernalia 183
   Introduction to the Concept of Shamanism 183
   The Instruction in Journeying 185
   Power-Song and Journeying 188
   Healing 190

Advanced Courses in Shamanism 193
Approaches to the Role of Shamanism in Modern Society 194
Manuals on Neo-shamanism 197

Chapter 5 The Revival of Shamanism in Other Cultures 208

Conclusion 216

Appendix   Advanced Courses in Shamanism 224
Nordic Shamanism and The Spirits of Nature 224
Shamanic Healing and Spiritual Ecology 234
Soul Retrieval Training 244
The Soul Retrieval 251

Bibliography 259

Subject Index 269

Name Index 272

LIST OF ILLUSTRATIONS

1. Map of Greenland 39
2. Séance 40
3. Séance 41
4. The Mother of the Sea 42
5. *Tupilak* 42
6. *Tupilak* 43
7. *Tupilak* 44
8. Amulet 44

Acknowledgements

I would like to thank the following: first and foremost, all the anonymous course participants who entrusted me with their spiritual experiences. Dr Schuyler Jones and Dr Donald Tayler of the Pitt-Rivers Museum, Oxford; Professor I.M. Lewis, of the London School of Economics; Kirsten Thisted, of Copenhagen University; Poul Mørk and Rolf Gilberg, of the National Museum, Copenhgen; author Jens Rosing; artists Ib Geertsen and Bodil Kaalund; Professor Lydia Black and Professor Richard Pierce of the University of Alaska, Fairbanks; the Librarian and staff of the Balfour Library, Oxford; the Librarian of the Tylor Library, Oxford; Bodil Valentiner, Librarian of the National Museum Library, Copenhagen; The Librarian and staff of the Bodleian Library, Oxford; the President and Fellows of Wolfson College, Oxford; and The Danish Research Academy. Last but not least, my partner, Richard Ramsey, for his patient support and proof-reading, and our two rescued greyhounds, Ricky and Missy, who contributed to keeping my spirits high.

Preface

When I decided to write on the shaman, I was aware that I was venturing into a difficult and very sensitive area of research. Although there had been an explosion of interest during the previous two decades in the role of the shaman in the West and numbers of books of various depth had appeared, I still felt that my special area of interest, the Greenlandic shaman or *angakkoq*, was not usually represented in the literature on shamanism which was available in English. I therefore set myself the task of writing on the Greenlandic shaman utilising some sources that had only appeared in Danish.

To capture the nature of the *angakkoq* is a challenge. What is available is a variety of sources produced by narrators who describe not only the behaviour of different *angakkut* but also voice their own 'approach' to the *angakkoq* and his relationship to the spirit world. I have, however, used descriptions that I hope through their diversity of opinions on the role of the *angakkoq* ultimately draw a picture of this mediator between his society and the world of the spirits.

My interest in the traditional Greenlandic belief system started with a chance visit to the Tukâk theatre in 1980. This theatre, situated on the rough west coastline of Jutland in Denmark, was created with the intention of educating young Greenlandic actors and helping them to re-establish contact with their roots, the traditional beliefs in spirits, and the mythology, but in a form that was a mixture of those old traditions and the experiences of the young Greenlander in the modern Westernised society that Greenland, in many ways, had become. As far as I have been able to establish, however, traditional shamanism has not been revived in Greenland.

The attempt of the Tukâk theatre to present a different kind of spirituality was an eye-opener to me. Participating in some of the theatre's courses, I became highly interested in Greenlandic mythology, in which the role of the shaman and the spirit world play an important part. In the early eighties I wrote a master's thesis in Danish literature where I analysed a modern Danish writer's usage of the Greenlandic spiritual world to illustrate our de-spirited modern society. My conclusion was that this writer, Vagn Lundbye, saw himself as a sort of modern version of a shaman, as a mediator between a non-inspired Danish society and a highly inspired traditional Greenlandic one. I was unaware as I wrote that a modern version of shamanism, known as core-shamanism, created by Michael Harner, was starting to spread in the United States.

As I followed the development of the interest in shamanism in the West during the eighties and nineties, as presented in journals, books and courses, it became clear to me that there were significant differences between the shamanism that had derived from the traditional Arctic region and neo-shamanism, especially where the relationship to the spirits was concerned. I therefore decided to participate in a variety of courses to examine that difference. The fieldwork material in this book is based on the courses of one particular course organiser. He was fully informed of my intention to conduct research and to compare the courses with the traditional shamanism represented by the *angakkoq*. I undertook my research with a sense of profound respect for the valuable experiences of the participants and was very careful never to take any notes during the participants' descriptions of their journeys where permission was not first given. The examples of journeys are therefore based on my own experiences and the accounts given to me during the interviews I conducted.

One of the aspects of New Age thinking that has caused me concern over the years is a reluctance to face the negative aspects of spirituality. There is an old Nordic legend which describes a saint who was carefully building a church during the day but each night a troll came and tore it down. After this had gone on for some time, the saint decided to hide during the night and find out who the culprit was. Hearing the troll's name, the saint managed to face the troll, using the name as his weapon, to put an end to the nightly destruction and get on with building his church. The un-named dark side can play all kinds of havoc or, in other words, the sense of power achieved in a course might 'overwhelm' the present-day healer as it did some of the *angakkut*.

Merete Demant Jakobsen
Oxford

INTRODUCTION

The otherness of the shamanic world-view has fascinated — and appalled — researchers and missionaries for centuries, just as it now fascinates modern urban Westerners. The increase in the number of shamanic courses over the last few years is just one indication of how much interest exists in the role of the shaman. I have chosen to focus on the concepts of mastery of spirits and healing from a shamanic perspective among the Greenlandic people, with a few examples from other Eskimo[1] peoples, and the New Age version of shamanism called neo-shamanism, core-shamanism or urban shamanism.

The reasons for choosing the Greenlandic *angakkoq* as an example of a shaman in a traditional society are manifold. First, most works, including those on Eskimo shamanism, do not make use of several interesting sources as these have only appeared in Danish; the chapter on the Greenlandic *angakkoq*[2] therefore includes many of these. Secondly, the East Greenlandic population was more or less untouched by Christianity until the end of the last century, and there exists a rich corpus of material dealing with this part of Greenland and their *angakkut*[3] which describes the early stages of a recent colonisation. Thirdly, as this is a more 'pure' form of shamanism untouched by other religions until very late, it leaves us with a possible indication of what shamanism might have been in other parts of the Northern Hemisphere before Christianity or Buddhism were introduced.

It is, however, important to keep in mind the fact that shamanism is a very flexible configuration of behaviour patterns, including magical flight, trance and, first and foremost, mastery of spirits. This flexibility has meant that shamanism adapted itself to the religions it encountered and it can be difficult to determine what is of Buddhist or shamanic origin among the shamans in Central Asia, as indeed shamanism influenced Buddhism in its turn. Shamanism as it appears in Greenland, and especially East Greenland, therefore serves as a credible example of traditional shamanism.

The second part of the book deals with New Age shamanism examined from the perspective of traditional shamanism. What is described as neo-shamanism or core-shamanism is a form of shamanism that has been created at the end of this century to re-establish a link for modern man to his spiritual roots, to re-introduce shamanic behaviour into the lives of Westerners in search of spirituality and, thereby, renew contact with Nature. The chapter on neo-shamanism also deals with the general spread of urban shamanism and briefly touches on the role of modern healers in traditional societies.

Although I have decided not to include the theories of C.G. Jung, even if they are easily applicable to neo-shamanism, the description of Western man as presented by Jolande Jacobi in her preface to Jung's *Psychological Reflections* serves well as an introduction to the aim of this book in explaining the growing interest in shamanism at present:

> Western man today, engaged in a mighty struggle outwardly and inwardly for a new and universally binding order of life, stands at a point where two worlds meet, amid an almost inconceivable devastation of traditional values. No clear orientation is possible, nothing can yet point to a way in this whirlwind of spiritual forces striving for form. Human existence itself in all its inadequacy and insecurity must submit to a new revision. (1953: xxiii)

Written in the shadow of the Second World War, it posits the view that modern Western people are continuously striving to establish a value system according to which their life experiences make sense. One of the questions this book asks is whether shamanism with its roots in traditional societies can be the 'new revision' and fill the spiritual void which seems to be the price of modernity.

The reason, however, for not including Jung's theories directly is that they would apply a 'prefabricated' explanation to encounters with non-ordinary reality, experienced both in traditional and modern societies, and thereby become a screen which may narrow important anthropological aspects. As difficult as it can be to extract 'the voice of the people' from accounts of traditional belief systems made by outsiders, adding a psychological explanation is not the aim of this book. Seen from a modern point of view, it is tempting to call the power-animal a symbolic representation of specific emotions and describe it as an archetype which has lain dormant in the subconscious of the super-ego driven Westerner and which is now released through shamanic courses, but it serves no immediate purpose in the understanding of the actual first-hand experience of individuals with the spirit world. My intention is to present the patterns of behaviour both in traditional and modern societies vis-à-vis the spirit world, not to query whether the spirits are projections of internal structures. The book is, therefore, concerned with the structure of the belief systems and their cultural implications, not the structure of the mind. It is, however, important to acknowledge the role of the shaman as the keeper of a psychomental balance in his society as well as the fact that many apprentices have started their work in a condition that has several elements in common with mental disease.

The social role of the courses in shamanism can be explained by using the theories of another intellectual of this century, Pierre Bourdieu. The network established by New Age adherents could be determined as a *field* in which each individual experiences certain *habitus* which might leave the individual participants in a double role: the one he or she experiences in the larger society, where there is little recognition of magical skills, and the one established within the *field* where the values, positions and hierarchy differ and where the individual can achieve a new status and thereby also gain financially by taking on an active organising and healing role. The change of status is achieved by creating a new view of spiritual values, and thereby of Nature, which ultimately leads to the creation of a new mythology of the universe in which we live. The interesting aspect of this, however, is that not only is there a *field* in ordinary reality; non-ordinary reality can, to a certain degree, be seen as a *field* in its own right. The role of the shaman in traditional society is to move between those *fields* on behalf of society and in the interest of his fellow human beings. The role of the course participants is to establish contact with a source of wisdom and guidance available in non-ordinary reality which ultimately can guide them in their daily undertakings in ordinary reality.

This book has drawn its major theoretical orientation from the work of one of the most important specialists within shamanism,

S. M. Shirokogoroff, whose *Psychomental Complex of the Tungus*, formed the basis of my approach to the role of the shaman as mediator between the visible and invisible world and as master of spirits. Mastery is crucial to the shaman's function in society. If he loses control over the spirits he simultaneously loses the respect of his fellow human beings. Mastery should therefore be understood in its broadest sense: an *angakkoq* masters his spirits insofar as he is able to use their power.

My role in the shamanic courses was that of participant observer. I have used my own journey experiences as examples as they were typical in their structure — and individuality — and not taken down other participants' journeys out of respect for their privacy. My information about individual experiences derives from the interviews I carried out and for which I am very grateful for the trust I was shown. My double role as participant and observer was clear from the beginning of the courses and did not seem to create any problems.

The source material used for the chapter on Greenland is comprised of the writings of a variety of authors who were either missionaries, explorers, scientists or ethnographers. I have tried to make it clear in the text when it was necessary to take the author's background into account. Missionaries like the Egede family were, in their descriptions of the Greenlanders, simultaneously interested in presenting a picture of Eskimo culture and in ridiculing the work of the *angakkut*. The Inspector of South Greenland, Heinrich Rink, on the other hand, tried to let 'the voice of the people' speak through their own stories which he collected, and blamed the missionaries for many of the social mistakes committed against the Greenlanders — partly because of a lack of respect for the role of the *angakkut*. Knud Rasmussen saw himself as the advocate of the Eskimo people and in his writings 'the voice of the people' is expressed very elaborately. Gustav Holm, a scientist, and William Thalbitzer, a philologist, again had different approaches. Thalbitzer attempted a scientifically based presentation of the people in his detailed description of the culture, which would give 'a more realistic assessment of the Eskimos' intellectual and cultural achievements' (Sonne 1986: 203). Undoubtedly it has been difficult not to be carried away by a fascination with the otherness of Eskimo culture and reading through the material I have, therefore, presented *approaches* to, if not the ultimate truth about the *angakkoq*. I hope, however, that an image has formed which gives a deeper insight into the relationship between the *angakkoq* and his helping spirits that is the main focus of my investigation.

The texts which form the basis for the Greenlandic part have mostly been written by outsiders to the culture. The material used for the New Age part is presented by participants not only in the culture but in the shamanic world-view. As several of the texts are manuals of instruction on how to become a shaman, they are to be seen as promoters of shamanism. The course organiser is a teacher in shamanic techniques. He might have been inspired by other cultures but he is predominantly representing his own. The core-shamanism taught by Michael Harner is a conglomerate of the approaches of different cultures to shamanism but ultimately it is meant to be universal, it is a neo-shamanism, an urban shamanism applicable to the life of modern people living worldwide under urban conditions. My role may be compared to that of the earlier writers on Eskimo culture, apart from the fact that I am part of the larger culture in which these shamanic courses take place. As much as the séance had an impact on Holm or Rasmussen, they were first and foremost messengers between cultures and, as far as my role as a course participant is concerned, this is to a certain degree true for me too.

Notes

1. I use the word 'Eskimo' throughout the thesis instead of 'Inuit' as this is the common term in both old and recent publications.
2. The spelling of Greenlandic terms varies from writer to writer. In quotations I keep to the spelling of the author; in my own writing, however, I attempt mostly to use the new West Greenlandic spelling. This applies to *angakkoq* sing., *angakkut* plur., *ilisiitsoq* sing., *ilisiitsut* plur., *toornaarsuk*. Names of persons also vary in spelling: Avko/Avvgo, Kaakaaq/Kâkâq, Maratsi/Maratse, Migsuarnianga/Mitsuarnianga/ Missuarniánga, and names of places such as Angmagssalik/Ammassalik.
3. Thalbitzer in his notes to Christian Rosing, *Østgrønlænderne*, writes that 'some interpret the Eskimo word *angákoq* as "one of the mother's brother's family" (from *angak*, "mother's brother"), others as a "visionary and dreamer" (from the verb. *angavoq* "roaming about"), because the spirits show themselves to him in his visions during his ecstatic experiences' (1906: 126 [my translation]). The Danish translation of *angakkoq* is 'åndemaner', spirit-invoker. I have referred to the *angakkoq* with the masculine pronoun 'he' as they were mostly male.

Chapter 1

SHAMANISM: DEFINITION AND DESCRIPTION

Shamanism is *strictu sensu* pre-eminently a religious phenomenon of Siberia and Central Asia. Although the concept derives from the Tungus of Siberia, the role of the shaman as a mediator between the human world and the world of the spirits is known worldwide and therefore justifies the use of shamanism as a more general term. 'There is more between heaven and earth than one can directly see. Some societies have accepted this and handed it over to some special human beings to take care of the society's relationship to the supernatural. Such specialists that have existed as long as there have been human beings are called spirit-invokers or shamans' (Gilberg 1978: 14 [my translation]).

The existence of mediators between the sacred and the profane seems to be as old as human society. We find representations of shaman-like figures in Neolithic paintings and in many cultures there are references to a distant past, when human beings were in much more balanced contact with the spirit world and every individual was capable of direct communication. It later became the specialist's task to contact the hidden world and the shaman became the spiritual leader of the society, with his knowledge of mythology, and healing, and his capacity as a mediator between spirits and human beings. The task of the shaman was to create cosmos out of chaos by travelling to the spirits and, through that encounter, to deal with crises in society such as lack of game, illness or failing fertility.

When Knud Rasmussen, the Danish explorer in the Arctic at the beginning of this century, asked Aua, an Eskimo shaman, why their society had all the taboo rules which made an already challenging life even more demanding, he replied, pointing at the tired men coming back from a hunting expedition, and the ill women and children, by returning the question: 'Why?' When Knud Rasmussen could not find any reason either, Aua answered that apparently the questioner himself did not know, when asked, why life is as it is. And that is how it has to be. All customs come from life and go to life. 'We fear hunger, the cold, illness, not death but suffering, dead peoples' and dead animals' souls, the spirits of earth and sky and because of this fear the rules exist built on the wisdom of our forefathers' (Rasmussen 1931a: 46 [my translation]).

Aua thereby expresses how a society which lives in close contact with Nature has to have a set of ways to deal with forces that are inexplicable and unpredictable. E.E. Evans-Pritchard describes what he calls the emotionalist explanation of primitive religion: 'However foolish primitive beliefs and rites may appear to the rationalist mind, they help rude people to cope with their problems and misfortunes, and so they eradicate despair, which inhibits action and make for confidence conducive to the individual's welfare, giving him a renewed sense of the value of life and of all the activities which promote it' (Evans-Pritchard 1965: 48).

The shaman's role is to reduce the fear of these forces and establish a balance in society as a whole. Some rites can be performed by ordinary members of society but often the shaman is the only one who can travel to the spirits because he knows the way. He is the mediator between the sacred and the profane. He is the messenger and the healer of individuals and of society as a whole.

The Origin of the Term

The obvious first source for determining the origin of the words 'shaman' and 'shamanism' is Mircea Eliade's major work, *Shamanism. Archaic techniques of ecstasy*. In this he states that the word shamanism 'comes to us, through Russian, from the Tungusic *saman* (Eliade 1989: 4). He discusses whether the term is derived from the Pali *samana* (Sanskrit ´*sramana*) through the Chinese *sha-men* (Ibid.: 495). The relatedness with Pali underlines for Eliade the closeness between Buddhism and shamanism and he refers to the work of Shirokogoroff, *Psychomental Complex of the Tungus*, another important contribution to the understanding of shamanism. Shirokogoroff states that: 'Several comparisons have been made of the Tungus word "shaman" with other languages, of which the first, namely, the indirect derivation of *saman* from the Sanskrit ´*sramana*, is correct' (1935: 270).[1]

Shirokogoroff proceeds to discuss the generalisation of the term shamanism which has taken place among ethnographers and the term *saman* that is now applied to groups in Siberia where it was previously unknown. 'The ethnographical elements, of which the complexes styled shamanism consisted, were also found in ethnical groups living in different parts of the world, and on this ground "shamanism" received a still broader application, in reference to the complexes which could not be styled by one of the terms already in use, as Christianity, Buddhism, Taoism, Lamaism etc.' (1935: 269).

Shirokogoroff wishes to narrow the concept down to its origin. He claims that 'Shamanism as a European creation has collapsed and we have to revert to the initial point of investigation – to the Tungus shamanism' (Ibid.: 269).

> However, I do not introduce a new term, because I hope that it will be possible to save the term 'shaman' to be applied to the phenomenon here discussed. Without wearing out this term by the use in reference to very broad generalizations, and at the same time clearing it from various malignant tumours – theories which associated shamanism with sorcery, witchcraft, medicine-man, etc. – the term 'shaman' shall still be preserved. (Ibid.: 271)

This is, as will be shown, a wish that has not been realised. The term shamanism has been broadened to cover almost any attempt to contact the spirit-world worldwide and at the end of this century is applied to weekend courses for Westerners in search of a new spirituality.

Definitions of Shamanism

I.M. Lewis explains the meaning of the word *saman* among the Tungus people as 'one who is excited, moved, or raised' (1971: 51), while Vilmos Diózegi refers to the root of *saman*, 'sa-', to know. The shaman is the one who knows. Either of these interpretations can be applied to the role of the Tungus shaman: in an excited state the shaman knows more than his fellow human beings about the world of the spirits. It is very striking that most writers either use the Eliade and thereby Shirokogoroff interpretation of the origin of the word 'shamanism' or do not mention it at all. The definitions of what characterises a shaman on the other hand are plentiful.

Eliade's interpretation of the concept of shamanism is in its shortest form: shamanism equals techniques of ecstasy, attempting to distinguish shamanism from other concepts such as 'sorcerer' and 'medicine-man'. Eliade uses the shamans of north and central Asia as typical examples of 'this magico-religious phenomenon' (1989: 6) and describes the role of the shaman vis-à-vis the human soul:

> The shaman is the great specialist in the human soul; he alone 'sees' it, for he knows its 'form' and its destiny.
>
> And wherever the immediate fate of the soul is not at issue, wherever there is no question of sickness (= loss of the soul) or death, or of misfortune, or of a great sacrificial rite involving some ecstatic experience (mystical journey to the sky or the underworld), the shaman is not indispensable. A major part of religious life takes place without him. (Ibid.: 8)

It is through the ecstatic journey to the other worlds dealing with major issues in society that the shaman finds his role. In doing that he communicates with the spirits:

> For a 'spirit' can equally well be the soul of a dead person, a 'nature spirit', a mythical animal, and so on. But the study of shamanism does not require going into all this; we need only to define the shaman's relation to his helping spirits. It will easily be seen wherein a shaman differs from a 'possessed' person, for example; the shaman controls his 'spirits' in the sense that he, a human being, is able to communicate with the dead, 'demons', and 'nature spirits', without thereby becoming their instruments. (Ibid.: 6)

The role of the shaman is to avoid becoming the instrument of the spirits, but Eliade does not emphasise the mastery of spirits and the relationship to the spirit world is of minor importance in his definition: 'A shaman is a man who has immediate, concrete experiences with the gods and spirits; he sees them face to face, he talks with them, prays with them, implores them — but he does not "control" more than a limited number of them.' (Ibid.: 88). Shirokogoroff on the other hand defines the shaman: 'In all Tungus languages this term refers to persons of both sexes who have mastered spirits, who at will can introduce these spirits into themselves and use their power over the spirits in their own interests, particularly helping other people, who suffer from the spirits; in such a capacity they may possess a complex of special methods for dealing with the spirits' (1935: 269). This leads to the following definition:

1. The shaman is a master of spirits.
2. He has a group of mastered spirits.
3. There is a complex of methods and paraphernalia recognized and transmitted.
4. There is a theoretical justification of the practice.
5. The shamans assume a special social position (Ibid.: 274).

Shirokogoroff emphasises the mastery of spirits as one of the major elements in the definition of shamanism. However, mastery of spirits is not enough to determine what a shaman is, as this may occur in other areas such as that of the magician. The magician might use his power over spirits for personal gain, while the shaman, ideally, is using his skills on behalf of other people, or society as a whole. The special social position of the shaman is necessary for him to function as a mediator between the world of the spirits and that of human beings. Other members of society might possess healing skills, magical songs, and so on, but the shaman acts on behalf of society as a whole and, to do that, his relationship to the spirits has to be one of control.

Hultkranz states that shamanism is no religion in its own right, but a configuration or a complex (Bäckman and Hultkranz 1978: 11). Shamanism is to be defined by reference to the elements of which it is comprised, and to its general motivation.

> The central idea of shamanism is to establish means of contact with the supernatural world by the ecstatic experience of a professional and inspired intermediary, the shaman. There are thus four important constituents of shamanism: the ideological premise, or the supernatural world and the contacts with it; the shaman as an actor on behalf of a human group, the inspiration granted him by his helping spirits; and the extraordinary, ecstatic experiences of the shaman. (Ibid.: 11)

The ecstatic magical flight or journey is not seen as the main element of shamanism. Ecstasy is only a part of a whole complex of behaviour patterns. The relationship with spirits and the supernatural world is seen as an important factor.

> We may thus widen the concept of shamanic trance to infer two distinctive experiences, one, the extra-corporeal flight of the shaman with the assistance of helping spirits, two, on the spot information passed to the shaman by helping spirits. In both cases the séance opens with the calling of these spirits. The trance-state is identical with the mysterious world where they appear. Shamanism is unthinkable without the helping spirits, as we have stated before. (Ibid.: 20)

Rolf Gilberg also emphasises the relationship to the spirits in his list of what the shaman's function in North Asia encompasses:

1. The shaman controls one or more spirits.
2. He has a group of helping spirits that are invoked at the beginning of each séance and who help him during his travelling to the world of the spirits.
3. He has a set of methods helped by equipment such as a garment, music, special language, imitation of the voices of the spirits, etc. All these can be handed over to the next generation.
4. He has a theoretical justification of his praxis through myth and the traditions of society.
5. The shaman gains a special position in society.
6. He uses ecstasy. (1978: 15 [my translation])

All the definitions above clearly have several aspects in common. As shamanism is a complex of behaviour, the actual difference lies in which aspects of the complex are stressed. Eliade stresses ecstasy and the journey, Shirokogoroff the mastery of spirits, Hultkranz includes four major aspects which do not emphasise the journey, but still underlines the relationship with the spirits and Gilberg clearly follows the line of Shirokogoroff and Hultkranz and treats shamanism as a complex.

In I.M. Lewis's article, 'What is a Shaman?', he points to the fact that ecstasy and the journey are an important part of Eliade's understanding of classical shamanism. He refers to the relevance that Eliade attributes to the role of the spirits in shamanism, that possession by spirits is 'universally distributed phenomena' and therefore not specific to shamanism. He makes a reference to the finding by Shirokogoroff that there is a difference between a person possessed by spirits and spirits possessed by the shaman. Lewis concludes that 'A shaman is an inspired prophet and healer, a charismatic religious figure, with the power to control spirits, usually by incarnating them. If spirits speak through him, so he is also likely to have the capacity to engage in mystical flight and other "out of body" experiences' (1981: 32).

Lewis does not include ecstasy in the definition but again the control of spirits plays a major role. He introduces the concept of incarnation of spirits, and states that 'Shamanism and spirit possession regularly occur together and this is true particularly in the Arctic *locus classicus* of shamanism. Thus, amongst both the Eskimos and the East Siberian Chuckchee, shamans are possessed by spirits' (1971: 51). Hultkranz, however, criticises Lewis's approach as Lewis 'refuses to believe that shamanism has any particular connection with any cultural stratum. His attitude reflects the general ahistorical attitude in British social anthropology' (1989: 46).

The shaman is, however, more than a master of spirit possession (as that would be applicable also to possession cults), he is a master *sui generis*. When the Greenlandic *angakkoq* travels to the spirit world, the travelling soul, the free soul,[2] is sometimes replaced by a spirit. As the soul is busy somewhere else, the spirit interacts with the audience. Instead of saying that the shaman is possessed, I would rather say that the shaman master spirits that might replace him when journeying to the spirit world. For Raymond Firth what distinguishes shamanism from spirit possession or spirit mediumship is that, 'Shamanism, as I use the term, applies to those phenomena where a person, either as a spirit medium or not, is regarded as controlling spirits, exercising his mastery over them in socially recognized ways' (1967: 296).

This focus on mastery of spirits is essential to my understanding of the role of the shaman in Greenlandic society. In the initial stages of apprenticeship the person exposes himself to spirit possession without having any control over the actions of the spirits. He experiences mental and physical dismemberment and through letting himself undergo the destruction of his human power, he gains the supernatural power that is necessary for him to fulfill the role of mediator between the world of humans and the world of spirits. Without this transformation no shamanism can take place. In this phase he might be in a state of 'insanity' and therefore be equated with any other mentally unstable member of society but his actions are perceived differently; if not he might be killed. It is only by taking control of this process that he can achieve the role

of shaman. In his first séance the Greenlandic *angakkoq* is forced by
the helping spirits to 'come forward'. The spirits that have initially
been his molesters are now incorporated as helpers, but they claim
public recognition. The new shaman might still be controlled by
them to 'come forward' as a shaman, but the trained and skilled
shaman controls his spirits, he is the master.

   This section on the definition of classical shamanism may be
concluded by quoting S. M. Shirokogoroff, who has produced one of
the most important pieces of work on shamanism and to whom
many of the above-mentioned definitions owe tribute. In
Psychomental Complex of the Tungus he writes: 'We have already
seen that the relations between the shaman and the spirits may be
defined as those between "master" and "servant". However, such
are the relations only when the shaman is really a good and strong
person while a weak person may easily become the prey and an
instrument of the spirits' (1935: 366).

Definitions of Shamanism by Two
Organisers of Shamanic Courses

As the second part of this book deals with the New Age concept of
shamanism, especially the core-shamanism created by Michael
Harner, two performers of core-shamanic courses are briefly
mentioned. Michael Harner, an anthropologist by training, refers
to Eliade in his article, 'What is a Shaman?' and defines a shaman
as 'a person who journeys *to* the spirits, seeking them out in their
own world and remaining in control during the time spent there'
(1988: 8). He states that the difference between a priest and a
shaman is 'that a shaman journeys and otherwise works in
another reality while in a substantially altered state of
consciousness, whereas priests work basically in ordinary reality'
(Ibid.: 9).[3] Using this in a New Age context leads to the statement
that, 'In shamanism everyone is his or her own prophet, getting
spiritual revelation directly from the highest sources. Such people
rock the boat; they are subversive' (Ibid.: 10).

   The altered state of consciousness and remaining in control are
clearly important in Harner's concept of shamanism. On the other
hand, Jonathan Horwitz, also an anthropologist, and an apprentice
and former member of Michael Harner's Foundation for Shamanic

Studies, for which he taught for several years, presented the following definition of shamanism at a symposium on Religious Rites:

> A shaman is someone who changes his or her state of consciousness at will, in order to journey to another reality, a 'non-ordinary reality,' the world of the spirits, where she meets with her spirit helpers to ask for help, power, or knowledge for herself and/or others. Mission accomplished, the shaman journeys back to ordinary reality where she uses or dispenses the newly gained knowledge and/or power.' (1991: 2)

What is significant here is that the relationship to the spirits is not that of mastery but that of recipient of help, power and knowledge. The organiser of the courses which forms the basis of the field research of this book, expanded on that view. When asked in an interview, in 1995, about his attitude to mastery of spirits he responded 'I think that mastery is not correct. Mastery is true for sorcery. The sorcerer attempts to master the spirits. If you want to play with the spirits they are happy to play, but they know the rules better than any sorcerer.'

This approach underlies the whole manner in which shamanism is presented at his courses and reflects the less confrontational experience of interacting with spirits for the course participants on the shamanic courses compared with that of the Greenlandic apprentice. The helping spirits are mostly instant helpers, the seeker a recipient not a master.

Trance/Ecstasy

The shaman is, as I have argued, first and foremost a master of spirits in the traditional society. His role is to contact and to possess spirits so that a communication on behalf of an individual or society as a whole can be established. The way of communicating with the spirits is mostly through ecstasy but there are also other less dramatic ways of establishing contact. The shaman is in charge of this communication. If he loses control, he risks losing his soul. It is, therefore, important that the procedure, even when the shaman is seized by ecstasy, is still part of a scenario that the shaman has initiated and ultimately of which he is in charge. He is the master and ecstasy is his tool. 'Shamanic ecstasy is identified as a specific class of ASC[4] involving: (a) voluntary control of entrance and duration of trance, (b) post-trance memory, and (c) transic communicative interplay with spectators' (Peters and Price-Williams 1980: 397). This points to what makes shamanic ecstasy[5] different from other forms of trance state: that it is voluntary, that it leaves the shaman able to communicate with his audience and that he remembers what he has said and experienced during the trance. This is mostly not the case in possession cults and mediumship. 'Basically, spirit possession involves a loss of memory and is, therefore, a dissociated state, whereas magical flight is not' (Ibid.: 403).

The mastery and control of the ecstasy is also mentioned by Shirokogoroff in connection with introducing spirits into the shaman himself. The Tungus or Manchus did not 'recognize anyone as being a shaman, if the person could not possess spirits' (1935: 271), i.e. master the spirits compared with other people who might be possessed and show some nervous and psychic troubles. 'A shaman who cannot produce the needed effects of extasy is considered a bad shaman; persons in whom an extasy turns into a fit (who cannot control themselves) are considered as possessed by the spirits and therefore cannot become shamans — they must be treated' (Ibid.: 363). Lewis writes about the Venda tribes of Southern Africa that 'the role of shaman is assumed by those women who, in full control of their own spirits, are considered to be capable of controlling and healing spirit affliction in others. Like the Tungus shaman, they "master" their own spirits and use them for the public good, or at least for the good of that public which consists of women' (1971: 93).

The shaman use of different levels of trance can be described as follows:

1. Light trance. A state of incomplete ecstasy. Only partial suspension of exterior influences. The vision is a waking vision. In this trance the guardian spirits and the helping spirits appeared. This state might be used in connection with healing or divination.
2. Nightly dreams. Dreams in which the spirits appear as helpers and informants.
3. Deep trance. The shaman appears as if dead. The stage for excursion into the other world, the drama not visible to the mortal eyes. Healing and journeying to the land of the dead. (adapted from Bäckman and Hultkranz 1978: 95ff).

As there is such a close connection between the behaviour of the shaman and that of the mentally ill, the shaman has been seen by some researchers as a mentally unstable member of society. Eliade writes 'the shaman is not only a sick man; he is above all, a sick man who has been cured, who has succeeded in curing himself' (1989: 27). Lévi-Strauss calls the shaman 'a professional abreactor' 'a neurotic' (1963: 181ff). Devereux, an ardent advocate for the neurotic elements in the behaviour of the shaman claims that 'Unless we assume that psychotic eruptions can arise ex nihilo, without unconscious antecedent, or that spirit possession (in the occultist sense) is a reality obliging the anthropologist to believe in the existence of spirits, we must assume that a person who briefly, lapses into a psychosis has an active, though latent and unconscious, psychotic core' (1961: 1,089).

The abnormal condition, both mentally and physically, of the new shaman is a worldwide characteristic. According to Lewis, the mentally ill and the future shaman have the same starting point. They both experience 'Involuntary, uncontrolled unsolicited possession (or other seizure, e.g., illness or other trauma)' (1986: 89). Lewis calls this the first phase of the shamanic career. It is the next phase, though, that sets the new shaman apart from the role of the patient as a 'domestication' takes place (acceptance of the spirits), and finally, in phase three, the shaman controls the spirits and the state of trance and, therefore, relates in a voluntary way to the calling.

Peters and Price-Williams also point to the state of the shaman as being that of an ill person becoming cured.

> Ideally, the shaman does not slip in and out of ASC unpredictably, his 'soul loss' is controlled and ritualized. What was once a spontaneous crisis is now a controlled ecstasy in which he has mastered the techniques and learned the parameters of celestial space. Yet magical flight is not only descriptive of the shaman's controlled soul journey; it is a psychotherapeutic device. Its practice and mastery may well be the means by which the shaman comes to 'master himself,' i.e., become cured. (1980: 405)

The 'wounded healer' concept of the shaman, as seen by Joan Halifax in *Shaman: The Wounded Healer*, and also described by Bogoras among the Chuckchee,[6] might in some cases be true but in others the apprentice, on his own initiative and wishing to become a shaman, seeks the necessary transformation of behaviour, challenges the spirits and thereby his own mental state. The alteration in behaviour, which can be compared with that of mental illness, is thereby voluntary. Several observers have perceived the Greenlandic *angakkut* as the more intelligent members of the society. Although a few shamans had psychotic behaviour patterns and even became murderers, most were insightful upholders of the belief system and the mental and social equilibrium. The role of a shaman in society is open to both these categories, the one inducing fear, the other trust.

The rites of passage for the shaman have to bring him into contact with spirits; first, through separation either psychologically or physically from his society; secondly, through an apprenticeship which will help him undergo mental transition to be able to deal with the spirits; and, finally, incorporating at will the spirits into his own body so that he is no longer possessed by the spirits but possesses them as helping spirits in his future work for his society.

The state of trance is clearly a product of an alteration in the brain. This can be induced by using drugs, as is seen particularly among the South and North American Indians, or it can be created by the intake of large amounts of alcohol, as among the Siberian tribes and the female shamans of Korea. But there is no doubt that drumming is the most important tool in inducing trance. Drumming, dance and the already established expectation of being in contact with defined spirits seems in many cultures to suffice as a 'drug'. The trance state and ecstasy are by no means limited to shamanism. In the case of the Holy Ghost people in West Virginia, the snake-handling congregation find themselves inspired by the Holy Ghost and, therefore, are in the power of the Spirit. Even the Christian clergyman sees himself as inspired but not as a master of the Holy Ghost.

Stewart Wavell writes about an encounter with a Malayan shaman who told him 'You cannot see spirits unless you are in trance.' Among the Akawaio in the Amazonian area Audrey Butt observed how the shaman would use tobacco juice, vomit and then go into a trance (Wavell, Butt and Epton 1966: 52) and generally speaking it seems to be common in South America to have the trance induced by using hallucinogens such as *ayahuasca, caapi, yaje*, whereas Shirokogoroff mentions the employment of music and words as trance-inducing in his description of the Tungus:

> In almost all forms of shamanistic performances, when the extasy of the shaman and the excitation of the audience are needed, i.e. with the exception of some cases where the shaman is alone,

several technical methods for bringing up a necessary psychic condition of the shaman and the audience are used. These are rhythmic effects, music of the performance, particularly rhythmic movements, dancing, drumming and productions of various noises with the costume, also singing or reciting, and the contents of the text of the performance, i.e. descriptions in words of the relations between the shaman and the spirits, the people and the spirits. (1935: 325)

It is worth noting that the trance takes place in the company of 'believers'. Shirokogoroff mentions that in some of his observations the trance did not occur because non-believers were present and showed disbelief or ridiculed the shaman. Some even interfered with the séance and stopped the shaman from getting into a trance. He also mentions the smoking of tobacco and drinking wine or breathing the smoke of *laedum palustrum* or any other plant with a pleasant smell. He points out that a strong person may drink more than a bottle of vodka during his performance (1935: 364).

When the Greenlandic *angakkoq* travels to the spirit world the audience is often asked to sing him along the way and therefore plays an active role in inducing the altered state of consciousness. There is an interplay between audience and shaman which is crucial for the success of his journey.

The Korean shaman, the *mansin*, generally a woman, is also a master of the spirits. In the *Kut*, the séance normally taking place in people's own homes, she calls down the spirits of the ancestors or the gods and in costumes representing the specific gods she dances and makes the audience dance.

The mansin dresses her [the daughter-in-law in the household] in the Seven Stars' white robe. She dances, faster and faster. Now the Chatterbox Mansin throws the yellow robe over the white costume. The Chatterbox Mansin discerns the influence of two personal Body-governing Gods, the Great Spirit Grandmother and the Seven Stars. The daughter-in-law dances to a frenzy. Okkyoung's Mother [another shaman] stands beside the dancing woman, beating the rhythm on her cymbals, tapping her foot in time, nodding her smiling face. The daughter-in-law finally collapses in a head-to-floor bow. The women in the hot-floor room nod consensus, 'The god ascended. Yes, the god ascended.' (Laurel Kendall 1985: 11)

There are two points to make about this trance situation. First, the costumes play an important part in the trance state. The costumes represent the specific god and the person to whom the *mansin* gives this costume is perfectly aware of which god has descended into her. The *mansin* is therefore creating a trance state in one of the audience by dressing this person up and asking her to dance on behalf of the household to establish a contact between this and the god. In the above quotation one of the audience is asked to participate and actually is seen to reach a trance-like state. Secondly, the shaman is not in trance, she is mastering the trance state of the daughter-in-law and therefore the descent of the spirits into her. If trance were the only indication of a shaman it would be difficult to assess the status of the daughter-in-law when the spirits have entered into her body.[7]

The daughter-in-law is clearly possessed by a spirit and possession and trance are intimately connected in the séance of the shaman. Spirit possession is the aim of the séance and inducing such possession is the tool of the shaman both in herself and also in the audience. William Sargant tries to make a clinical analysis of the state of trance and possession. It is, according to him, the brain of man and not his soul which is affected by mystical techniques, though the possessing deity or spirit will be identified differently against varying religious backgrounds (1973: 76).

> But possession has also very often been deliberately induced to give a human being the most direct and immediate possible experience of a deity by becoming its living vessel and to enable him to act as a channel of communication between gods and spirits and their worshippers on earth. The effect of this experience in creating and maintaining faithful adherence to systems of belief has been profound and far-reaching. (Ibid.: 44)

With this interpretation of possession it becomes even more clear how important it is to see the shaman as the master of spirits. In her observation of the *mansin* in Korea Laurel Kendall gives an example of a *mansin* breaking off her trance to ask for a pair of shoes. As the state of possession and the state of trance are interlinked it is important for the shaman to establish with the audience that she is in a state of trance because the atmosphere then creates a trance-like state among the audience and the following contact with spirits is more readily accepted. 'When a subject goes into trance or shows an increased state of suggestibility, it becomes much easier for him to accept beliefs which he would have regarded critically in his normal state of mind' (Ibid.: 53).

According to Sargant several religious cults use trance/ecstasy in their worship. The Samburu in Africa dance themselves into a state of trance and collapse to lose fear of fighting. A trance-state is also induced to perform healing. The Macumba worship in Brazil or Voodoo in Haiti are prime examples of the congregation getting into a state of trance through dancing and drumming. This has, however, in my view nothing to do with shamanism, because, although the worshippers are giving themselves over to the spirits and are becoming possessed, they are not mastering them. They are without will and often cannot remember any of their actions. Indeed, it is important not to confront them with their behaviour while they were in a state of trance. These worshippers are losing control, not only of their actions but, within that, also of their moral code. There is a close link between ecstasy and sexuality (Sargant 1973: 115, 126, 176).

When Werner Jacobsen, the Danish explorer, in the 1930s visited the lamaistic monastery Han-kir-va Sume, he experienced the reverend lama Djamserong's 'performance'. When Jacobsen arrived the lama was surrounded by a temple orchestra, which consisted of enormous drums, oboes and conch horns and long copper trumpets. He had just started the process of being possessed by supernatural forces. In an impressive costume he was dancing round in wild ecstasy and Jacobsen described his impression of the scenario in the following way:

> It is as if he is suddenly struck to the ground by invisible lightning. For minutes he is lying lifeless. Oboes, trumpets and the chant of the monks have stopped. Only the drums continue in a still increasingly wild rhythm. The great spirit has arrived and has struck Djamserong to the ground. But now it possesses his body and he jumps up completely possessed by unrestrained savagery. His face is twisted. The pupils have disappeared up under the eyelids, and the bloodshot eyeballs are staring without direction into space. The incredibly long tongue hangs down over his chin, and blood-flecked foam bubbles from his wide open mouth. (1965: 42 [my translation])

This could very easily be a shaman in a séance, the only difference being the surrounding temple and the status of the lama. But most importantly, the lama is not believed to master the spirit. The spirit masters him and he is totally given over to the trance.

The interaction between the séance, the shaman and the researcher is naturally of importance to the description of the séance. Lewis points to this in his criticism of the anthropologist's approach:

> On the contrary, the majority of anthropological writers on possession have been equally fascinated by its rich dramatic elements, enthralled — one might almost say — by the more bizarre and exotic shamanistic exercises, and absorbed in often quite pointless debates as to the genuineness or otherwise of particular trance states. Their main interest has been in the expressive or theatrical aspect of possession; and they have frequently not even troubled to ask themselves very closely what precisely was being 'expressed' — except of course a sense of identity with the supernatural power. (1971: 22)

I will try in what follows to clarify what the people, including the shaman, believe in, what impact this belief has on the equilibrium of society and what measures are taken to establish and sustain this belief system. The séance is first and foremost the work of the shaman. He knows his audience, he knows the use of paraphernalia and he knows how to create the atmosphere in which the spirits can be approached.

Émile Durkheim describes the expression of magico-religious life:

> We have seen that if collective life awakens religious thought on reaching a certain degree of intensity, it is because it brings about a state of effervescence which changes the conditions of psychic activity. Vital energies are over-excited, passions more active, sensations stronger; there are even some which are only produced at this moment. A man does not recognize himself; he feels himself transformed and consequently he transforms the environment which surrounds him. In order to account for the very particular impression which he receives, he attributes to the things with which he is most directly in contact properties which they have not, exceptional powers and virtues which the objects of every-day life do not possess. In a word, above the real world where his profane life passes he places another which, in one sense, does not exist except in thought, but to which he attributes a higher sort of dignity, than to the first. Thus from a double point of view it is an ideal world. (1976: 422)

Whether Gilberg, quoted at the beginning of this chapter, who expresses an acceptance of the supernatural forces, or Durkheim who sees the existence of a belief in exceptional powers as a construction, are right, there is no doubt that the shaman — either reducing or inducing fear among members of his society — feels himself transformed and thereby transforms the environment within which he functions.

NOTES

1. Åke Hultkranz discusses this conclusion (1973: 26ff) claiming that there is no reason to expect that the word should be of Indian extraction and refers instead to Diószegi's suggestion of the closeness to the Tungus-Manchu verb sa, 'to know'.

2. Hultkranz mentions the concept of 'soul dualism': the body souls that 'impart life strength, mobility and consciousness to man' and the free-soul that 'is man's excorporeal form of manifestation in dreams, trance and coma' (1973: 30).

3. In this Harner disagrees with Hans Findeisen, who writes that *'In wirklichkeit sind die Schamanen keineswegs in erster Linie Zauberer, sondern priesterlich-väterliche Seelenführer, Heiler und Künstlerr'* (1957: 14) [In reality the shaman is not first and foremost a magician, he is priest-fatherly soul-guide, a healer and artist]. The distinction between priest and shaman as presented by Michael Harner is a valid one.

4. ASC is an abbreviation for Altered State of Consciousness.

5. In the literature that I have consulted, it seems as if the two words 'trance' and 'ecstasy' are used indiscriminately. The usage is not clear. Bäckman and Hultkranz claims that 'the term "ecstasy" is being used by students of religion and ethnology while the term "trance" is used by psychopathologists and parapsychologists' (1978: 19).

6. Bogoras writes: To people of more mature age the shamanistic call may come during some great misfortune, dangerous and protracted illness, sudden loss of family or property, etc. Then the person, having no other resource, turns to the 'spirits,' and claims their assistance. It is generally considered that in such cases a favorable issue is possible only with the aid of the 'spirits' therefore a man who has withstood some extraordinary trial of his life is considered having within himself the possibilities of a shaman, and he often feels bound to enter into closer relations with the 'spirits,' lest he incur their displeasure at his negligence and lack of gratitude. (1904-1909: 421)

7. Shirokogoroff also mentions the importance of the dress and the trance. Among the Tungus the shaman wears an elaborate costume: 'In fact, the costumes and other paraphernalia are needed by most shamans for the production of self-excitement, self-hypnosis and hypnotic influence over the audience' (1935: 287).

Chapter 2
EARLY ENCOUNTERS BETWEEN EXPLORERS, MISSIONARIES AND SHAMANS

Fascination with the discovery of remote corners of the world and the excitement of the encounter with the unknown have always been an important impetus behind exploration, although the actual reason for some of the journeys undertaken has been of a political nature. Some of the missionaries venturing into the same areas as the explorers might have been driven by a similar curiosity but their main purpose was the conversion of the 'savages'. The narratives of their encounters with the belief systems of these peoples thus reflect the interaction of an alien world-view with that of Christianity.

The shaman, and especially his séance, in the literature before the nineteenth century has generally been described either as an extraordinary exotic display, using jugglery, or the work of the devil. The first more thorough descriptions of the shaman coincided with the decline of interest in magic and alchemy in Europe. The official persecution of witches had disappeared only a short time before explorers participated in séances and made accounts of shamanic practices. It was, according to Gloria Flaherty, no easy task to describe such an experience to the authorities in the homeland: 'If their reports did not treat shamanism as a form of diabolic demonology, they were listed on the *Index librorum prohibitorum*; they were refused license to appear in print; or, even worse, they incurred accusations of heresy' (1992: 21).

It was, moreover, tempting to make a comparison between shamanism and the European concept of witchcraft and some of the explorers actually alluded to this in their writings. Joseph Acerbi, an Italian explorer, who travelled in Scandinavia in 1778-79 was not blind to the obvious parallel. He writes in *Travels through Sweden, Finland and Lapland, to the North Cape in the years 1798 and 1799*: 'The belief in spirits (witchcraft), not less absurd, even the vigorous mind of Dr. Johnson was not exempt from. But these ridiculous, mischievous, and cruel delusions, are happily banished almost from the inhabitations of the most ignorant, and we already begin to wonder at the credulity of our ancestors' (1802: 313).

As a late eighteenth century enlightened European, Acerbi is prepared to look critically at his own society through his encounter with the people of Lapland. He compares the belief system of the Laplanders with the representation of Christianity in medieval Europe, highlighting the perversity of the latter. 'The gloom and darkness which almost incessantly hang over Lapland, has not communicated to the religion of its inhabitants either that moroseness or dejection, which too much pervaded the perversion of our most holy system of divine faith and worship during the dark ages' (Ibid.: 299).

He is also aware of the impact of the missionaries on the population of Lapland. Perhaps inclined towards the concept of the 'noble savage', he gives a not very favourable description of the impact of the messengers of Christianity on the life of the Laplanders.

> When the king of the North, animated by a spirit of religion and piety, sent missionaries into those forlorn regions to preach the Gospel and propagate the Christian religion, the missionaries did not only make the poor natives pay the expenses of their journey, but also gave them to understand that they were to be remunerated for their trouble. That wandering people had hitherto lived without priests, and without any kind of burthen; in fact, because they were too poor to pay the exigencies of state. They worshipped in their own way, just how and when they pleased, a number of gods, who cost them nothing, except now and then a sacrifice, which they themselves ate up, and of which they left nothing to their deities but the bones and horns. (Ibid.: 54)

Acerbi states that the reason that the missionaries achieved an impact on the Laplanders stems from the 'indolence and idleness' (Ibid.: 54) of the people, which results in no opposition to the missionaries and a readiness to believe anything they are told. The missionaries, on the other hand, operate by depriving those who had some animals of this little wealth, promising them happiness in the other world, which in Acerbi's view would 'consist of drinking brandy from morning to night' (Ibid.: 55).

On the one hand he expresses an understanding of the balance between the lifestyle and the original religion of the Laplanders and on the other gives a condescending description of the character of the people. This attitude is also to be found in another travel description covering the same period. Martin Sauer in *An Account of a Geographical and Astronomical Expedition to the Northern Parts of Russia* in 1785 and 1794 makes the following presentation of the lifestyle of the Yakuti:

> The situation is well calculated for the Yakuti; for, placed beyond the reach of intruding visitors, they pass their time in savage indolence, and like the bears, their neighbours, are only roused from their lethargy by the absolute calls of nature, when they prowl about in quest of animals...
>
> But above all I was enchanted by the manly activity of my guides, their independence and contentment. Satisfied with the limited productions of nature, where nature itself seems to forbid the approach of mankind, their astonishing fortitude, keeping in full force every lively sensation of the mind, and surmounting all difficulties, until they obtain the interesting object of their pursuit, inspired me with ardent desire to participate in their dangers and delights. I pronounce them 'great Nature's happy commoners'. (1802: 46)

The comparison between the bear and the Yakuti reflects the thinking of the enlightened European. The people are in closer contact with Nature, their behaviour reflects that closeness and their concept of spirituality has therefore to be seen in that context. It might not be contaminated by the dark age terrors of superstition, and of doctrines of eternal punishment, 'which are repugnant to humanity and common sense' (Acerbi 1802: 300), it might even reflect some sound natural approach to spirituality but the adherents of shamanism are poor, indolent, idle and 'Nature's happy commoners'.

Hans Egede, a missionary sent out by the Danish King, Frederick IV, to Greenland, arrived in what was to be called Godthåb on the west coast of Greenland in pursuit of the descendants of those

Norwegians who had settled there in the middle ages and of whom nothing had been heard since. He did not encounter any descendants of these people but he did instead settle among the Eskimos and started a mission. In 1741 he recounted his work among these people. His description of the character of the Greenlanders is very similar to that of Acerbi's of the Laplanders and Sauer's of the Yakuti: 'The Greenlanders are commonly of a phlegmatic temper, which is the cause of a cold nature and stupidity: they seldom fly into a passion, or are much affected or taken with anything, but of an insensible, indolent mind' (1818: 122).

Hans Egede is of the opinion that this state of mind is due to a lack of education and, like Acerbi and Sauer, is aware that there are positive aspects in the kind of life that these Eskimos are leading. He cannot help but admire how 'peaceably, lovingly, and united they live together; hatred and envy, strifes and jars are never heard among them' (Ibid.: 123). Egede also finds it appropriate to compare animals and people and make a clear comparison between the dogs and their masters. 'Tame or domestic animals there are none, but dogs in great numbers, and of a large size, with white hairs, or white and black, and standing ears. They are in their kind as timorous and stupid as their masters, for they never bay or bark, but howl only' (Ibid.: 63).

This kind of ambiguous attitude to the character of the people who were encountered, is also reflected in the description of their belief system, the shaman's séance, the healing, the burial rituals, and so on. Some of the explorers and most of the missionaries interpreted the séance as the shaman's interaction with the devil. It was no doubt, as other later accounts admit, awe-inspiring to participate in such a performance and to proceed to interpret the experience of the shaman's skills as the work of Satan was an obvious deduction.

Johan Gottlieb Georgi in his description of the different peoples of Russia, *Beschreibung aller Nationen des Russischen Reichs, ihrer Lebensart, Religion, Bebräuche, Wohnungen, Kleidungen und übrigen Merkwürdigkeiten,* 1776, reflected on the connection between Satan and the shaman's séance. He stated that, although one could find little sense in the delusion and conjuring of the shaman, the shamanistic heresy gave great power to Satan through its description of nature and the fate of human beings. There were evil spirits everywhere which bothered everybody and the priests were boasting about the close connection with Satan. The drum was one way of establishing contact and through this intercourse one acquired information about the reason for the anger or good will of the gods, how one could appease them, one's fate, the power to change good luck and misfortune, and how to interpret dreams and undertake divination. 'This mistaken understanding is due to the shamanistic heresy and the reputation of the priests. Partly barefaced impostors, partly deceived fanatics, who believe in what they do, so that a small but not important difference is present in the performance' (1776: 392 [my translation]).

John Bell in his *Travels from St. Petersburgh in Russia, to Diverse Parts of Asia*, from 1715 – 38 described the interaction of the shaman with the devil in the séance.

> The Barabintzy, like most of the ancient natives of Siberia, have many conjurers among them, whom they call Shamans and sometimes priests. Many of the female sex also assume this character. The shamans are held in great esteem by the people; they pretend to correspond with shaytan, or devil; by whom, they say, they are informed of all past and future events, at any distance of time and place. Our ambassador resolved to inquire strictly into the truth of many strange stories, generally believed, concerning the shamans, and sent for all of fame in the places through which we passed. (1788: 248-50)

Bell proceeds to give a more detailed description of an encounter with a female shaman whose skills are only displayed when encouraged by drink and tobacco and whose divining powers are delivered 'very artfully, and with much obscurity and ambiguity'. Bell has this attitude confirmed by more encounters with shamans and has very little respect for their work. He sees it as an example of the worst kind of heresy and seems also to view Buddhism with the same kind of attitude:

> The religion of the Buraty seems to be the same with that of the Kalmucks which is downright Paganism of the grossest kind. They talk indeed of an Almighty and good being, whom they call Burchun, but seem bewildered in obscure and fabulous notions, concerning his nature and government. They have two high priests, to whom they pay great respect; one is called Delay-Lama, the other Kutuchtu. (Ibid.: 302)
> The 10th we were entertained with a famous Buratsky Shaman, who was also lama or priest, and was brought from a great distance. (Ibid.: 309)

The rituals of Tibetan Buddhism and shamanism have much in common and it is understandable that Bell does not discriminate between the two in his critique of shamanic behaviour. Both employ a trance-like state and many of the rituals of tantric Buddhism are derived from the close interaction with shamanism in the early stages of the introduction of Buddhism to shamanic societies. This is discussed by Shirokogoroff who claims that the shamanism among the Tungus has derived some of its rituals from Buddhism (1935: 278). As the two belief systems have existed side by side for centuries it might be difficult to determine which rituals are derived from shamanism and which from Buddhism.

Hans Egede also speaks of 'the farce of the imposture' (1818: 189), and then proceeds to give a thorough description of the séance. The spectators assembled in one of the houses after dark and then the *angakkoq* is tied, his head between his legs and his hands behind his back and the drum next to him. The light is put out and, while the spectators sing a song that they claim was made by their ancestors, the shaman begins conjuring and conversing with *toornaarsuk*, the great spirit. 'Here the masterly juggler knows how to play his trick, in changing the tone of his voice, and counterfeiting one different from his own, which makes the too credulous hearers believe, that this counterfeited voice is that of Torngarsuk, who converses with the angekkok' (Ibid.: 190).

The shaman manages to work himself loose and is believed to ascend into heaven through the roof of the house to meet with the souls of the *angakkut puullit*, the chief *angakkut*[1]. Hans Egede, although giving a detailed description of the séance, carefully establishes his own detached attitude to the performance. He has no doubt about the conjuring and falsity of the shaman's work.

And if by chance any one, who has been under these jugglers' hands, recovers, they do not fail to ascribe it to the virtue of their juggling tricks. At times they use this way of curing the sick; they lay him upon his back, and tie a ribbon, or a string, round his head, having a stick fastened to the other end of the string, with which they lift up the sick person's head from the ground, and let it down again; and at every lift he communes with his Torgak, or familiar spirit, about the state of the patient, whether he shall recover or not; now, if his head is heavy in lifting it, it is with them a sign of death; if light, of recovery. Notwithstanding all this, I am loth to believe, that, in these spells and conjurings, there is any real commerce with the devil; for to me it clearly appears, that there is nothing in it but mere fibs, juggling tricks, and impostures, made use of by these crafty fellows for the sake of filthy lucre, for they are well paid for their pains. (1818: 193-4)

Hans Egede is not prepared to condemn the people as influenced by the devil, but rather interprets the séance as proof of a lack of education in Christianity. He even points to the fact that although the Greenlanders have not been enlightened about Christianity they behave in certain circumstances as if they knew the law.

✗   Most missionaries and some explorers of the eighteenth century considered that the belief system of the people they encountered might be the work of the devil and therefore should be suppressed. Others might think, like Hans Egede, that it only showed a lack of education and perceived it as mis-information and pure jugglery. But explorers like Joseph Acerbi and Martin Sauer were aware of the negative influences on the people in their encounter with the representatives of European culture. Sauer, as secretary to the expedition arranged by Catherine the Great, was brave enough to let the people speak in his writing although he must have known the very energetic way in which Catherine the Great tried to ridicule and destroy the shaman and his séance. The experience of the people in the transition period between the old belief system and the introduction of Christianity is expressed through the voice of the man encountered by Sauer among the Khamtshatkas:

Our Sorcerers (said he) were observers of omens, and warned us of approaching dangers, to avert which sacrifices were made to the demons: we were then wealthy, contented and free.' He continued his discourse thus as nearly as I could translate: 'I think our former religion was a form of dream, of which we now see reality. The Empress is God on earth, and her officers are our tormentors: we sacrifice all we have to appease their wrath, or wants, but in vain. They spread disorder among us, which has destroyed our fathers and mothers; and robbed us of our wealth and our happiness. They have left us no hope of redress; for all the wealth that we could collect for years would not be sufficient to secure one advocate in our interest, who dares present our distress to our sovereign. (1802: 308)

This criticism of the methods of the missionaries and officials sent out by the enlightened court of Catherine the Great is echoed by the words of Acerbi observing in the same period the works of the missionaries sent out by the Danish king. He voices the same concern: innocent people living a life in close contact with Nature and adjusted to this life were facing hardship in the encounter with mercenary missionaries. There was little respect for their lifestyle and only contempt for their belief system.

Hans Egede in Greenland also sees the Greenlanders as a credulous group of people never questioning what they are taught and forgetting it rapidly. As they behave in a silly and childish way, the methods used by Egede are those that he would use in instructing children about Christianity. 'It is a matter which cannot be questioned, that if you will make a Christian out of a mere savage and wild man, you must first make him a reasonable man, and the next step will be easier. This is authorised and confirmed by our Saviour's own method' (1818: 216). According to this principle the whole lifestyle of the Greenlanders needed changing and it was necessary to make them settle in one place so that the teaching of Christianity could take place and 'little by little accustom them to a quiet and more useful way of life, than that which they follow now' (Ibid.: 217).

> They should also be kept under some discipline, and restrained from their foolish superstitions, and from the silly tricks and wicked impostures of their angekkuts, which ought to be altogether prohibited and punished. Yet my meaning is, not that they, by force and constraint, should be compelled to embrace our religion, but to use gentle methods. Is it not allowed in the church of Christ to make use of Christian discipline at times and seasons, with prudence and due moderation; which is a powerful means to advance the growth of piety and devotion? (Ibid.: 217)

At the end of his description of the Greenlanders Egede expresses concern about the changes that may come about for these people and a hope that they may preserve the good aspects of their life while changing to the lifestyle of a Christian. It is a concern well-placed. It is clear that Egede had already seen some of the pitfalls of the work of the missionary and the interaction with the world outside.

There were no epidemical or contagious diseases known among them as plague, small-pox, and such like, till the year 1734, when one of the natives, who with several others were brought over to Denmark, and together with his companions had the small-pox in Copenhagen, coming home again to his native country brought the infection amongst them; of which there were swept away in and about the colony about two thousand persons. (Ibid.: 120)

The attitude to the work of the *angakkut* on Greenland has been described in detail by the two sons of Hans Egede and I will therefore now devote some space to their observations.

The Work of Poul and Niels Egede in Greenland

The two sons of Hans Egede, Poul and Niels Egede, both continued in the footsteps of their father. Poul Egede, born in 1708 in Lofoten, arrived as a child in Greenland and therefore came in close contact with the population at a young age. He later studied at Copenhagen University and passed his theological exam in 1734, then returned to Godthåb. Two years later he moved to Christianshaab, north of Godthaab, where he worked until 1740, after which he had to resign because of health problems. In 1758 he became warden of the Greenlandic Mission and, in 1779, Bishop. He published in 1750 the 'Dictionarium groenlandico-latinum'.

He continued the writings of his father in the *Continuation of the Relations concerning the Condition and Nature of the Greenlandic Mission. Written as a Journal from Anno 1734 to 1740*.[2] In this he gives several detailed reports of encounters with the belief system of the Greenlanders and the work of the *angakkoq*.

The *angakkut* are presented as ignorant impostors filling the credulous Greenlanders with superstition and fear which give the *angakkut* a strong hold over them. When Poul Egede relates to the Greenlanders, whom he calls 'the savages', the end of the world, they ask him if there is not a support under the sky because they have heard the sky groan between Godthåb and Christianshåb. 'Their Angekut had told them that it was almost putrefied and when the sky collapsed it would kill all human beings' (1939: 27). They were apparently already well-acquainted with the fear of the doomsday prophecy, although in a different version.

Poul Egede described how several Greenlanders came to him to be helped because of what they have been told by an *angakkoq*. A man thinks that he is pregnant with a seal and says that he can feel the head in his stomach. He had this information when he consulted a *angakkoq* because of stomach ache. Poul Egede gives him a glass of brandy which he claims will drive out the foetus of the seal (Ibid.: 28).

The *angakkut* are believed to be able to take away parts or all of people's souls. The daughter of Poul Egede's host has been told that she has no shadow. As Poul Egede tries to prove that she indeed has one he is told that it is not that kind of shadow, but the innermost part of a human being, the soul. If they lose this they wither and die. Another girl has lost part of her soul and an *angakkoq* has tried to repair it with the soul of a sea-bird, a black guillemot, but a different *angakkoq* has torn it out again and given her another soul. 'The angekut can make anyone believe that they have no Tarrak: a part of the soul, they are believed at once and get a gift so that they will repair the soul with a new Tarrak' (Ibid.: 57).

Angakkut are the only ones who can see and deal with souls. When Poul Egede asks the Greenlanders how they deduce that people have souls, they answer that the *angakkut* say that they arrive in the dark and stand outside the houses. They cannot be seen by anyone except the sharp-sighted *angakkut* who describe the souls in the following way:

> They are pale and sallow, when they touch them, they have neither flesh, bone nor sinew but are totally soft as if they were almost nothing at all, but the reason why they are looking so badly, they pretend, is the strong turning and movement of the sky, which exhausts them so that they cannot get fat. Therefore the Greenlanders will prefer to have their dead friends travelling down than up. (Ibid.: 68)

The *angakkoq* is also the one who determines who is a witch.[3] Some old women are thought to induce misfortune and are savagely killed. An old woman complains to Poul Egede that she has been accused of being a witch and that the custom is to stone her to death. She claims that when the *angakkut* mumble in the dark they alone can see and they say that all *Hexe-kierlinger*, witches, are black from the elbow out to the fingers and have horns' (Ibid.: 49). It is a lie, she insists, and she believes that Poul Egede knows it.

Generally the detection of witches is by stabbing to see whether they contain blood, as a witch is believed to be bloodless. An old woman was stabbed and killed to see if she was a witch. She was then carried up on a mountain and cut into pieces. It is the *angakkoq* who points the finger but the killing is done by the bystanders. When Poul Egede reproaches an *angakkoq* for having accused an old woman of witchcraft he says that her soul had been seen by him travelling through the ground when she was still living and he did nothing more than push her to the ground, but the other people hated her and killed her (Ibid.: 77).

The *angakkut* have also the right to sleep with any man's wife if they please. Anyone who denies them that right is told that they will not live for a long time. Once, Poul Egede tried to set an *angakkoq* right on this point by saying that he smelled *angakkoq* and fornication stench. The *angakkoq* replied that he instead smelled a medical stench (Ibid.: 63). There is a constant battle of power going on between the *angakkut* and the missionary Poul Egede and the latter tries to expose the *angakkut* as impostors and jugglers. He therefore often challenges them to show him their *Luftspring*, a jump high into the air, and convince him of their special powers. Once he visits a settlement where the inhabitants expose their *angakkoq* to Poul Egede while he is reading to them and describing *angakkut* as liars and impostors. He is told that the *angakkoq* is actually sitting next to him without saying a word.

> The others said: Yes certainly he is a great angekok and can travel to the sky, to the moon and to Torngarsuk (the great spirit) when he wants to. I therefore asked him if he would make a jump in the air so we all could look at it, then he would be and should stay an angekok. Come to me, he answered, in the winter, when the sun has gone, then I will do it. It is too light now. His country-men wanted him to perform while I was there. If they had any secret hatred to him I do not know, because they seemed to get at him now they had a chance. (Ibid.: 29-30)

The ambiguity in attitude among the Greenlanders to their *angakkoq* seems to be characteristic of the many encounters that Poul Egede meticulously reports. On the one hand they are seen to have great respect for their *angakkoq* and his skills, whilst on the other they seem to take any chance to get back at him because of the fear he induces and the power he possesses. It is naturally important to keep in mind that the description of the role and skills of the *angakkoq* are seen through the eyes of a missionary. Some *angakkut* just repudiate the attempt by Poul Egede to disclose them as impostors whilst others are more easily frightened. Egede describes a meeting with an *angakkoq* who had not dared to go out and meet him as he thought he would skin him. Egede, who never missed a chance to ridicule an *angakkoq*, tells him that all *angakkut* are liars and impostors and the people believing in them are fools. The *angakkoq* gets help from his fellow men: 'All the other men came in and asked this great man to practise his witch-craft so that I would have good thoughts about him, but he could not make himself do it' (Ibid.: 43).

In the accounts of the conflict between Poul Egede and the *angakkut* the former often emerges as victor and manages to prove his point that the *angakkut* are conjurers and impostors. When a group of people claim that their *angakkoq* can control the weather, Poul Egede states: 'Nobody can control the weather except God; they answered: that some of their angekut can do it.' As he then asks them to show it, they reply: 'The best angekut are dead, and the living do not function, therefore they do not dare come to you. You are better to deal with, because you can tell us a lot that we have not heard before' (Ibid.: 47).[4]

Poul Egede also gives an account of the initiation[5] of the *angakkoq* and the travel to the Devil's Grandmother, the name he gives to the spirit which in other accounts is called the Mother of the Sea. Although his attempt is to ridicule and reveal the fraud of the *angakkoq* he also gives a detailed description of the belief system. He mostly battles with the *angakkut* but sometimes he even finds unwanted allies as some *angakkut* realize that it can help their reputation to side with him. An *angakkoq* claims that what Poul Egede relates about the sky is true, 'to make himself more credible'. The *angakkoq* insists that there are plentiful people and reindeer but the road is long if one goes straight up, whereas the road at the sea is shorter. Poul Egede is not surprised to hear the stupidity of the *hexe-mester*, the master of witchcraft, and contradicts this description by explaining that the Heaven he is talking about cannot be seen by the bodily eye in this life (Ibid.: 90).

To create distance from the *angakkut* is very important for Poul Egede. Christianity and the belief of the savages ought to be kept strictly apart and the *angakkoq*, whether in the role of enemy or attempted friendship, is to be defeated and kept at an arm's length. To underline the ridiculous behaviour of the *angakkut* he narrates an incident he has been told where three *angakkut* run after an *Angiak*, a spirit which they think is the reason for a fish, the capelin, staying in deep water. They run with the sole of a boot in front of their eyes. One has been careful enough to make holes for the eyes. 'The others fell over again and again as they were running as if in rage to catch this invisible Angiak in the air. One of them, they said, at last caught it and ate it. According to the description plentiful fishing arose (Ibid.: 108). Poul Egede concludes this description by narrating the reaction of the audience. Some believed the story while others agreed that the *angakkoq* must have used the method that Egede had revealed to them.

Poul Egede is aware that he might be seen as another *angakkoq* or a sorcerer and tries to deter that impression. Naturally, his aim is to demystify the skills of the *angakkoq* and to introduce the mystery of the Divine Truth in its place. The fear that some *angakkut* employed as a tool to suppress their fellow countrymen seems to serve him in good stead in his work as a missionary.

The quest for correction of the misconceptions of the Greenlanders is also shared by Poul Egede's brother, Niels. In the foreword to his *Third Continuation of the Relations concerning the Condition and Nature of the Greenlandic Mission. Written as a Journal from anno 1739 to 1743*,[6] the publisher, Johan Christoph Groth, expresses the following attitude:

> One can here see the ideas of the Greenlanders, both through reading and through conversations, which show their understanding of religious matters; and although it is but poor and often mixed with childish and carnal thoughts, their high esteem for God and the divine truth shines through along with contempt for the lies and fraud of the angekut of which they gradually become more and more knowledgeable. (1939: 127)

Niels Egede was born in 1710 and, like his brother, spent part of his childhood in Greenland. He remained in Greenland and became a merchant in Godthaab. He went back to Denmark with his parents in 1736 but could not settle and returned to Greenland in 1739, where he became a merchant and accountant in Christianshåb. He had to leave in 1743 because of health problems, but returned again in 1759 and became the founder of 'Egedes Minde', a settlement on the west coast of Greenland south of Christianshåb. He died in 1782 in Copenhagen.

The impression is that Niels Egede is more corporal in his methods of persuasion. He is aware that he is feared by the *angakkut* and not afraid to use force. He several times describes how he threatened them with a beating. Like his brother, he is keen to ridicule the *angakkut* in front of their fellow countrymen and takes every opportunity to get them to show their skill. In the winter period Niels Egede is visited by a group of Greenlanders as there is a lack of seals. An *angakkoq* offers to go to the sky and find the reason:

But I asked him to let me know when *Himmel-Farten*, the Sky-trip, was taking place, but he laughed at me, as I talked about the wonderful deeds of God! Therefore, I let him know that if he would not be persuaded by the good but despised the word of God he would get the same treatment from me as the other angekoks and liars have been given. As he realized the sincerity he slipped away and the others said that it was appropriate as he would suppress us all and they therefore asked me to stay and tell about the creation of the world and how the Son of God walked about curing illness, which they had heard from the previous vicar. I told them about it all and they said, now we feel as if we had just arrived in this world. Visit us often and you will find that we believe. (Ibid.: 146)

Niels Egede's experience is that the Greenlanders are prepared to believe anything they are told and that the *angakkut* use that to get their way both materially and in sexual matters. He is several times visited by people who are worried about either sickness or the condition of their souls. Niels Egede is uncompromising. If they do not give up their belief in the *angakkut*, he is not prepared to help. As with his brother he is met with fear by the *angakkut*. Three of them have even practised witchcraft against him to make him weak. They are afraid of corporal punishment or being killed by Egede. Niels Egede has a couple of times been shot in the head with no major wound and is therefore believed to be invulnerable (Ibid.: 187). Others are less frightened and ask why he is so much against their methods, since a vicar is doing the same sort of witchcraft. Niels Egede answers that his work is by the command of Christ and he adds that he did not consider it necessary to let this man know more. However, not all *angakkut* are against his arrival. Some try to side with Niels and even claim that they have seen God:

You have to believe everything he [Niels Egede] says, but this one thing he is lying about, that there are no seals in Heaven, because I was a quarter of a year ago in Heaven and talked with God who has given me the knowledge I have. As I asked him what God was like, he said that it is not for you as a learned man and half an angekok to ask about, your father has first taught me something about God and as I trained to be an angekok, I saw him as your father has taught. He is big and shiny as the sun and has the sound of thunder, and sometimes as strong wind, and was difficult to understand for other unlearned. (Ibid.: 131)

Niels Egede punishes him (it is not clear whether he uses a corporal method here), and tells him that it is impossible for him to travel to Heaven.[7] The only answer Niels Egede receives is that if he teaches the *angakkoq* his skills the *angakkoq* will teach him his. There is no doubt that some of the *angakkut* are acutely aware of the impact this missionary can have on their role and try to stem the tide. One even claims that he has been in Copenhagen and met the king and the prince. He has gifts to confirm this trip: butter, bread and a lock of hair from the prince's wife. He has been told by the king that a big ship will come to Greenland to take away a piece of the land and take it home and build on it. The king will also prohibit pirates from coming to Greenland (Ibid.: 177-8).

When Niels Egede is told this story, he asks whether he can have a message sent to Copenhagen next time the *angakkoq* goes there. This irony is wasted on the Greenlanders because when he asks if they believe this *angakkoq* he is told that they have seen the proof of the travel, the butter, bread and hair – confirming for him, how credulous they are.

Niels Egede is also confronted with the belief in the *Tupilak*. This is an evil magic creation of the *angakkoq* meant to kill a person. A man has disappeared in his kayak and is believed to have been killed by a ghost sent out by the *angakkoq*. Niels Egede tells them that such a thing does not exist but one of the persons present informs him that when he was a child he was playing with some other children when they saw an *angakkoq* at the beach. He packed half a sleeve with hair, grass and mosses and mumbled over it. When he had left the children went and observed that the sleeve was creeping and as they were about to leave out of fright the *angakkoq* came back and said: transform and become a *tupilak*, a ghost, and straight away it sprang into the water. Niels Egede tries to convince them that this was not possible but gets nowhere (Ibid.: 153).

Although he sometimes comes up against the stubbornness of the Greenlanders in relation to their old belief system, Niels Egede generally gives the impression that he manages to persuade them about the truth of the word of God. He even finds allies among the old women. One woman whose husband is ill is visited by a *heksekælling*, a witch, but turns her away and is praised by Niels Egede. In his presence another woman attacks an old man and reproaches him about his ungodly behaviour as an *angakkoq*: 'I have in the past been as bad and ungodly as you are, you will go to the devil, because you are still an angekok although for many years you have heard the Word of God and have not become any better'

(Ibid.: 185). The old man becomes scared and excuses himself saying that he is old and cannot learn new ways, but Niels Egede informs him that this does not depend on memory but good will.

As the link between the *angakkoq* and the powers of healing is important for the Greenlanders, Niels Egede also finds himself in situations where he is expected to take on that role. A young woman has denied the *angakkoq* his right to sleep with her and has been told that she will give birth to a seal instead of having children that could have been *angakkut*. Niels Egede is called to her bedside and asked to feel her stomach: 'I said that it was not my profession to feel the stomach of women, and that it was impossible that it could be true' (Ibid.: 204). He then asks whether she had eaten anything unusual and is told she had eaten raw barley. He suggests that she should drink water and the woman is well next day and convinced that he is stronger than the *angakkoq* as he can make seals disappear.

As mentioned above, Niels Egede had to leave Greenland in 1743 because of health problems and therefore his rather 'heavy-handed' methods of conversion stopped. He, his brother and father all worked to replace the power of the *angakkoq* with that of God but interestingly the young Poul and Niels do not seem to be concerned about the impact of the mission on the life of the Greenlanders. At the end of Hans Egede's description he voices a fear of the possible negative effects on the attitude and behaviour of the Greenlanders.

In a manuscript by Niels Egede from 1769, more than 25 years after his first writings, it becomes apparent that he is much wiser about the effects of his work on the lifestyle and culture of the Greenlanders living in contact with the mission. He writes of his disappointment that the Greenlanders are not strong believers in Christianity: 'No one is stronger in his belief than you can daily change it, if you say to them, you have to believe this or the other, they believe it for a while, until somebody else tells them something different, therefore I can hardly believe that many Greenlanders worship God in the right way and in the true spirit' (Ibid.: 242).

Niels Egede describes how young Greenlanders who have been at the mission start to doubt and lose faith as soon as they have lived some time away from it. He describes the Greenlanders as a strange people, that one cannot understand: 'obstinacy and cool-

headedness are reigning strongly among these people'. Niels Egede
sees no change in the last forty years in a positive direction but
more so in an evil one. He even claims that the un-baptised are
better than the baptised as the former have become thieves and stay
close to the colony thinking that they do the Danes a favour by
being able to read and write. They are just using the Danes, he
states, and their worship of God is based on the hope of getting
clothes and food at the colony without having to work. They insist
that they believe in Christianity but their *angakkut* tell them to
believe in the old ways.

> We angekut show our knowledge through art and miracles so that you
> can see and hear it visibly and realize it. The vicars say that you shall
> believe their words, because it is the word of God; but you can never see
> God or his Son or find any fruit of what you have heard, therefore our
> teaching is the right one. (Ibid.: 243)

This manuscript not only shows a changed attitude and
disappointment on the part of its author, it also deals with different
aspects of Greenland and is a general description of the country
where the presentation of the religion only takes up a part. The
young crusader for Christianity in the 1740s has become wiser and
his view of the *angakkoq* changes to that of some respect for his
opponent. He even uses an *angakkoq* as informant and states: 'that
if any among them is found to be sensible, it has to be one of their
angekoks, or wise-men, because they seem to have some idea about
everything' (Ibid.: 246).

This confession would have seemed unlikely in his earlier writing
and as a sign of openness of mind, Niels Egede participates in a
séance. He gets hold of an old *angakkoq*, Kannak, whom he asks to
tell him about his art. Kannak answers that now he is old and he
was able to do more previously but he has a contact still with a little
dwarf under the ground, *Ingnersoak*, who will answer his
questions. Niels Egede wants to reveal this man's mistaken belief to
others and invites him into his sitting-room. Kannak takes his drum,
places a flat lamp-stone next to him, and takes his dress off. He
starts to mumble and snort, grinds on the stone, calls *Ingnersoak*
and asks him some questions. He then questions the others as to
whether they can hear the underground being, but Niels Egede
answers no, which makes Kannak shout with terrible gestures. As

no one can hear the dwarf, Kannak becomes angry and says that he will not know the dwarf, while singing a strange song.

Niels Egede's comments show that he is now the one who conceals the truth: 'But something was not right. I, who am now a bit deaf, felt as if something blew under me, and the rest of the audience also thought there was something, but could not hear any words clearly, so I let him stay in the belief that his performance of witchcraft did not work' (Ibid.: 262).

This last manuscript from the hands of the Egede family is very interesting as it shows a slight openness of mind to the work of the *angakkut* and at the same time confirms the earlier fear of Hans Egede that the work of the mission has had a negative impact on the culture of the Greenlanders. The result of moving to a stationary position near the mission has obviously changed their pattern of living and resulted in a dependency on hand-outs. The readiness to believe in what you are told if food is available is understandable, but there is also another explanation to this willingness to adjust one's belief. The religious system of the Greenlanders is a highly individualised one. The work of the *angakkut*, although dealing with a known set of spirits and performing in a specific pattern in the séance, is very open to new inventions and, as has been shown above, there is plenty of space to include the Word of God in the universe of the *angakkut*. The aim of the work of the *angakkoq* is first and foremost to make the individual happy in this life, a sort of opportunism in the relationship to the surrounding spirit-world, which obviously is alien to the Egede family who are dealing with the eternal bliss of the soul despite the hardship of life on earth.

The Egede family's writings are an important source of information and observation on the 'untouched' belief system of the Greenlandic Eskimos. There had been whaling boats along the shores of Greenland for decades before Hans Egede arrived in 1721. Although the Greenlanders believed in the magic powers of what were called Dutch dolls (Ibid.: 188), the powers and belief in the *angakkut* were more or less as they had been before European intervention.

The Egede family were not the only observers of shamanism in Greenland in the eighteenth century but they were the first. David Crantz wrote a detailed description on the mission of The United Brethren in *The History of Greenland: including an account of the mission carried on by the United Brethren in that country*. This was translated into English from German in 1820 but the first edition came out in 1767. In his chapter on the Greenlandic belief system Crantz points out that it is difficult to obtain any information on the superstition of the Greenlanders 'on account of their extreme ignorance, thoughtlessness, credulity, and especially their diversity of opinions, as each is perfectly free to adopt what tenets he pleases' (1820: 181). He includes in this statement the views of the mariners who had earlier reported on the beliefs of the Greenlanders and, unable to speak the language, had misinterpreted their behaviour. When a Greenlander went out in the morning to look at the weather conditions, the mariners interpreted this as a morning prayer. Although aware of the mariners' lack of understanding of the 'otherness' of the Greenlanders Crantz persisted in his own fixed opinions: 'There are indeed some who believe, that their souls are not immortal or different from the living principle in other animals; but these are either the most stupid sort, who are ridiculed by their companions, or else wicked cunning men, who profess such opinions for their own private emolument' (Ibid.: 184).

He continues to describe the concept of soul among the Greenlanders. The soul is divided into parts and some of these 'materialists' even believe in the existence of two souls, a shadow and the breath. The shadow is thought to leave the body at night and go hunting, dancing or visiting. This, according to Crantz, is what gives the *angakkoq* his sustenance 'since it is their business to repair damaged souls, bring back those which have gone astray, and even change them when diseased past cure, for the sound and healthy souls of hares, reindeer, birds, or young children' (Ibid.: 185).[8]

However, although Crantz is clearly ridiculing the gullibility of the Greenlanders, he, like Niels Egede, admits that some of the *angakkut* have real talent and penetration. He suggests that they are visionaries 'whose understanding has been subverted by the influence of some impression strongly working on their vivid imagination' (Ibid.: 196). He even proceeds to say that 'their unblamable deportment and superior intelligence have made them the oracles of their countrymen, and they may be deservedly considered as the physicians, philosophers, and moralists of Greenland'.

This praise of the skills and intelligence of the *angakkut* is balanced by the statement that they themselves are aware that their 'intercourse with the spiritual world is merely a pretence to deceive the simple, and that their frightful gesticulations are necessary to sustain their credit, and give weight to their prescriptions (Ibid.: 197). The *angakkut* are seen as intelligent manipulators of their stupid fellow countrymen who are credulous and easily persuaded by any trickster's performance. This simplified insight into the Greenlanders' concept of the world is sustained through the nineteenth century and again expressed by Dr Helms in *Grönland och Grönländarne. En skildring ur isverlden*. He states that 'Everybody thinks what pleases him the most' (1868: 89ff [my translation]).

Helms maintains that it is completely unimportant for the *angakkut* what the Greenlanders believe about them, whether they are seen as higher beings with an influence on the spirits, as long as they are well paid. The *angakkut* tell many stories to increase the esteem in which they are held. There are good *angakkut* who try to help but there are also witches who kill people and are therefore resented by their fellow countrymen. The description by Helms is almost word for word the same as that of the Egede family and of Crantz and does not add any new perspective to the religious life of the Greenlanders, although written a century later.

If one tries to give an overall view of attitudes to the work of shamans in the seventeenth and eighteenth centuries, it must be concluded that attitudes towards the 'savage' people and their shamans are not very homogeneous, even by observers such as Acerbi, Georgi and Sauer, writing in the same decade. There is an attempt to be open-minded and academic but at the same time the 'savages' are described with characteristics that are also applied to animals. This ambivalent approach has to be seen in the context of Christianity but also in the Eurocentrism of the beholder. Being explorers and not missionaries, Acerbi and Sauer are not blind to the negative aspects of the encounter, as seen from the perspective of the native, but cannot on the other hand escape the prejudice of their own background.

The Egede family are missionaries and therefore have the purpose both of exploring Greenland and converting the Greenlanders. Much space is given to the descriptions produced by Hans, Poul and Niels Egede, because their writings offer a unique view of the 'untouched' shamanism where the inhabitants had hardly been in contact with the outside world and of the attitude of the missionaries to this belief system of the Greenlanders. Here also we find this ambiguous approach: on the one hand the 'savages' are credulous, stupid, and easily persuaded to any kind of belief; on the other they are seen as 'nature's happy commoners'. But in the words of Margaret T. Hodgen: 'an unfavorable verdict upon the newly discovered peoples was far more often employed than a favorable one' (1964: 361).

NOTES

1. As a missionary Hans Egede is inclined to ascribe a hierarchy of spirits to the belief system of the Greenlanders. Birgitte Sonne describes the tradition of *angakkut puullit* in her article 'Angakkut puullit i Grønland og Alaska', that these *angakkut* had a special position as their helping spirits were polar bear or walrus (1986: 143). They were not tied up during the séance and they were believed to be able to cut up and re-assemble a human being (Ibid.: 146).

2. I have used the unabridged version of the manuscripts which were published in *Meddelelser om Grønland* Bd. 120, 1939. The Danish title is *Continuation af Relationerne betræffende den Grønlanske Missions Tilstand og Bekaffenhed. Forfattet i form af en Journal fra Anno 1734 til 1740*. The quotations from Poul and Niels Egede's writings are my translation.

3. The concept of the 'witch' will be dealt with in Chapter 3.

4. The view that the best *angakkut* are dead is preserved up to the twentieth century. The living *angakkut* cannot perform to the standard – or rather the account of the standard – of the dead *angakkut*.

5. The section on 'The Initiation of the *Angakkoq*' deals with this process in detail.

6. The Danish Title is *Tredie Continuation af Relationerne betreffende den Grønlandske Missions Tilstand og Beskaffenhed, forfattet i form af en Journal fra Anno 1739 til 1743*.

7. In Danish the word *Himmel* covers both sky and heaven. Where it is clear that the conversation between the *angekkok* and Niels Egede is dealing with the Christian concept I use the translation 'heaven'; in all other cases I use 'sky' as the Greenlandic concept has not derived from Christianity. The *angakkoq* in this case is relating what he has been taught by Hans Egede and therefore knows the Christian concept.

8. The actual description of the quality of the soul resembles that of Niels Egede mentioned above and there is no doubt that Crantz was acquainted with the work of the Egede family.

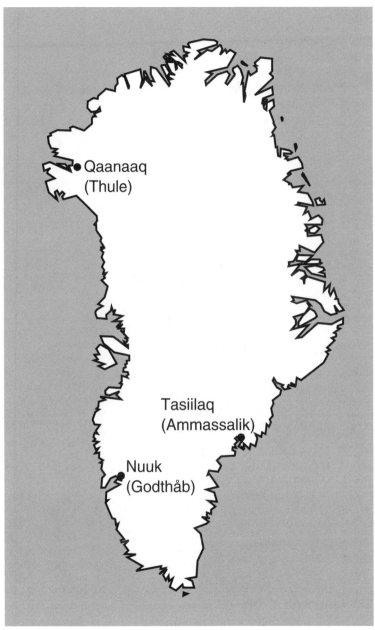

Map of Greenland

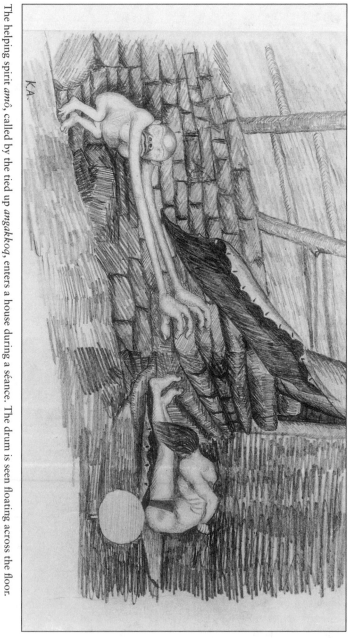

The helping spirit *amô*, called by the tied up *angakkoq*, enters a house during a séance. The drum is seen floating across the floor. Kârale Andreassen, The National Museum of Denmark. From Ib Geertsen (1990): *Kârale Andreassen. En østgrønlandsk kunstner*, Atuakkiorfik, Nuuk.

The helping spirit *ajumâq* enters during a séance. Its legs and arms are black and everything it touches much die. Kârale Andreassen, The National Museum of Denmark. From Ib Geertsen (1990): *Kârale Andreassen. En østgrønlandsk kunstner,* Atuakkiorfik, Nuuk.

The Mother of the Sea. The *angakkoq* is trying to cleanse her from the
transgressions committed by human beings so that she will release the game again.
Kârale Andreassen, The National Museum of Denmark. From Ib Geertsen (1990):
Kârale Andreassen. En østgrønlandsk kunstner, Atuakkiorfik, Nuuk.

Tupilak being harpooned by a man in a kayak. Above the water line the *tupilak*
looks like a seal but under the surface its true nature is revealed as its limbs are
from different animals. This is the manifestation of a wish to kill.
Kârale Andreassen, The National Museum of Denmark. From Ib Geertsen (1990):
Kârale Andreassen. En østgrønlandsk kunstner, Atuakkiorfik, Nuuk.

Female *tupilak* from Ammassalik, east Greenland. Wood. 12.4 cm. 1900. Donated by Therkel Mathiassen. The National Museum of Denmark, Department of Ethnography.

Tupilak from Ammassalik, east Greenland. Wood. 12.3 cm. 1900. Donated by Therkel Mathiassen. The National Museum of Denmark, Department of Ethnography.

Amulet from Ammassalik, east Greenland. Head and foot of raven. Length: 24 cm, width: 7 cm. Donated by P. Rüttel 1903. The National Museum of Denmark, Department of Ethnography.

Chapter 3
THE GREENLANDIC
ANGAKKOQ

I know nothing, but continuously life confronts me with forces that are stronger than me! As it is difficult to live we have the knowledge of our forefathers, and it is always the inexorable that becomes the fate of man and woman. Therefore we believe in evil. The good we do not have to consider as it is good in its own right and does not need to be worshipped. The evil on the other hand, which is lurking in the great darkness, threatening us through storm and bad weather and sneaking up on us in dank fog, has to be kept away from the path we walk. Human beings are capable of so little, so little, and we do not even know whether what we believe is true. The only thing we do know for sure is that what has to happen will happen. (Rasmussen 1921b vol. 1: 9 [my translation])[1]

These are the thoughts that an old East Greenlandic man shared with Knud Rasmussen in an attempt to explain his outlook on life. In a few words he expresses the attitude to life among a people living under Arctic conditions. The forces of nature are merciless and therefore play a major part in the composition of the belief system. As another Greenlander expresses it:

Our country carries secrets in its womb, that no man has any idea of. We up here live two kinds of life, in the summer under the torch of the sun and in the winter under the scourge of the northern wind. But the cold and the darkness is what makes us think. And when the great darkness covers the land many hidden things are revealed and then the thoughts of human beings go along pathless ways. (Berthelsen 1914: 33 [my translation])

Under such conditions the natural and the supernatural are intertwined, and the concept of the forces involved in the fate of human beings handed down through generations, making it possible for each individual to relate to the conditions of life in accordance with the wisdom of their forefathers. The belief system of the Greenlanders derives from a holistic view of the visible and the invisible existing side by side (Birket-Smith 1927: 176). 'The person living in close contact with nature does not see any chasm between himself and nature. Unsurprisingly, he interprets everything he sees in his own image. As he lives, everything surrounding him has life too' (Birket-Smith 1946: 14 [my translation]).[2]

This life is known as the 'owners' of the visible world or *inue*, singular, *inua*. This concept is applied to nature, things, even to emotions.[3] The *inua* can move outside the thing it represents, but it is always closely connected with its place of origin (Schultz-Lorentsen 1951: 40). The interconnectedness between human beings and surrounding nature has an impact on the relationship, especially with respect to animals. They are providers of food and garments. 'But the eskimo hunter also regarded his game animals from another point of view, for they occupied a central place in his way of life and philosophy. He had to defer to them, propitiate them, ward off their vengeance, ingratiate himself with them, and please them so that they and their fellows would permit him to kill them' (Søby 1970: 43). As Aua, the Iglulik shaman told Knud Rasmussen: 'The greatest peril of life lies in the fact that human food consists entirely of souls' (1929: 56). Among the Chuckchee, Bogoras points out that animals are men covered with skin garments; men might on the other hand transform themselves into animals (1904-1909: 279). There is an inter-relationship between animal and man.

The weather is equally important for survival. The concepts of *sila* cover two main areas: 1. the free space outside the house, the air, the weather and the world, 2. intelligence and wisdom (Thalbitzer 1926: 39).This is, according to Birket-Smith, 'an impersonal magical energy. This force is dangerous. Man knows so little, he is so helpless and commits so many mistakes. He must be careful not to get in touch with this power' (1924: 433 [my translation]). Taboos are therefore created to prevent this contact.

According to this world-view fear plays a major part in the attempt to protect human beings from retaliation by these powerful forces. 'The Eskimos aim at performing a magical reign over nature and the "supernatural" more so than they try to please the powers' (Birket-Smith 1927: 186 [my translation]). Sacrifices were, therefore, not so common.[4] If a human being wanted to live without fear he had to be careful all the time, being cautious of his words and deeds, as there were many spirits which could take offence (Doro 1985: 11). To prevent this, the Inuit had taboo rules, magic prayers and songs,[5] amulets,[6] and, first and foremost, their *angakkut*. They were people of major influence on the social life, health and prosperity of their fellow human beings. 'The laws and customs were, moreover, mostly closely connected with the religious opinions of the people, which were again acted upon by the angakoks' (Rink 1877: 140). They were often the more insightful and intelligent people in the community (Mylius-Erichsen: 1905: 13) and the disappearance of their art when Greenland was colonised was lamented by several researchers. Rink comments on the disappearance of the *angakkut*:

> One of the first reformatory steps was that of doing away with the angakoks. As a matter of course the high priests of paganism could not exist in friendly harmony with the propagators of the new faith. But here two peculiar circumstances have to be kept in view. In the first place, on account of the amalgamation of religious observances with the social customs and laws, totally subverting the authority of the angakoks was the same as abolishing the only institution that could be considered to represent appointed magistrates and law-givers. Secondly, the class of angakoks comprised the most eminent persons, both as regards intellectual abilities, personal courage, and dexterity in pursuing the national trade. In so far as individuals can always be found who misuse their authority to promote their own selfish aims, the Eskimo, in this respect, exhibit nothing peculiarly distinguishing them from any other nation. (Rink 1877: 142)[7]

When Europeans arrived there was an openness in the belief systems of the Greenlanders to include Christianity as part of the existing spirit world. There were also benefits to be derived from being a Christian because it was no longer necessary to keep the old taboo rules, which complicated life. 'The power of the angakut which now and then could have unpredictable outlets was also broken. But, on the other hand, the baptized was involved in a new norm system with strict rules of behaviour, that could be equally difficult to adhere to' (Kleivan 1983: 223ff [my translation]). The segregation of the sexes by the Herrnhut missionaries, the prohibition against drums, song and dance all of these had been an expression of joy in the community, but were now seen as sinful and eliminated. Consequently, there were some incidents of fanatical movements based on religious enthusiasm leading to an overwrought state that the Herrnhut missionaries had difficulty controlling (Kleivan 1983: 231). Rink, who was inspector for South Greenland recognised that Christianity might have lessened the manifestation of passions in violence and thereby created more personal security, 'but this did not so much happen by leading passions in a better direction as by blunting them in self-contempt vis-à-vis strangers' (Rink 1868: 253 [my translation]). There is no doubt that the belief in the existence of spirits lived alongside Christianity and that the *angakkut* continued to perform secretly after the introduction of Christianity. King Christian VI wrote a formal letter to the Greenlanders in 1746 to complain about their continuing use of the *angakkut* and lack of attention at the school to hear the words of God (1934: 305).

Some missionaries, however, approached the people with sensitivity and Rasmussen praises Enok Kristiansen's way of sharing the conditions of the people of Kap York by being both a friend and a teacher. He is not perceived as having any 'missionary honour that wishes to boast of quick and tangible results' (Rasmussen 1918: 14 [my translation]). The mission started the process of 'civilisation' but modernity finished it off. As Greenland after the Second World War had become open to the world, the Danish state in 1953 decided to change its status from that of colony to being on equal terms with Denmark, a sort of Northern Denmark. The change that Greenlandic society has undergone with the introduction of industry and a more vigorous school system has been immense, but by that stage most *angakkut* belonged to the past.

Undoubtedly the skilled *angakkut* of former days had a huge influence on their society. Rasmussen describes their role:

> In everyday life they share the fate of their fellow human beings, now skilled hunters, now average, exposed like everyone else to the small and greater tribulations of life; they are never surrounded by cult status before that very moment some kind of event puts the magic drum in their hand and lifts them from earth into space, where nobody can follow them. Then they can work at arresting the approach of evil towards human beings and perform in the eyes of their countrymen the highest form of goodness; or they become the henchmen of darkness in

the service of a bad cause and commit evil against their fellow human beings. (1921b vol. 1: 15 [my translation]).[8]

Rasmussen comments on the sincerity of the *angakkut* by claiming that most of them were seen as decent people, who believed in their conjuration and felt a strong devotion to their work. Although aware of some trickery and ventriloquism the *angakkut* truly believed that the spirits talked through them (1921b vol. 1: 21). This concept of the decency of the *angakkut* is far from being shared by many other observers. Several sources point to the fear that the Greenlandic people had towards these mediators to the powerful forces surrounding them. Naturally the *angakkut*, by the mere fact that they communicated with these forces, were inducing respect but also a sense of an unpredictable power.[9] Rüttel, a missionary, describes the insecurity created by the many murders among the people on the east coast of Greenland and especially their fear of the *angakkut*. He describes in detail how two *angakkut* kill a man, who was a murderer himself, and how the body is cut up to avoid retaliation from the dead. He refers to well-known *angakkut*, both the famous Migsuarnianga and Maratsi, as the murderers, and also narrates how they wish to convert to Christianity (1917: 65, 76, 112).[10] Chr. Kruse gives a detailed description of Maratsi:

> Maratsi (Maratuk), who is now (1902) 50 years old, is absolutely the most interesting man in the district. He is tall (162 cm), strongly built, thin with a marked face of mixed type where especially a pair of restless, flashing eyes makes a strong impression. He is courteous in his behaviour towards the European, calm, of few words and modest. When you see him for the first time, you get the impression of facing an outstanding personality and this first impression is completely favourable. The information you get about him is therefore surprising; he is at the moment the most skilled and feared angakok in the district, the apprentice and heir of the famous Avgo. (1912: 35 [my translation])

Kruuse continues to explain how Maratsi is sought by the people in connection with illness and solving murder cases. He is praised for his power over the spirits and although he himself claims when with Europeans that he does not possess such skills, he does believe in them. He has a difficult personality and has committed murders, theft, threatening women who will not sleep with him with soul stealing,[11] and so on. Kruse describes the transformation of Maratsi during a song fight. He comes across as wild and evil, his eyes wide open and his teeth protruding: 'over his whole figure was something so wild and misanthropic that I fully understood the demonic fear that he induced in his fellow countrymen' (Ibid.: 40 [my translation]).[12] This power could, however, turn against the *angakkoq* and he could become a murder victim himself (Rasmussen 1908: 156).[13] The predictions of the *angakkut* could also create a murderous mood and contribute to the deeds of revenge which swept through the East Greenlandic society around the time Europeans arrived at the close of the last century (Ejnar Mikkelsen 1939: 19; 1960: 119). Their arrival ended the reign of the *angakkut* either by their conversion to Christianity or by making most of their skills redundant. Mikkelsen describes such an *angakkoq*. He had been feared and powerful, now however, 'he was a harmless, hunched up old man', living in utmost poverty with his family (1960: 108 [my translation]).[14]

The change of personality taking place under a séance or when an *angakkoq* was communicating with the spirits leads to a consideration of a possible neurotic personality trait. The *angakkut* comprised people of high intelligence and integrity as well as disturbed and even evil-minded murderers. The art of the *angakkoq* was open to both categories. A. Berthelsen, a medical doctor in Umanâk, writes about the mystical religiosity among the Greenlandic people, that they are impulsive and easily suggestible and thereby susceptible to the megalomania of a paranoiac (1914: 17). Birket-Smith describes the condition of the *angakkoq*: 'Behind all the mad behaviour of the angakok, which by outsiders often denounce as simple fraud, there lies a disposition of a sick mental life. It is first and foremost highly strung individuals, hysterics and epileptics that perform as angakut' (1950: 719 [my translation]). Birket-Smith states that the work of the *angakkut* is the only outlet in society for such people (1950: 721).[15]

This is a rather simplistic and sweeping statement that does not include the behaviour of all *angakkut*. The ability to achieve different levels of trance is not necessarily connected with mental illness although it might initially resemble that to the audience.[16] Arctic hysteria was not the prerogative of the *angakkut* but could afflict anybody. Rasmussen describes a young man, Qitdlugtôq, who is overcome by hysteria. Knife in hand he walks straight out in a lake. His fellow men do not take this incident very seriously but shout with laughter: 'He passed me quite closely, his eyes staring wildly around, strangely scared, as if he does not see any of us. He sings a spirit song, constantly, with feverish passion. It is the song of the dead, I am told, he sings with the spirits of the dead. He is believed to be happy and that is why his voice is trembling.' He balances on a cliff and walks up to a tent with small children. The owner of the tent then calmly takes the knife away. It is the spirit of his dead mother who is believed to have caused this attack of hysteria (1915b: 109 ff. [my translation]).

People in a vulnerable social position might choose to become *qivittut*, hill wanderers, to escape the pressure of society, be it threatening to one's life, ridicule, shamefulness, or wrongdoing by others. Sometimes *qivittut* were hoping to achieve supernatural skills. In modern times it was believed that they were in contact with the devil (Rasmussen 1918: 6). It is possible to return within five days after which the society believes that the person has achieved special skills, such as the capacity to run very fast, to fly, and to hit everything that he aims at (Parbøl 1955: 453).

The *angakkut* only left society to acquire helping spirits in the wilderness. They were powerful personalities who might take advantage of the readiness of their fellow human beings to believe in their powers, they might even be ruthless murderers, or they might be well-intentioned individuals who truly wanted to help society against the onslaught of evil forces. Naturally, the evil doers, as in most societies, were the ones whose tales were told with most vigour.

The readiness to believe in the power of the *angakkut* can be seen as gullibility (Birket-Smith 1927: 177) or, as Rasmussen describes the attitude:

> The great majority of course believe blindly in the magician's capacity to make use of supernatural forces, and the few sceptics who, in an ordinary way, represent a certain opposition, are equally keen adherents of the mysteries at crucial moments. The magicians themselves are undoubtedly self-deceived in the conduct of their incantations; I do not believe that they consciously lie. Otherwise, why should they, when they themselves fall ill, seek the help of the spirits? But their magic arts are degenerating, and growing more and more simplified. (1908: 156)

Rasmussen believed that decline among the Polar Eskimos was due to the fact that they were not suffering any more than those on

the east coast. This last bastion of the *angakkoq* fell as late as the
first part of this century. This leaves us therefore with outstanding
material collected by researchers and missionaries among a people
who were more or less untouched by other belief systems until 1884.

Apprenticeship and Initiation

The East Greenlandic *angakkoq* was first thoroughly described by
Gustav Holm who, on his *Konebaadsexpedition*[17] to the east coast
of Greenland from 1883 to 1885, made a study of the people around
Angmagsalik. In this, Holm gives a description of the different spirits
which are believed to have an impact on the life of the East
Greenlanders and states that the *angakkut* are the only people who
can see and interact with these. Becoming an *angakkoq* is open to
everyone but those who want to acquire a reputation as skilled
angakkut have to be especially ingenious and cunning.[18] To become
skilled it is necessary to learn from an older *angakkoq* 'where they
should search for that which puts them in connection with the spirit
world', as the East Greenlanders express themselves according to
Holm (1888: 121). There are often two apprentices at the same time.

> The apprentice starts at a specific lonely place, in a cleft or cave, to rub
> a stone upon another stone round in the direction of the sun. This is
> done for three days consecutively and then, so they say, a spirit emerges
> from the cleft. It turns its face against the sun-rise and asks what the
> apprentice wants. He then dies under the most terrible pains, partly
> from fear, partly from exhaustion, but the following day he revives.
> (Ibid.: 121 [my translation)

This is repeated for three or four years. Through this the apprentice,
according to Holm, comes in contact with several spirits,[19] *tartoks*,
which then serve him. Among those are the *tarajuatsiaks*, which are
shadows smaller than human beings with a pointed bald head. These
are the ones that the *angakkoq* uses for getting the wind to blow,
retrieving a sick person's soul or stealing a soul. He is also in contact
with the *timerseks*, who are spirits that live inland and are as tall as the
length of a woman's boat and who have a soul as big as a human being.
They can help the *angakkoq* to steal and abduct souls. The *inersuaks*
can, as the spirits of the sea, make the animals of the sea come close to
the coast. Most *angakkut* have an *amortok* as *tartok*. It appears during

the séance as a sort of oracle, bringing news from afar and answering questions. It has black arms and is dangerous to approach when it enters the house. People who touch it will themselves become black and die. It walks with heavy steps and cries 'Amo'.[20]

The *angakkoq* apprentice obtains a whole set of spirits such as the *angakkoq bear*, the *toornaarsuk* and *apertek* which all function as his helping spirits. When the apprentice tries to get into contact with these spirits he has to follow a special diet and not eat entrails; he must not work with iron and first and foremost he must not tell anyone about his apprenticeship. Holm presents an account of an East Greenlander, Sanimuinak, telling how he became an *angakkoq*. In a footnote Holm states that the version is considerably abbreviated.

When I was quite a small boy, I once made a sledge, for which I was beaten up by my mother with the upright of the sledge. I then made up my mind to become an *angakok*.[21]

We were living in those days at Umivik, having previously had our home at Norsit. I then went out to Norsit to a certain cleft in the mountain which faces sunrise, laid a large stone over the cleft, and another on top of it. I now began to rub the upper stone round against the lower 'the way of the sun', and continued till I was almost lame in the arms.[22] I now heard a voice from the depths of the cleft calling to me; but I understood not the words, grew numb with fear, and my bowels jumped up into my throat, but I had no strength left to bear me up on my way home. Henceforth I ate no more entrails, hearts, nor livers of seals, nor did I work in iron.

The next day I went out again to the cleft, and ground the stones against each other, as on the previous day. Once more I heard the voice from the depths of the cleft; my bowels and heart flew up to my throat, and I was seized with the most horrible pains. The following day all went in the same manner as before but that I now heard the voice say: 'Shall I come up?' I was numb with terror, but said: 'Yea, come up!' The stones lifted and a 'sea-monster armed with claw-like shears' came up and looked towards the sunrise. It was much larger than those which are to be found in the sea.[23] Presently the monster vanished, and I travelled back home. This was my first spirit (*tartok*). The winter waned towards its close, and when it was spring again, I went back to the same spot and rubbed the stones; and when I grew tired and had no strength in me to rub them any longer, the stones went on of themselves moving round 'the way of the sun'. There came a little man up from the ground; he looked towards the sun-rise. He was half as long as a man, was clad in a white frock, and had black arms. His hair was curly, and in his hand he carried a wooden implement, with which he caught salmon. I lost consciousness, and when I came to myself again, the man had gone. He was my second spirit.

The following year I repaired to a place where a brook was flowing from a little lake. A little man with a pointed head, which was quite bald, came up from the stream. He cried like a little child: '*Unga! Unga!*' He was my third spirit.

Next year I went inland to *Tasiusak*. Here I cast a stone out into the water, which was thereby thrown into great commotion, like a storm at sea. As the billows dashed together, their crests flattened out on the top, and as they opened, a huge bear was disclosed.

He had a very great, black snout, and, swimming ashore, he rested his chin upon the land; and, when he then laid one of his paws upon the beach, the land gave way under his weight. He went up inland and circled round me, bit me in the loins, and then ate me. At first it hurt, but afterwards feeling passed from me; but as long as my heart had not been eaten, I retained consciousness. But, when it bit me in the heart, I lost consciousness, and was dead.

When I came to myself again, the bear was away, and I lay wearied out and stark naked at the same place by the lake. I went down to the sea, and, having walked a little, I heard someone coming running after me. It was my breeches and boots that came running, and, when they got past me, they fell down on the ground, and I drew them on. Again I heard something running. It was my frock, and when it had got past me, it fell down, and that too I put on. Peering down the river, I saw two little folks, as big as a hand. One of them had an *amaut* on, in which there was a little child. Both the bear and the three little folks became my spirits.

Once when I was standing by the shore at *Umivik*, I saw three kaiakers coming in, dragging a narwhal. When they came in to shore, the kaiaks flew up in the air like three black guillemots, and the narwhal sank like an *ovak* (cod).

At *Pikiutdlek* I got me two spirits, one of which was called *Kuitek* and shrieked: '*Unga! Unga*', like a new-born babe. The other was called *Amortortok* and shrieked: '*Amo! Amo!*'. They were both *Tarajuatiaks* (tarajuadat = shades). *Amortortok* is from the south, and speaks the same tongue as the *Kavdlunaks*. At *Tasiusak* too I met a spirit with a pointed head and without hair living in the sea, which is as big as a man. His second spirit is *Amok*, who dwells in a crumbling stone, and his third spirit *Ungortortok*, who barks like a fox, dwells in a dried-out lake, and is as big as a hand (a frog?).

Once I have seen *Tornarsuk*.[24] He was sitting bent over with his back towards me, holding his privy parts with both hands. I leapt up on his back, and then lost consciousness. When I came to myself again, I was lying on a large stone. (1914: 298ff)

It is necessary to keep in mind that the behaviour of the *angakkoq* is highly individualised. The presentation of the initiation differs in each case from that of other *angakkut* in the same area but naturally there are similarities as other accounts will show. It is significant that Sanimuinak decides to become an *angakkoq* on his own initiative. He is beaten by his mother and following the possible anger and humiliation he makes up his mind to become an *angakkoq*. He does not state that anger is the reason but it is a tempting deduction to make from his narration. The reason for becoming an *angakkoq* might be that the *angakkoq* has power and can frighten people.

As no teacher is mentioned, Sanimuinak seems to conduct the whole process on his own account. He goes to the cleft, he turns the stone and he gets in contact with the spirits. Overcoming his fear, he is introduced to his helping spirits one by one. They are described as *Tartoks* and adhere to the traditional spirits in that they have the qualities known to the members of society. The second helping spirit is clearly a *Amortortok*, which will help in future séances and the third spirit is a *tarajuatsiak*, whose function is mentioned above.[25]

Sanimuinak is all the time the agent, seeking places for encounters with the spirits. The encounter with the spirit of the bear is very significant in the process of becoming an *angakkoq*.[26] The whole appearance of this enormous bear will challenge the strength of the apprentice and the pain and fear which have to be endured show his ability to endure hardship in his future work as *angakkoq*.

The process of dying and being revived is a well-known part of the initiation of the shaman worldwide. It is necessary to die and thereby be transformed in order to overcome the fear of death and dealing with the world of the dead people. Sanimuinak's nakedness and the animation of the clothes emphasise that a transformation has taken place and he now observes more spirits and can state that the bear and the spirits 'became my spirits' (Ibid.: 300). It is important to this analysis of the shaman as the master of the spirits that, from being a victim, he transforms himself into manipulator. Sanimuinak can now gather a number of spirits and once he even sees *tornarsuk*. The significance of the privy parts is known from the creation of the *tupilak*.[27] The genitals are one of the centres of a man's strength.

But not only men became *angakkut*. Women could also become apprentices and learn the skill of mastering spirits. Thalbitzer describes the initiation of a female apprentice in *Memories of Youth of a Female Angakok* by Teemiartissaq (Thalbitzer 1923: 455ff).

Teemiartissaq is told by her father to train as an *angakkoq* and one day she sees a bloody butterfly, which possesses her and she begins to whistle. A person comments on her behaviour saying: 'Now she is training diligently for an angakok, she "begins to whistle"; she is becoming one who can descend to the deep sea; I wonder if she will visit the godhead of the sea when she has become a fully trained angakok.' Then she recovers consciousness. Later she is asked whether she wants helping spirits and proceeds up a mountain where she encounters two foxes talking about the food of the land and the food of the sea. Another day she ascends again and meets a human monster. 'I then let him teach me.' The spirits instruct her that if she gets a husband she should use magic, by cutting a piece of his hair and throwing it after him when he goes out in his kajak or putting dogs' hair between the soles of his boots. 'If you place them there he will be robbed of his soul. When he has been robbed of his soul he will die.'[28]

She continues to ascend and this time she gets to see some *Taarajuätsiaqs*[29] which tell her that 'When you begin to summon your spirits, those who are in the eyrie of the "falcon", all, you must exert yourself to see them. When you have seen them all, you will know how to begin to summon spirits with the drum. You shall be able to do everything' (Ibid.: 458).[30] Teemiartissaq is betrayed by her stepfather who reveals her attempt to become an *angakkoq* and thereby transgress the rule of secrecy. Teemiartissaq decides to end her apprenticeship. 'Thereupon I ceased to search for visions, like people who are ashamed of themselves, although I had kept (my searching for them) secret (Ibid.: 458).

Teemiartissaq thereafter has a dream in which she sinks into the interior of the earth. She meets two persons; one, an assistant spirit, places himself under her and helps her to ascend through the ocean where she sees the tents of the dead. 'The other, his attendant, addressed me: "Remain here! he will procure you the spirit. If you (afterwards) begin to summon the spirits (by means of the drum), then you will be able again to get out there"' (Ibid.: 459). With the help of these two spirits she meets up with her elder brother and is told how he died by capsizing. She informs him that she had thought of becoming an *angakkoq*, but was hindered through the actions of her stepfather. Weeping, she leaves her brother as he descends and she ascends to the boundary of this world. She finds her husband trembling and informs him that she has been with her dead relatives.

Teemiartissaq proceeds to go to the grave of a dead person and helps the ghost ascend by putting her arm in the grave. The ghost tells her: 'The foundations of the *angakkoq* arts are the ghost of the dead' (Ibid.: 465). This ghost becomes an assistant spirit. She keeps it a secret 'because I so greatly desired to become an *angakkoq*. It is told that when women are fully trained *angakkut* they can do all things – fly through the air and "whistle" for their assistant spirits.'

She again goes up to the mountain and there meets a spirit. It is a terrifying sight. His face is blood-red all over and she wants to flee but cannot. When this spirit appears for the first time some people exclaim, 'There is someone whistling – it whistles – it whistles! There is one about to become an *angakok*.' After he has been up a short time, he disappears. Teemiartissaq exclaims that she has had a dreadful sight and a house-mate says, 'It was the whistling spirit, do not speak of it.' Again, Teemiartissaq underlines the importance of keeping her plan to become an *angakkoq* secret.

She goes up to the sinister grave where the flat top-stone is rocking violently. It is according to her 'the starting point of an angakok apprentice'. She is afraid but the fear leaves her and the dead person comes out of the grave. She is now ready to appear as an *angakkoq* but is still filled with fear. Her stepfather, who also is an *angakkoq*, tells her, that so was he. Teemiartissaq starts to seek for her assistant spirits and goes inland where she throws herself on her back and shouts:

> 'Who indeed will come to me?' She hears a singing voice asking her to rise from below. Then (I) said: 'I will not come forth so that he sees me, let me not risk being frightened to death (fainting from fright)!' At this he appeared in all his horror – oh, bluish black (or green) – then I lost consciousness. As he had begun to devour, he devoured it (my body) entirely. When I regained consciousness, I had no clothing. My clothes (I put on) (and) down I went (to our dwelling). (Ibid.: 469)

According to a footnote following this description Teemiartissaq never succeeded in becoming a thoroughly trained *angakkoq*, nor to obtain helping spirits. Teemiartissaq's account of her apprenticeship, however, follows the 'rules' of initiation: searching for encounters with spirits in remote areas, the mountain and the grave site, receiving teaching from possible helping spirits, losing consciousness through interaction with the spirits, dreaming a travel to the underworld and meeting her dead brother, interacting with ghosts, facing fear of the spirits and being devoured and returning to life naked. She does not practise her knowledge in a séance of her own and therefore does not master the spirits. In her account she mentions how as a very young person she takes up healing but it does not seem to continue into her apprenticeship. The healing and retrieving of souls through the help of the spirits is here kept apart from the initiation to become an *angakkoq*. Compared with the account of Sanimuinak she is less coherent in her description and more frightened of her encounter with the spirits. She does not grind any stones and thereby invoke the encounters; she is, on the other hand, getting a ghost out of the grave. In Sanimuinak's case no ghost is present, the spirits are all non-ancestral whereas Teemiartissaq let the ghost tell her that it is a very important part of the art of the *angakkoq* to interact with ghosts. Both Sanimuinak and Teemiartissaq have the experience of being devoured and waking up without clothes.

These two accounts, although collected within two decades of each other, have obvious similarities but the differences point to the fact that the *angakkoq* is very much a creator of his own spiritual world. Some of the helping spirits are the same and, importantly, are known to all by their name, but the encounters differ widely on several points and the description of the spirits equally so. As the concept of even one of the major spirits, *toornaarsuk*, differs within the same community the possibility of the addition of various spirits by the individual *angakkoq* to his own universe is largely in his or her own hands. What can be said to be a common feature is that the *angakkoq* has to encounter spirits, overcome his fear and turn them into helping spirits, be devoured and rise again. These features are known worldwide for the apprentice shaman.[31]

Teemiartissaq's brother has also trained to be an *angakkoq* and she explains the purpose of the training.

> They train for angakok, all our guides and warners both such as know incantations (*serhrat*) and such as understand magic (*iliseeneq*) concerning the means of making them (the magic expedients) strong (and) concerning the issue (or elements) of spells and (other) magic prescriptions (and) concerning rocking movements of the drum, – by questioning about these subjects they learn them; in a retired spot the angakok [who accompanies them] gives them tuition. Thus they grow up and amount to something both those who rub the stone and those who

are infected by the vapours from the crevices in the inland ice – (and) those who are occupied in wandering on the inland ice. (Ibid.: 473)

Teemiartissaq narrates how her brother goes to the inland glacier to meet spirits. It is a struggle. He said, '"Come, boldly forth, ye two!" Then they came boldly towards him, he said, here at the entrance to the inland glacier. He then said, "Now, then, would you kindly let one of you come out and be at his service, when one (here) will begin to be angakok." At the entrance (to the inland ice) he exclaimed in a loud voice: "It is I," said he – "Stamp (on the ground)!" the two said. "Now I might begin to conjure my assistant spirit." His spirit, a giant, then beckons him to come into the glacier as the sunlight is dazzling him. The brother goes. In the darkness he encounters a growling bear[32] that the two spirits ask him to leap over, he admits that he is afraid but the spirits answer: "I thought you were an angakok pupil, leap over them. You who will soon begin to conjure your spirits shall become invincible."' In the end the brother 'flew like a spirit through the air he could not fall into the sea' (Ibid.: 475ff).

He goes to visit a house with three house-fellows at the inland ice. One of the fellows asks him if he has come to stay and he answers, 'I shall not remain here, as I am an angakok pupil, one who moves always further.' If he had not answered like that he would have been eaten; he is then warned against being snatched by one of the female inhabitants of the house and is urged to escape. His assistant spirits help him by puffing at him, the same way as the *angakkoq* puffs at a person so that he becomes healthy, and he gets away. The parents are showing anxiety at their son's strange manners. 'His son had become an angakoq pupil with his secret angakoq training. Keeping it secret we learn this skill and wisdom' (Ibid.: 477). Again it becomes clear that it is important to seek spirits in their dwelling place and to overcome the fear of entering into another realm. The brother reacts in a bold fashion and overcomes his own fear. In the end he is rewarded with helping spirits and the ability to fly – one of the characteristics of the *angakkoq*.

Holm states that the apprentice also has to learn a special language (1888: 122). He does not describe this in detail but Poul Egede gives a short presentation of the mechanism of the language on the west coast of Greenland. The language consists of transcriptions such as:

Tarub tunga: which faces the darkness: the North
Mangersoak: the great hardness: stone
Negovia: his creator: father
Akitsok: the soft: water

These are obviously used as a secret language only to be communicated between the *angakkoq* and the spirits. To secure this secrecy they also reverse the meaning of the words: *Niviarsiarak*, literally 'a little girl' is 'a grown man' (1939: 41). Secrecy seems to be the rule for the apprentice who has to take great care that his knowledge is not made available to other people in the community. If, after ending his apprenticeship, the apprentice does not make clear to the community that he is now an *angakkoq*, he cannot become one and has to try to become an *ilisiitsoq* instead. They are mostly feared and hated.[33]

It often takes about ten years to become an *angakkoq* and to be skilled it is necessary to let as many *Tartoks* be present as possible. Therefore, according to Holm it is important to be a good actor, have dexterity, have answers instantly ready and make a demonic, mystical, thrilling impression on the audience (1888: 123).

Holm questioned the *angakkut* on their performance, after having participated in one himself, and states that the *angakkut* he approached first asked whether he believed in them. If Holm said that he did not know what to believe the *angakkut* would tell him lies; if, on the other hand, he said that he did not believe any of it, the *angakkut* themselves were prepared to reveal all their tricks and admit that it was only a game. They themselves believed that other *angakkut* were capable of interacting with the spirit-world. Sanimuinak, mentioned above, came to Holm to get help against some enemies by asking for a magic word from Holm. When Holm states that he cannot help him with magic he does not believe him and answers:

> That he would not say anything to anybody about my help; but I had to help him, because he would confide in me that he was neither capable of witch-craft nor to speak with the spirits or healing people. It was all something that he made people believe; but he was convinced that others could interact with the spirits. (Ibid.: 127 [my translation]).

Sanimuinak, who has described his initiation in detail is apparently prepared to renounce his skills when threatened by someone else. This apparent contradiction between presenting one's own skills as useless and trickery and on the other hand believing that somebody else has the gift of communicating and mastering spirits is a well-known phenomenon. One has, however, to take into account that understatement of cleverness is common among the Greenlanders.

Rasmussen gives a detailed account of such apprenticeship (1938: 104ff). In this description the apprentice is often chosen as a child, in most cases beginning by seeing a ghost or something supernatural. This applies to Teemiartissaq, as she starts as a child. This was the first and an important step towards becoming a shaman.[34] The apprentice might be an orphan child whom an old shaman took pity on and encouraged to go and seek for the mother. The boy might leave for a lonely place and stay away for two or three days; when he returned people would know that he had started to become a shaman and not ask any questions.

Knud Rasmussen describes why a shaman starts searching for contact with the spirits. As with Sanimuinak the reason for starting a career as a shaman springs from frustration and humiliation:

> I was still a boy when I began to train to be a shaman, the reason being that the people in the settlement often tried to scare me and make me afraid, or shame me and mock me; I wished to cease fearing the things of which I was afraid. My father had died before I had begun to remember; when I was a small boy my mother was one of the two wives of the man *Nôrsît* (*qavseraq*: second wife). The man was cruel to my mother, and he tormented and mocked me in every way he could think of. I was most afraid when this man began to stab my mother in the thighs and abdomen with his knife; I thought he was going to kill her, and I, being only a little boy, was afraid he would begin to stab at me with his knife. Later this man drove my mother out of his house, and we went to the people at Sermilik. I was unable to forget all the cruelty we had put up with, and this is the reason why I began to seek. (1938: 110)

According to Rasmussen the apprentice would go to a lonely place inland and meet his helping spirit by crying out and hearing his own echo. Finally, after three days, the echo might be followed by a voice that would come nearer and a human being would appear. If the voice was a shaman the boy was allowed to touch him. This would be repeated for three days and the boy would then have a helping spirit. This spirit had to be informed that the apprentice was seeking to become a shaman. If the spirit were a shaman he would

invite him to his home where he was not to eat anything if he were
to return. This invitation to the home of the spirits is similar to that
of Teemiartissaq's brother, but the description of the echo is not
mentioned by Teemiartissaq or Sanimuinak.

Rasmussen states that the period of apprenticeship could be as
much as eight or nine years. That period would involve the
collection of helping spirits. The apprentice might go to a cliff, call
and hear the echo and then he might hear the voice of a crying
child. If that was the case he would have to turn round and run. He
was not to turn and look at the spirit, but the spirits would instead
touch him, and he would lose consciousness whereupon the spirits
would help him back to life. This infant spirit would then be his
helping spirit. In collecting his spirits the apprentice would have to
experience an encounter with the new spirit three times.[35]

Rasmussen points to the fact that the first time the apprentice
experiences something supernatural he is seized with fear, but he
will get used to it. When an apprentice had reached that stage he
was ready to go to a lonely place and turn the stone, as we have seen
in Sanimuinak's description. Rasmussen adds a detail as he
mentions that the shaman would have to lie on his back and that
the stone would have to be black if the apprentice was a man and
white if a woman. The apprentice might do this for days without
anything happening but one day waves would rise in the lake and a
great bear would come out 'a lean monster, dog or bear, with short
legs and a tremendous head, much too large for its body, with a
long snout' (Ibid.: 107). It would approach the apprentice and
throw him up in the air three times. Then it would eat him and he
would lose consciousness. His helping spirit would bring him back
to life and he would lie stark naked. Then he would start to run
back home and would be seized by fear by his own clothes coming
running towards him as Sanimuinak describes it.

When the shaman had been eaten by the bear it was time for
him to appear among his fellow men as a shaman. He would
practise on his own first. Rasmussen gives an account of a meeting
between a shaman and a ghost which is identical with that of
Teemiartisaaq's. The shaman would, beside having all his helping
spirits, have another remarkable skill which was called
silanigtalersarput, which meant that he had the capacity of seeing
clearly in darkness and could even see through the clothing, skin
and flesh of his fellow-beings into their very innermost being.[36]

Not every shaman could achieve all these skills and there was a physical manifestation of it:

> It was said of a person who had no special wisdom, i.e. one who did not understand magic and could not see into the hidden things, that his intestines had no horn; but if a person understood magic, the length from the breast up to the throat was quite dark.[37] And so all the shamans said: The life of man is frail; to those who can see it it is as if their souls were about to glide from their body all the time. It is no hard matter to do them harm by taking their soul from them. Human life is very very frail. So frail is it that one could deprive a man of his soul just for fun. (Ibid.: 110)

West Greenlanders had been exposed to the influence of the missionaries for more than 150 years when Holm encountered the East Greenlanders in 1883-85. The earliest more thorough accounts on the initiation of the *angakkoq* are made by the Egede family. According to Hans Egede writing in 1741, the *angakkut* pretend that they have their knowledge from *toornaarsuk*. If a person wishes to become an *angakkoq* he must retire to some remote place, where he must find a large stone and invoke *toornaarsuk:* 'This presence so terrifies the new candidate of angekutism, that he immediately sickens, swoons away, and dies; and in this condition he lies for three whole days, arises in newness of life, and betakes himself to his home again' (1818: 188).

Hans Egede's son, Poul, gives a more detailed account. He asks how one can become an *angakkoq* and is given the following description:

> You have to go away into an area where there are no human beings, there you shall search for a big stone and sit yourself on it. Then call the Devil[38] and say that you want to be an angekok, then he comes to you. But when you have first seen him, you will get heavy pains and eventually die and will lie like that for three days. Then you will become alive again. Then go home and you are instantly an angekok. The first time you will fly to the Sky, it has to happen at the Autumn Solstice, because then the nearest Sky, the rainbow is near the horizon. And then you have to let yourself be bound with a thick string (such as the Greenlanders use for their harpoons when they shoot seals). Head between the legs and with the rest of the string the whole body must be tied up. A drum shall be put next to you. When the light is put out and the windows are covered completely so it is totally dark in the house, you must start on the second

song, as our ancestors have done, then you are immediately free again, and go straight up through the roof and through the air until you come to the first Sky. (1939: 14 [my translation])

In the upper sky there are many different animals and *angakkut puullit* which are *angakkut* with bags, their souls. Poul Egede then asks how one can become an *angakkoq puullit* and gets the explanation that one has to proceed as with an *angakkoq* but not be bound.

Then a white bear comes though the entrance and bites the *HexeMæster*, the witch-doctor, on his big toe, drags him out into the ocean and throws him into the water. A walrus instantly appears, which grabs his genitals, eats him and the bear. After that his bones, one after the other, will be thrown onto the floor where he has been sitting. When all of them are there, he will rise up through the ground and become alive again. (Ibid.: 14)

As will be seen, there is a correspondence between the description of Hans Egede and Poul Egede as far as the procedure and the length of time are concerned. The simplicity of the procedure and the shortness of time, only a few days compared with years at the east coast, make one wonder if the Egedes have got their information right or if the informant has been telling the whole story.[39] As on the east coast, the initiation is highly individualised. The apprentice makes himself available to the spirits by sitting in a lonely place. The encounter with the spirits is in the other accounts frightening and the description of becoming an *angakkoq puullit* [40] clearly has a parallel to that of Teemiartissaq and Sanimuinak, both of whom die in the process and are resurrected. The magic bear and walrus, which are present in the account of the successful *angakkoq* apprentice, show the closeness between the *angakkoq* and animals, a closeness understandable in a hunting society where much of the work of the *angakkoq* is to deal with the well-being of the society and thereby its food resources. What is striking, however, is how available the role of apprentice is. It is open to everyone. There is no description of a dream or special characteristics in the behaviour of the person seeking to become an *angakkoq*. The choice is made by the person and the election is made by the spirits. The skill achieved is the mastering of the spirits and the performing of the séance, where the shaman is tied up.

To make a comparison with another Eskimo area, the observations made by Knud Rasmussen on his Fifth Thule expedition among the Iglulik Eskimos in Canada are described.

A young man wishing to become an angakoq must first hand over some of his possessions to his instructor. At Igdlulik it was customary to give a tent pole, wood being scarce in these regions. A gull's wing was attached to the pole, as a sign that the novice wished to learn to fly. He had further to confess any breach of taboo which he might have committed, and then, retiring behind a curtain with his instructor submitted to the extraction of the 'soul' from his eyes, heart and vitals, which would then be brought by magic means into contact with those beings destined to become his helping spirits, to the end that he later met them without fear. The ultimate initiation always took place far from all human dwelling; only in the great solitude was it possible to approach the spirits. Furthermore, it was essential that the novice should start young; some, indeed, were entered to the profession before they were born. Aua himself was one of these, his mother declaring that her coming child was one that should be different from his fellows. His birth was attended by various remarkable features, special rites were observed, and strict discipline imposed on him during childhood and early youth; 'nevertheless, though all was thus prepared for me, I tried in vain to become an angakoq by the ordinary methods of instructions.' Famous wizards[41] were approached and propitiated with gifts, but all in vain. At last, without knowing how, he perceived that a change had come over him, a great glow of intense light pervaded all his being (this is a recurrent feature in the process) and a feeling of inexpressible joy came over him, and he burst into song. (1927: 126)[42]

The apprentice might have had to spend from a few days to a decade to achieve the skills and control his fear. The prime purpose, however, was that he would be able to collect his helping spirits and perform the séance, which is the most important aspect of the *angakkoq*'s work.

The Pantheon

As mentioned in the previous section, the possibility of becoming a fully recognised *angakkoq* is dependent on an ability to interact with the spirits. The *angakkoq* has to go through fearsome encounters with several spirits and, through these encounters, be able to transform his interaction with them from that of possession to that of mastery. The pantheon of spirits is divided up in terms of both function and residence. The major spirit, the Mother of the Sea, as she is sometimes called, resides on the bottom of the sea and has control of the sea animals. She is, therefore, responsible for good fortune in the hunt and, hence, for the survival of the settlement. The *angakkoq's* capacity to deal with her is of the utmost importance. The Moon Spirit is another major spirit with whom the *angakkoq* has to interact. He is among other things responsible for fertility and the transgression of taboo rules. He is naturally resident in the sky. *Toornaarsuk,* mentioned in almost all the accounts of the spirits of the *angakkoq,* is sometimes described as the great spirit, at other times as one among others and is often thought either to help the *angakkoq* on his travels or to reside with the Mother of the Sea. The following accounts of *toornaarsuk,* the Mother of the Sea and the Moon Spirit will show the variety of interpretations that are characteristic of a society such as the Greenlandic where the inhabitants live in small scattered settlements. The belief in these spirits is perceived as an inheritance from the wise forefathers and therefore of importance to the equilibrium of the living.

Hans Egede gives a description of *toornaarsuk* in his chapter on 'Religion, or rather Superstition, of the Greenlanders':

> moreover, as they are addicted to different kinds of superstition, and that they hold there is a Spiritual Being, which they call Torngarsuk, to whom they ascribe supernatural power, though not the creation or the production of creatures (of whose origin they tell many absurd and ridiculous stories), all this, I say, supposes some sort of worship; although they do not themselves, out of their brutish stupidity, understand or infer so much, or make use of the light of nature and the remaining spark of the image of God in their souls, to consider the invisible being of God by his visible works, which is the creation of the world. (1818: 183-4)

The belief in *toornaarsuk* is here interpreted as a crude version of a monotheistic world-view, as there is some kind of hierarchy among the many spirits which makes one the greater but not the creator. This spirit is closely related to the Mother of the Sea, which Egede describes as 'his grandame, or (as others will have it) his lady daughter, a true termagant and ghastly woman' (Ibid.: 201).

The grandson of Hans Egede, Hans Egede Saabye, writes in his diary the following about the belief in *toornaarsuk*:

> The Greenlanders believe in a supernatural being and the immortality of the soul. This being, which they call Torngarsuk, is according to the description rather evil than good. Eternal it cannot be as it has a great grandmother – a terrible woman, ruling over the animals of the sea, often calling the animals to her and thereby robbing the inhabitants of their food. It is not seen as the creator of the world either; as the world has been created on its own account, and the first Greenlanders are grown out of the earth. Some describe Torngarsuk as a man, others say that he looks like an animal, and others again that he is like a human being. Some describe him as big, others as small. Some say that he is immortal, others that a certain sound can kill him. His residence is deep under the ground, where it is rather good to be and the food is plentiful. So different are the opinions of this being; but they do not love it, and they do not fear or worship it.[43] When they are well and lucky in hunting, and nothing else goes against them, then they are completely indifferent to Torngarsuk. Only if they are ill or unlucky, or the animals of the sea leave the coast then they follow – not Torngarsuk but their angakok who is in connection with him. (1942: 57-8 [my translation])

Egede Saabye is here presenting a description of *toornaarsuk* which consists of such a variety of interpretations by the Greenlanders themselves that it seems almost impossible to give a unified picture both of his appearance and the attitude toward this spirit. It shows how the interpretation of the power of the spirit over the fortune of the individual and the settlement is more or less believed to be of the same character, the *angakkoq* being the actual interpreter, but that the concept of the spirit is so individualised as to make it almost impossible to talk of the same spirit except by name.

Crantz, from the same period as that of Egede Saabye, writes an account of *toornaarsuk* which parallels that of the former:

> Their account of his person differs very much. According to some he is of small stature. Some affirm that he resembles an immense white bear; others a giant with one arm; while others again contend that he is no bigger then a man's finger. He is, however, allowed by all to be immortal, but yet might be killed, were any one [to] break wind in a house where witchcraft is carrying on. The other great but mischievous spirit is a female without a name [the Mother of the Sea]. Whether she is Torngarsuk's wife or his mother is not agreed. (1820: 190)

As becomes clear also from this description a unified picture of the great spirit does not exist. Crantz adds the bear, which has been seen to play a major part in the initiation of the *angakkoq*, to the appearances of *toornaarsuk*. It is a likely deduction for the missionary that the ultimate transformation of the *angakkoq* should be attributed to the great spirit. Crantz adds in a footnote that the soul of man is called *tarngek*, *torngak* is the spirit in general and *torngarsoak*, *torngarsuk* abbreviated is the great spirit. This might indicate a connection between the concept of the soul and the great spirit, which seems to reside in the land of the dead. *Torngak* is the name of the *angakkoq's* helping spirits. The *torngak* helps the *angakkoq* in his work with the souls of the dead, and is therefore closely related to the *tarngek*, this *torngak* might even be a former *tarngek*.

Henrik Helms confirms the above accounts by stating that the description of *toornaarsuk* shows that 'Every one believes what suits him the best' (1868: 89ff [my translation]). Gustav Holm gives a very different picture of what is called *tornarsuk* in East Greenland. He lives with his helper, *aperketek*, in the sea. They are animals that can be seen not only by the *angakkoq* but also by other people.

> Tornarsuk is described as long as a big seal, but heavier. Its head and hind limbs are like the seal's, but the front limbs are longer, that is the length of a man's arm, but thicker than such and ending in fins. It often is described as having red arms and being red around the mouth. Tornarsuk swims rapidly at the bottom of the sea. (1888: 115)[44]

Holm mentions that *toornaarsuk* is at the service of the *angekkut* and neither *toornaarsuk* nor *apertek* are good or evil spirits but are obeying their master. This is clearly a completely different concept of these spirits from that found on the west coast. It is not even described as being greater than any other spirit, but ranges at the level of the other spirits available to the *angakkoq*. The description has something in common with that of the *tupilak*, which is also a seal created by the *angakkoq* – and other members of the settlement – to kill an enemy. The connection between the Mother of the Sea and *toornaarsuk* is closer as both of them reign and reside in the sea.

Kruuse is interested in making the image of the great spirit clearer and yet achieves a confusing description of several versions of *toornaarsuk* (1912: 44). Rasmussen also describes more than one *toornaarsuk*. '*All* shamans had a *tôrnârssuk*. A *tôrnârssuk* had very long arms, reaching right down to the knees, the body was broad, the legs short. Some shamans asserted that their *tôrnârssuk* was like an animal with many legs, a thing that was not like anything else' (1938: 114ff). He narrates a story told by an *angakkoq*. In this it is clear that the *toornaarsuk* for the *angakkoq* is just another helping spirit. He encounters it at the sea shore. As it spots the *angakkoq* it runs away and the *angakkoq* is almost at the point of leaping forward. As the *toornaarsuk* runs, the *angakkoq* follows it and receives it as a helping spirit.

The missionaries in West Greenland might have been more inclined to perceive *toornaarsuk* as a greater spirit – or the devil – than the rest of the spirit world because it would make a crude parallel to a monotheistic cosmology; it might also be possible, as there is a reference to the bear as *toornaarsuk*, that this can be seen as an example of at least some recognition of hierarchy in the pantheon of the spirits.[45] The East Greenlandic concept is not homogeneous either and according to Kruuse's observation a unified concept is not possible with regard to *toornaarsuk*. The conclusion must be that the concept of spirits as such is highly individualised and varies from settlement to settlement and from person to person. Birgitte Sonne points to the complexity of the approaches to *toornaarsuk* and focuses on the different backgrounds of the explorers and missionaries in their interpretation of the influence of that spirit: 'With the greatest probability, *toornaarsuk* has been a qualifying denotation, and nowhere a *nomen proprium*. Thus, the hypothesis that *toornaarsuk* was a deity is not tenable' (1986: 215). Erik Holtved writes that the 'Eskimos once regarded Tôrnârsuk as a powerful deity who, however, outside Labrador was forced in the course of events into the background by the Sea-woman. Yet, in Greenland it is still Tôrnârsuk who helps the angakkut and gives them power to subdue the Sea-woman' (1963: 165). Holtved admits that evidence here and there seems faint, that 'What position he may have held in relation to other co-existing deities in the past is, however, difficult to establish with certainty. He seems above all to have been the grand teacher and source of power to the shamans, the "primordeal shaman,"' (1963: 169).

The attempt by the Greenlanders to fit in with the ideology of the missionaries and other foreigners added to the variety of interpretations among the Greenlanders themselves. As I have already said in respect to the initiation of the *angakkoq* there is also a variety of concepts regarding which spirits are to be encountered for the initiation to have been successful.

One spirit, however, seems to have a more unified presentation and that is the Mother of the Sea. Hans Egede gives the following description of her:

> She is said to dwell in the lower parts of the earth under the seas, and has the empire over all fishes and sea-animals, as unicorns,[46] morses [walruses], seals, and the like. The basin placed under her lamp, into which the train oil of the lamp drips down, swarms with all kinds of sea fowls, swimming in and hovering about it. At the entry of her abode is a corps de garde of sea dogs, who mount the guard, and stand sentinels at her gate to keep out petitioners.[47]...

> Round the infernal goddess's face hangs the aglerutit[48] which the angekkok endeavours to rob her of. For this charm, by which she draws all fishes and sea animals to her dominion, which no sooner is she deprived of, but instantly the sea animals in shoals forsake her. (1818: 202, 204)

Poul Egede gives the same description of the Mother of the Sea which he calls the Grandmother of the Devil. He adds some details which make the encounter between the *angakkoq* and the Mother of the Sea more dramatic. The *angakkoq* has to drag her around by the hair until she becomes faint. He also has to pass through several challenges before he gains entry to the house of the Mother of the Sea. This will be dealt with in more detail in the section on 'The travels of the *Angakkoq*'.

Rasmussen describes the same woman seen through the eyes of the Polar Eskimos in North Greenland. They tell him that in the old days the *angakkoq* used to go down to *Nerrivik* (The Food Dish), the ruler of the sea creatures. It is said that she has only one hand and, therefore, the *angakkoq* would help her to plait her hair and to arrange it on top of her head. In gratitude she released the sea animals. This relationship seems to consist of a friendly exchange of services rather than violence. The Mother of the Sea has also got a name, which is unusual, in that in most accounts she is not named which may be due to the fact that the name itself contains power (1908: 151).[49]

On the east coast, according to Rasmussen, she also was in charge of the animals and it was dangerous for the *angakkoq* to get near her. Only the most skilled *angakkoq* could undertake such a journey, and when he managed to get into her house he would encounter the following sight:

> she was all covered with dirt, and her hair was matted together with filth. The moment he entered she seized him, and they fought; she was very strong, and he would have been unable to manage had his helping spirits not come to his assistance. At length they got the better of her, and started to wash the squirming woman, afterwards combing her hair, which was a difficult task, for the hair was all entangled. (1938: 127)

When the dirt has been cleared away, the woman moves her lamp and animals are released. This description is obviously different in the narration of the relationship between the *angakkoq* and the Mother of the Sea. In Egede's presentation there is a robbery taking place and no indication of friendship. In the above situation the *angakkoq* is on friendly terms with the Mother of the Sea having removed dirt from her hair and helped her. The end result and the purpose for the dangerous undertaking of encountering her are that the creatures of the sea are released and become available to the community.

The Moon Spirit is in East Greenland called *Aningáhk*. He is regarded as a hunter who catches sea animals and who has his house, his hunting grounds and his implements of the chase in the sky (Thalbitzer 1908: 448ff). The Moon Spirit is a powerful punishing spirit with influence on weather and fertility. He might remove men's souls as punishment for breach of taboo rules and is especially concerned with those relating to birth. When the *angakkoq* visits the Moon Spirit he has to pass the 'eater of entrails' who will attack him if he laughs at her ridiculous movements. The Moon Spirit is easily angered and therefore feared (Thalbitzer 1926: 58).[50] The three above-mentioned spirits are the ones that the *angakkoq* mostly deals with concerning the interests of society, but as seen in the preceding section there is a whole range of different spirits residing in the mountains, in the sea, in lakes, in the air, and so on.[51]

The *angakkoq* may also have the souls or spirits of dead people as his helpers. Rink describes the relationship between the dead and the living: 'The dead are tutelary spirits for their grand children and especially for those who are named after them' (1868: 213). The presence of a dead person's soul might be detected though a whistle or a ringing in the ears. The same relationship is described by Rasmussen in his travel diary: 'He [Uvdloriaq] had dreamt about his dead father, just before he left. He thought that it meant unfailing luck for us for a long time ahead. The dead always prepared the road for the living that they cared for' (1915a: 197 [my translation]).

The number of spirits is large. The Greenlanders lived in an animated world surrounded by mostly hostile and dangerous spirits and the *angakkoq's* task was to master these on behalf of his society.

> An evil man was the worst enemy of man and life. But nature too was full of horror and dangerous problems. There were the mountain spirits, sea spirits, underground spirits, giants and goblins, who were only too willing to come and help when evil called and gave them a chance. All these spirits were stronger and mightier than man himself and he would perish inevitably if his forefathers had not arranged life so well by means of amulets and magic words, and if certain people had not been given the power to rule the hopelessness of darkness. These people were shamans, and they were regarded almost as deities in frail human shape. The shamans, who in their daily existence shared conditions and fate with their fellow-men, sometimes skillful at hunting, sometimes only moderately so, exposed like others to life's great and trifling troubles, and who never surrounded themselves in any cloak of cult until some event forced sorcery upon them and elevated them from the ground into the skies where no other mortal could follow them. Then they laboured to stop evil on its way towards mankind thus in the eyes of their fellow-Eskimos practising the highest form of goodness. (Rasmussen 1938: 69)

Although he admires the work of the *angakkut* in an attempt to present the Eskimo culture favourably, they were not all seen as kind-hearted and beneficent. Several were, no doubt, tempted to use the power given to them by the belief in their mastery of spirits, to further their own self-interest, but there were also people who truly had devoted their lives to the service of their fellow-men. On Greenland and among other Eskimos it depended on the single *angakkoq* and his personality in the same way as it does in any religious setting. To create good hunting luck, to heal, to divine, to judge transgressions, the *angakkoq* had to be the master of the spirits.[52] These helping spirits were only visible to the initiated. They were either nature spirits or spirits of dead people or animals, 'invisible spirit people that lived and moved in the vicinity of the settlement, under the earth, under the rocks by the sea or inland' (Thalbitzer 1926: 18). This was an animated world into which the *angakkoq* had direct access.

Paraphernalia

Compared with shamans from other cultures, the Greenlandic *angakkoq* did not use elaborate paraphernalia. The Tungus shaman, the Mongolian shaman and the Korean *mansin* all use special costumes for the séance, which are seen as a powerful part of the success of the shaman's interaction with the spirits. The Tungus shaman dress is adorned with implements and thereby a symbolic representation of the powers of the spirits invoked. The Korean *mansin* undergoes transformation through dressing up in different garments representing the invoked spirits, and the Mongolian shaman is afraid of handing over his costume because the spirits inhabiting it might get out of control. Dress and spirit control are interlinked. The Greenlandic *angakkoq* is not dressed in a special garment, but is often semi-naked, with only a loin cloth or belt.[53] The séance almost always takes place in darkness so that it is the senses such as hearing and feeling which are affected. The drum is, therefore, the most important item of paraphernalia.

Rasmussen gives the following description of the drum:

> The magic drum consisted of a round ring of wood over which was stretched the skin of a bear's bladder or the gut of a bladdernose sewn together. Before use the drum skin was moistened and gave out a booming note when the wood ring was struck with the stick, which as a rule was of wood. When the interior of the house had become quite dark, the shaman performing the invocation would often be seized with an inexplicable feeling of fear, and some have told that they trembled so violently at something unpleasant and unknown that they had a feeling of being about to die. It was thought that the drum in the hand of the shaman possessed mystic and supernatural power which helped to summon the spirits. It would become alive in the course of the séance, and floated freely about the house without being touched by the shaman's hand. (1938: 95)[54]

The *angakkoq* stone[55] was used to invoke the spirits, the *angakkoq* grinding it. The method of using the stone has been described in Sanimuinak's account: 'I now began to rub the upper stone round against the lower "the way of the sun", and I continued till I was almost lame in the arms. I now heard a voice from the depths of the cleft calling to me' (Holm 1914: 298).

Whether there was a use of masks during séances in Greenland is not clear. Thalbitzer reported that an old woman, Aleqajik, told him, 'that before the arrival of the Europeans the masks were often used in the house-games (*uaajeertut*) when they tried to represent the spirits of the angakut. The angakut themselves did not use them during their ceremonies. When worn out they were not preserved but thrown out on the refuse-heap' (1914: 639).

The skin that was placed in front of the entrance to the house during a séance might be mentioned as another item of paraphernalia as its rattling indicated the arrival of the spirits. Holm writes about the beginning of a séance that 'the angakok places himself in front of the house entrance feet pointing towards the entrance and resting on the lower part of the dry skin, that is hanging in front of it' (1888: 123 [my translation]). There are very few items of paraphernalia in use at the séance of the Greenlandic *angakkoq* and it is therefore all the more important to use voice and touch as invoking elements.[56]

The amulets were also part of the *angakkoq's* paraphernalia. They were not necessarily used during the séance but were used to protect the *angakkoq* during his ordinary life, where he might expose himself to more dangers than other members of the settlement. Amulets were naturally used by everybody, the most famous example being the boy's dress collected by Rasmussen during the Fifth Thule expedition. This dress was adorned with over eighty amulets. Thalbitzer describes the function of amulets among the East Greenlanders in the following way:

> The effect of the amulets goes partly in the direction of frightening or luring the spirits away or in other ways to avert the persecution of evil persons, partly in directly assisting the wearer of the amulet by giving him vigorous growth and good hunting. The amulet does more than merely represent the animal or human being which it imitates or by which it is made. The amulet is alive because it has been made during the recitation of a charm or spell, when the dominating qualities of the animal or the part of the body have been invoked; the power of these qualities is at any rate potentially present in the amulet. (1914: 630)

Men often wore amulet straps which were never taken off. 'The main object of these straps is, naturally, to be the bearer of the man's protecting amulets on both sides of the body in its upper part, so that no evil spirit may be able to penetrate to his soul within' (1914: 625). Thalbitzer mentions that similar straps have been noted among the West Greenlanders. The amulets were made of either 'copies of human-figures (wooden dolls, seldom animals) or even sometimes consist of parts of dead human beings, animals or plants, or even remnants of broken implements. Small dried animals or parts of animals, e.g. crustacea, bees, birds, raven-heads, fox-jaws, whiskers, claws, nails, teeth, are placed on the body or the implements' (1914: 630).[57]

The use of amulets continued after the conversion to Christianity. Peter Freuchen describes how Navarana, his wife, is wearing both a crucifix, made of an old record, and 'in the case the crucifix did not work Navarana had an "old fashioned" amulet, a ball of a piece of drift timber. It could resist water and hunger and cold, it was not disturbed by pains resulting from being hit and was altogether good to carry if it could transfer some of its characteristics to its carrier' (1963: 224 [my translation]).[58]

Another magical aid for the *angakkoq* was the *tupilak*. As with the amulet it could be created by ordinary members of society but, when invisible, the *angakkoq* was the only one able to see it during the séance. It was made of bones of various animals, moss, skin, seaweed, a kayak sleeve or an old mitten. It was created near water and animated with magical songs. It sucked the sexual organs of the maker to give it strength. It is the physical manifestation of revenge. When, however, it has been sent out against a victim it blindly obeys orders. 'Should the prospective victim prove to be a greater magician, he can order the tupilak to turn against its maker, who then becomes the hunted victim' (Robert Petersen 1964: 75). The role of the *angakkoq* is to realise the existence of the *tupilak* during a séance and perhaps manage to destroy it.[59] The amulet and the *tupilak* are available to all and therefore the *angakkoq* is also using them. They are, however, not necessarily connected with his work as *angakkoq* although his special skills make it easier for him to achieve them.

The Séance

The earliest encounter with a séance of a west coast *angakkoq* happened for Hans Egede a year after he arrived in Godthåb in 1722. A bottle had been stolen from the captain of a boat and a man approached Egede stating that he could discover who had stolen the bottle. As Hans Egede felt some interest in the 'monkey-tricks' this man could perform, he let him go ahead (1925: 18). The Greenlander immediately started to mumble and grind on the floor and to make strange gestures laughing and touching his toes and other limbs, as if he felt very much pain, and sometimes he exchanged a word or two with his friends. When the man got up he told Hans Egede that none of the people present had committed the theft but gave the name of a man who had just left the area. After having seen this performance Egede concluded that there was superstition among the Greenlanders, although he had not thought so. The man, apparently seeing Egede as another kind of *angakkoq*, tried to tell him how difficult his work was and pointed up at the sky. Egede's lack of language was a barrier for more detailed conversation but he was aware that the man saw him as capable of doing similar things.

It is an interesting account because the *angakkoq* performed without being under the kind of threat that was later introduced into the relationship between the Egede family and the *angakkut*. Apart from performing in full light and without his drum, the *angakkoq* is using the same technique as that among the East Greenlanders and the Polar Eskimo, the laughing, the mumbling and the grinding. He might have been restricted from more elaborate sounds because of the environment. Egede is now aware that something superstitious is going on among the Greenlanders and attends the first full performance in October 1722 when he is invited to a house in the evening:

> When I came in they were sitting preparing monkey-tricks, which one of them, who now came to them, and whom they praised as a skilled man, was going to perform. I had to sit down with the others and look at what this *Hexen Mester*, master of witchcraft, would do. Then the light was put out and the aforesaid person sat down on the floor together with other persons and the women started to sing a strange song, which I could not understand, thereafter he hit a thing looking like a drum, shouted and rumbled the dry seal-skin, which they had put on the floor, sometimes he talked to the others and asked I don't know what. They had also ordered another outside the house which had to answer him on what he asked inside. I pretended that I did not understand and asked the person sitting near me what it meant. He said that it was a dead person they were asking several questions about themselves, and asked me whether I was afraid. (1925: 57 [my translation])

Egede tells them that he is not afraid and that it is all a lie but the people present deny this. He gives here a description of a séance which conforms to those in other parts of Greenland for, although there is no mention of the tying up of the *angakkoq*, the sound effects and the drumming are the same.

These accounts of an encounter with the *angakkoq* are interesting because they represent Egede's first impression. In his later writing he gives a more detailed description based on his experience with the séances:

> The farce or imposture is thus acted: a number of spectators assemble in the evening at one of their houses, where, after it is grown dark, every one being seated, the angekkok causes himself to be tied, his head between his legs and his hands behind his back, and a drum is laid at his side; thereupon, after the windows are shut and the light put out, the assembly sings a ditty, which, they say, is the composition of their ancestors; when they have done singing the angekkok begins with conjuring, muttering, and brawling; invokes Torngarsuk, who instantly presents himself, and converses with him (here the masterly juggler knows how to play his trick, in changing the tone of his voice, and counterfeiting one different from his own, which makes the too credulous hearers believe, that this countefeited voice is that of Torngarsuk, who converses with the angekkok). In the meanwhile he works himself loose, and as they believe, mounts up into Heaven through the roof of the house, and passes through the air till he arrives into the highest heavens, where the souls of angekkut poglit, that is, the chief angekkuts, reside, by whom he gets information of all he wants to know. All this is done in the twinkling of an eye. (1818: 189-91)

It is clear from this description that Egede has now attended more séances and can add the tying up and the actual spirit to his information about the séance. He mentions that the *angakkoq* works himself up and possibly some sort of trance is meant by this. The *angakkoq* is now also described as travelling to the upper world, so Egede, apart from having an insight into the jugglery, as he calls it, also has an understanding of the cosmology which is part of the séance.

When Rasmussen visited the Eskimos of the Polar north on the 'Danish Literary Expedition', commencing in 1902 he encountered Sagdloq who had the reputation of being the greatest and oldest *angakkoq*. Sagdloq decides to conjure up spirits because his wife is ill and is helped by Kale, another *angakkoq*, who has learned his skill from Sagdloq. Sagdloq sits in his house with a drum, the audience sitting outside: 'Every face bore the imprint of earnest reverence (1908: 16). The role of the *angakkoq* is ambiguous and Rasmussen observes:

> Sagdloq came of an old and much feared family. His paternal uncle and his nephew had both been murdered, as soulstealers, and Sagdloq was the only one still living, said his countrymen, who had inherited the wisdom from his forefathers. For instance, no other magician[60] could crawl out of his skin, and then draw it on again; but he could do that. Any man who saw a magician in this state, 'flesh-bare',[61] would die, they declared. (1908: 17)

As the séance is about to begin Rasmussen is looking into the house where Sagdloq is sitting playing his drum on the raised stone sleeping place. 'When he saw my face at the window he stopped beating the drum, laughed up at me, and said: "All foolery, silly humbug! Nothing but lies!"' This understatement of the powers of the *angakkoq* is a common feature: 'A magician always precedes his conjurations with a few deprecating words about himself and his powers. And the more highly esteemed he is, the more anxious he is to pretend that his words are lies' (Ibid.: 18).[62]

The old Sagdloq starts to sing his spirit song and his apprentice, Kale, sits on the roof of the house, more and more affected and involuntarily joining in the singing. Sorqaq, who is also a 'magician' stands in the middle of the crowd and gives vent to approving grunts. All the rest stand mute and motionless. Suddenly Sagdloq shrieks: 'Ow! Ow! It is impossible! I am underneath! He is lying on me. Help me! I am too weak, I am not equal to it!' The shrieks die away in convulsive sobbing. Old Kale on the roof sings his spirit songs with tears in his eyes. Sagdloq says: 'Make haste! Put out all your strength!' Silence and no drumming follows. Then drumming starts again and, 'The Evil Fate – misfortune-bringing spirits – the white men!' After a long howl, 'The white men brought the Evil Fate with them, they had a misfortune-bringing spirit with them. I saw it myself, there are no lies in my mouth; I do not lie, I am no liar, I saw it myself!' Sagdloq continues to explain that the misfortune-bringing spirit has touched Moltke's sledge, one of the participants in the Expedition, and brought illness also among the dogs. The house now seems full of people wrestling. He continues to shout that only the dogs are ill and therefore nobody can eat dog-meat. He then inquires among the audience. He cannot save his wife, as she had eaten dog-meat.

> Then a savage roar was heard from within the house, and the drum began again: Too-too-to-too, repeated interminably, and with extraordinary vigour. It was like the snorting of a locomotive engine. Sagdloq was in a state of complete ecstasy; the rheumatic old man sprang about the floor like a wounded animal. His eyes were shut and he moved and twisted his head and body in remarkable contortions to the music of the drum. Then he uttered one long howl, with peculiar refrains. Human laughter seemed to be mingling with the lament, which ended at last in a quiet sobbing. He could not save his wife! (Ibid.: 21)

The description of this séance gives a vivid impression of the drama involved in the communication between the spirits and the *angakkoq*. The different voices represent the appearance of different spirits involved in clarifying the fate of the old woman. Evil spirits have arrived with the white men, a statement which could have a dangerous overtone, but the *angakkoq* then transfers the evil to the dogs of the newcomer and the eating of dog-meat, which is an explanation for the unavoidable death of his wife. She has committed an act which has put her in contact with evil spirits and her husband cannot save her. Needless to say, the wife actually died the following summer.

The dramatic use of sound effects to represent the different spirits is common in all the Greenlandic séances. The spirits' voices are heard either speaking normal Greenlandic or speaking the so-called '*angakkoq* language'. The use of the drum and songs are also an important part, probably inducing a light trance.[63]

To understand the importance of the *angakkoq*'s work in society it is necessary to look at the concept of the nature of a human being.

> Every person consists of a soul, a body and a name. They believe that a human being has a soul, or a spirit, which is immortal. The soul is outside the person, but follows it, as his shadow follows a man in the sunshine. Although the soul is thus not inside the body, the body and the soul are nevertheless inseparable as long as a person is to continue alive; for when the soul leaves the body, the body pines away and dies. Only great magicians can see the soul. They say that it looks exactly like a person, only that it is smaller. Consequently a man's soul can be stolen by a magician, who can bury it in the snow; the hole in the snow must be covered with the fleshy side of a dog's skin. And then the person will inevitably die, unless another magician, favourably inclined to him or

her, can find the soul that has been stolen and bring it back to the body. After death of the body, the soul ascends into heaven or goes down into the sea. It is good to be in either place. (Rasmussen 1908: 106)[64]

As the environment is inundated with souls and spirits,[65] the life of the Greenlander has constantly to be conducted according to the character of these. Most of them are regarded as evil and therefore dangerous. The *angakkoq's* task is to keep the relationship between the souls, spirits, and human beings in balance. The division of the human being into body, soul and name, shows the vulnerability of the person's well-being as the soul can leave the body or be stolen and the name can also disappear. The name is, according to Holm's observations (1888: 112), the size of a human being and enters into the child when, after birth, it is smeared round the mouth with water while the name of the deceased person which is to be given to the child is mentioned. The name can leave a human being if it gets offended, whereupon the person becomes ill.

Among the Polar Eskimos the name was originally regarded as a kind of soul which, after the death of a person would take up its abode in a pregnant woman's womb. When the child is born it cries out for a name but only a magician or a 'wise woman', *ilisîtsoq*, must be appealed to, and his or her helping spirits say what the child's name is to be (Rasmussen 1908: 116).

The soul among the Angmagsaliks is described by Holm (1888: 112) as small, not bigger than a finger or a hand. The soul can become ill and die and so the person will become ill and die. The soul can also be stolen by an *angakkoq* or *ilisiitsoq*. The person will then have a heavy head and will become ill. It is the task of the *angakkoq* to retrieve it either from the underworld or from the people living inland. It can also have been eaten by another *angakkoq's* helping spirit.

The concept of the soul varies within the same area. The catechist Hanserâk, who followed Holm on his expedition, writes in his diary: 'A human being has many souls. The biggest are situated in the larynx and the left side of a person and are tiny people the size of a sparrow. The other souls are situated in all the person's other limbs and are the size of a joint of a finger' (1933: 116 [my translation]).[66] Hanserâk then continues to state the same fact that a stolen soul makes a human ill and might cause death. A Polar Eskimo describes the soul in the following way: 'The soul is what makes you beautiful, makes you a man. It is that alone that makes you act and be busy. It is what directs your whole life; and therefore the body must collapse, when the soul leaves it' (Rasmussen 1908: 106).

The *angakkoq* is a retriever of souls, and thereby a healer, a giver of names, a mediator between the spirits and the community and a judge of transgressions of the rules of taboo. He has to be good at his job because he is holding the welfare of individuals and the society as a whole in his hands. He must have overcome fear of the spirits and of death to journey to the bottom of the sea to encounter the Mother of the Sea or to the land of the dead. He is therefore also feared as he can turn precisely those same skills against society as a whole or against single individuals.

One of the most famous accounts of a séance among Greenlanders is made by Holm. It is important to bear in mind that the East Greenlandic community had been more or less isolated until Holm's arrival in the early 1880s. This description is thus presented in full as it represents a first-hand account of a séance by an observer with no apparent agenda of his own. Holm explains that when the séance takes place in the house, the *angakkoq* sits with his feet resting on the lower part of the dry skin in front of the entry. The arms are bound so hard that sometimes wounds are created round the wrists. His head is placed between his legs and a thong is tied round it and, according to the *angakkoq's* account, he then experiences a sense of light. The drum with the drumstick is placed next to the *angakkoq* and is used by the *tartok*[67] during the séance. The drum sometimes dances round the head of the *angakkoq*. The less skilled *angakkut*[68] are not tied but summon the *tartok* and get the drum to dance by hitting a piece of seal-skin.

After an hour's waiting, during which the Angakok lay quite calmly in darkness behind the platform, everything was made ready. New, bone-dry watertight skin was hung at the house doorway, other skins over the window above the door, whereas the other windows were not covered, at any rate not the one opposite which we were sitting. After the floor round the passage had been carefully swept and rubbed, and all dirt removed between the floor stones, a double-layered skin with the hair on was placed carefully in front of the door-curtain. A large flat stone was laid to the right of the door to cover hollows in the floor-stones. After the drum had been wetted it was placed with the drumstick on the flat stone. A long seal-thong with the hair on was then softened very carefully by means of rubbing, stretching etc.

Finally, *Sanimuinaq* came forward. He walked as in a dream, almost martyr-like, looking neither to the right or the left, and sat down on the skin on the floor. The flat stone and drum he placed very meticulously. His hair was bound at the back and a thong was pressed down over his forehead. The man who had pressed the thong down now pinioned the Angakok with it from the hands up to the elbows and pulled it so tight that the hands became quite blue. During this process the Angakok was puffing and groaning as if he succumbed to a great power. When he noticed that I was watching the lashing of his arms carefully, he said to me in a pitiful voice, that I could see for myself that it would be impossible for him to loosen them. I was shown a seat on a skin on the floor, where it was the coolest to sit, while all the others gradually crawled up on the platform. The lamps were then put out, first the one which was the furthest to the left of the Angakok, then the next in the line and finally the one furthest to the right was extinguished.

Immediately the spirits were invoked with the cries: '*Goi! goi goi goi*'– now one voice, now more, sometimes from one end of the house sometimes from another. During this the Angakok grunted, puffed and sighed loudly. Suddenly, the skin at the door started to rustle as if it was moved by a strong wind. The drum began to beat first slowly then gradually more rapidly. All kinds of noise and racket followed: rattling, swishing, clattering sounds. Sometimes like the noise in a machinery workshop, sometimes like locomotives,[69] and again as of large flying beings. During the most terrible noise the platform and the window-sill were sometimes shaken. Now the Angakok was heard lying under a heavy superior force, groaning, wailing, screaming, whining, whispering, now the spirits were heard some of whom had coarse, others tiny, others lisping or whistling, voices. Often a demoniacal, screeching, mocking laughter was heard. The voices sometimes came from above, sometimes from under the ground, now from one end of the house, now from the other, now outside the house or in the entrance passage. Cries of: '*hoi! hoi! hoi!*' faded away as if into the remotest abyss. With immense skill the drum was beaten, often moving round in the house, and especially hovering above my head. The drum often accompanied singing, which at times was subdued as if coming from the underworld. Beautiful singing by women sometimes came from the background. After a deafening, clattering and swishing noise everything suddenly became quiet, and then in came the fearsome monster *Amórtortoq*. It has, as mentioned, black arms, and whoever it touches becomes black and must die. It went with heavy steps about the house and on the platform and roared: '*a–mo! a–mo!*' Everybody fled to the farthermost corner of the platform for fear that the monster should touch one of them. It was particularly lingering round me, roared at me in the ears and tried to pull the skin on which I was sitting away as if to get me up in the corner with the others, but it succeeded only in tearing the skin. After this spirit another came which screamed like a fox. One of the *Tartoks* expressed that it smelled as if there were *Kavdlunaks*[70] present and made very careful inquiries about us. Apart from that nothing was understood of the spirit language. (1888: 124-6 [my translation])

At this point the host, *Kutuluk*, no doubt 'prompted' by the *tartok*, asks Holm whether he is tired. As the séance has lasted about an hour, Holm admits that he is. The *tartok* then starts to retreat and after a while somebody asks if the lamps can be lit, but *Sanimuinak* answers that the *tartok* is still present. The drum is not heard any more and it was thought that the *tartok* had left.

> Soon the drum started again, and the retirement proceeded to the rattling of skins and the dying away of the singing. The lamps were lit in the opposite order to that in which they had been extinguished, and everybody sat as before the performance. The Angakok sat bathed in sweat in the same place as at the beginning. His hands were still bound behind him in the same fashion as before but not nearly as thoroughly. (Ibid.: 126)

Holm's detailed description gives an insight into the effects of the *angakkoq*. The careful cleaning and preparation of the house, the binding of the *angakkoq* so as to show that he is not the manipulator but that his *tartok* is the actual agent, the silent waiting before the storm of noises and voices, the frightening arrival of the monster; all obviously is meant to create an atmosphere of awe and fear. The *angakkoq* is the master of the events and his word is the law as the *tartok* ultimately is at his service. This description does not contain details of travel but is more focused on the actual dramatic effects involved in the séance.[71]

The description of Sagdloq's seance earlier in this chapter is different in two major aspects: the *angakkoq* is alone in the house and it is broad daylight. Compared with the East Greenlandic *angakkoq* the

> Polar Eskimo magicians are exceedingly gentle and make but little ado. They themselves say that all the great ones are dead. Once upon a time it was customary among them, too, to fly up to the heaven and down to the bottom of the sea in a soul flight; a magician could take off his own skin and draw it on again, and in the hearing of many people the spirits could assemble, when the lamps were extinguished, just as on the East

coast. Now this magic art is dead together with the old men; the last of them was Sagdloq. (Rasmussen 1908: 149)

This description of the old kind of séance is given by a Polar Eskimo, who states that 'now, as before, they are the masters of their helping spirits':

> When an Angákoq becomes 'inspired,' he groans, as if he was near fainting, begins to tremble all over from head to foot, and then suddenly springs out on the floor and strikes up a monotonous spirit-song, to a text which he improvises to fit the special case that he has to treat. He sings the chant loudly and more loudly, and gradually, as the conjuration progresses, he grows more and more unrestrained in his antics and his cries. He sighs and groans, as if invisible powers were pulling at him, and he often makes it appear as if he were being vanquished by a stronger power. But further than this, the auditors see nothing of the spirits. The angákut themselves declare that they suffer agonies in every limb while the spirits communicate their prophecies to them. And, during the song, which is accompanied by beats on a little round drum, they sometimes work themselves up into a peculiar state of ecstasy, during which, with their closed eyes, long floating hair, and anguished expression, they sometimes produce an overwhelming effect on their auditors. (Ibid.: 150)

The drumming and the sound effects are obviously identical but the *angakkoq* of the Polar Eskimos is apparently not tied as is the custom both on the east coast and on the west coast of Greenland.[72] Trance is alluded to as something induced by the singing and drumming but to create the sound effects one would imagine that a light trance was induced. The way of inducing such a trance by controlling the breath is described in the attempt of the great *angakkoq*, Mitsuarnianga, to commit suicide by using this technique after suffering the loss of his wife and in deep pain from a knee wound. His son Kârale Andreassen experienced the attempt as a young boy:

> 'Listen my son, you must not get afraid, when I try to leave my body, I am tired of suffering so much. When it is possible I will tell you first, before I leave my body for good.' As he said this he started to diminish his breathing like during a séance, lowering his voice more and more until it could only be heard at the solar plexus, and there it rested for some time. During this he was still breathing lightly with long intervals. Suddenly his spirit left his body (a faint humming sound was heard) and then he stopped breathing. The sound moved deep, deep down and then started to wander

in different directions; sometimes by the house entrance, sometimes at the opposite side of the house. After having circled like this it gradually became clearer, as if it was spiralling upwards and at last it was heard at the solar plexus, and the breath had returned. (1935: 108ff [my translation])

The father does not succeed in his attempt and is later converted to Christianity.[73] The description of the breathing technique is revealing for the skills of the *angakkoq* in connection with persuading the audience in the séance of the presence of spirits.[74] It also underlines the belief by the *angakkoq* in his powers even over his own death.

The influence of the new culture on that of the East Greenlanders is well described in Therkel Mathiassen's account of the performance of Salomon, the grandson of the great *angakkoq* Avgo, who

held a séance with lamps extinguished and for two hours filled the air with the most remarkable sounds, knocking, drumming, singing, screaming, wheezing, howling, hissing, and distorted speech – and then when the lamps were lighted and a company of about seventy people in cotton anoraks, woollen sweaters, and cloth trousers roared with laughter at Salomon's weirdly amusing performance, and he demanded a packet of rolled oats as his fee – certainly, the old days have gone for ever in Angmassalik. (1933: 144)

Travels

An important part of the séance is that it instigates the *angakkoq's* travels with his helping spirits on behalf of his society. This is mostly done in a deeper trance, where the *angakkoq* is oblivious to physical reality (Merkur 1985: 110, Bäckman and Hultkranz 1978: 95ff) The three main areas he is travelling to are the realm of the Mother of the Sea, The Moon Spirit and the Land of the Dead.

It is a difficult task to travel to the Mother of the Sea and it demands courage and knowledge from the *angakkoq*. There are different accounts of the level of danger involved in this undertaking, but the *angakkoq* and his helping spirits are the only ones who can approach her. In Hans Egede's description the *angakkoq* and his helping spirits first have to pass through the 'mansion of all the souls of the deceased, which look as well, if not better, than ever they did in this world, and want for nothing'

(1818: 203). The *angakkoq* and his helping spirit then continue the journey which takes them to

> a very long, broad and deep whirlpool, which they are to cross over, there being nothing to pass upon but a great wheel like ice, which turns about with a surprising rapidity, and by the means of this wheel the spirit helps his angekkok to get over. This difficulty surmounted, the next thing they encounter is a large kettle, in which live seals are put to be boiled; and at last they arrive, with much ado, at the residence of the devil's granddame, where the familiar spirit takes the angekkok by the hand through the strong guard of sea dogs. The entry is large enough, the road that leads is as narrow as a small rope, and on both sides nothing to lay hold on, or to support one; beside that, there is underneath a most frightful abyss or bottomless pit.[75] Within this is the apartment of the infernal goddess, who offended at this unexpected visit, shows a most ghastly and wrathful countenance, pulling the hair off her head: she thereupon seizes a wet wing of a fowl, which she lights in the fire, and claps to their noses, which makes them very faint and sick, and they become her prisoners. But the enchanter or angekkok (being beforehand instructed by his Torngak, how to act his part in this dismal expedition) takes hold of her by the hair, and drubs and bangs her so long, till she loses her strength and yields; and in this combat his familiar spirit does not stand idle, but lays about her with might and main. (Ibid.: 203ff)

The *angakkoq* then gets hold of the *aglerrutit*, a piece of material that a woman has aborted on and is therefore clearly unclean, and by this frees all the animals so that they can be caught by the Greenlanders. The return journey is smooth and a proud *angakkoq* with his *Torngak* makes an easy journey back. Sitting waiting for him are his fellow-men awaiting the result of his journey. Sometimes they are taken to task for having transgressed the taboo rules and have therefore caused the Mother of the Sea to withhold the game, but nevertheless they know what dangers the *angakkoq* has faced on their behalf and they appreciate it. As can be seen from the above description of the journey, an *angakkoq* without his auxiliaries would be in grave trouble. He is encountering dangerous challenges en route and only through his courage can he venture on and complete his task. If he fails, it might mean famine and the likelihood of death for the waiting audience.

In this west coast version of the journey by Hans Egede, the relationship between the *angakkoq* and The Mother of the Sea is one of battle. The *angakkoq* has to prove himself stronger than her and there are no comforting elements. The spirit and the *angakkoq* are at war over the ownership of game. No sacrifice is being made, no combing of hair, it is a mere combat of strength. The helping spirit takes an active part in this battle and the *angakkoq* has to rely on this spirit to be able to help him both on the journey and in the encounter.[76]

On the east coast this encounter is described slightly differently by Rasmussen. The journey is so dangerous that only a highly-trained *angakkoq* could undertake it. Having survived the dangers similar to those described by the Egedes on the west coast he says:

> The shaman arrived at the house of the great woman, and there it was their real difficulties began; the road into the house was as sharp as a knife edge, and on both sides was deep sea with strong currents and heavy swells. The entrance-passage was not always open, but was in constant motion, opening and closing, and when the walls met, the whole house shivered. Inside the house the shaman could hear the furious woman scolding. There he would stand at a loss, not knowing what he should do; even the helping spirits did not know; but after some hesitation he let himself slide inwards just as the passage opened, and heard the woman cry: 'Who dares come here, where he has no business to be; perhaps he thinks that I will allow him to live!' The shaman now balanced himself along the sharp edge with his helping spirits after him, and, on entering the house saw a woman on her platform; she was all covered with dirt, and her hair was matted together with filth. The moment he entered she seized him, and they fought; she was very strong, and he would have been unable to manage had his helping spirits not come to his assistance. At length they got the better of her, and started to wash the squirming woman, afterwards combing her hair, which was a difficult task, for the hair was all entangled. Thus they worked with her and tried to soothe her, and they removed the dirt and straightened her hair. When this was done the woman became quite different; now her face was one big smile, and she said: You are welcome, and with what can I pay you? (1938: 127)

She then removes her lamp and all the game pours out. The *angakkoq* makes his way back and the return journey is easy. There are clear similarities in the trials of the east coast *angakkoq* with those of the west coast *angakkoq* but the attitude to the spirit is different. On the east coast the encounters result after a fight in a friendly exchange of services and the *angakkoq* and The Mother of the Sea form a good relationship. The Mother of the Sea donates the game to the settlement because of the caring treatment rendered by the *angakkoq*.[77] No doubt the west coast description by the Egede family is coloured by their attitude to the role of the spirits as representatives of negative forces and the battle therefore emphasised.[78]

Travelling to the Mother of the Sea is, as has been shown, one of the most dangerous and important journeys undertaken by the *angakkoq*. Although the versions differ the concept of danger is predominant. A similar dangerous journey has to be undertaken to the Moon Spirit/The Moon Man mainly to deal with the fertility of the society. Rüttel describes this journey in his diary. It started at dusk from the settlement of the *angakkoq* down to the sea and from there to the beginning of the sky where there again is land and stone. After walking for a while there is a byway that leads to a star, where the man,[79] who tears out the entrails of the people he can catch, lives. He is not worth a visit and the *angakkoq* therefore stays on the Moon road. On that he encounters three dangerous crevices, that the *angakkoq* easily passes as he is floating over the soil and only touches it now and then. After passing the evil star man and the stilts on which the sledge of the Moon Man rests the *angakkoq* reaches the Moon Man himself. The journey lasts all night until dawn (1917: 39).

The other travelling he has to perform is the journey to the Land of the Dead, to make contact with the deceased or to bring back souls which have gone astray. According to Helms (1868: 95), the concept of life after death among the Greenlanders on the west coast is not altogether clear. Some believe that the good, that is the skilled hunters, come to the land of bliss or of the souls, which is situated deep down under the bottom of the sea, the entrance to which is found in some big holes in the cliff. Here *toornaarsuk* and his mother live in eternal summer with eternal sunshine. There is plenty of water and game, but before the good souls can arrive in this land they have to fight for five days outside a steep cliff. The cliff is very bloody as the battle is tough. It is therefore worse to die during the winter. The bad, that is, evil hunters, witches and such like go to the sky, where there is great need of food, which is connected with the constant movement of the sky, resulting in the souls being famished and becoming pale and feeble. But other Greenlanders believe that the land of bliss is situated in the sky and the good souls enter there instantly after death. Here one is entertained with dance, game and hunting.[80]

The two versions of belief in the role of the sky in the afterlife might indicate the influence that Christianity has had on the interpretation of the place of the dead as being that of the sky.[81] Teemiartissaq, Thalbitzer's informant (1923: 459ff), describes how she encounters her brother in the land of the dead. This is situated under the earth and she has to travel with the assistance of her helping spirits through the ocean. The original concept of the land of the dead was probably situated at the bottom of the sea, in close contact with the game and the Mother of the Sea; the reversal of this concept must, it is submitted, be due to the influence of the missionaries.

The *angakkoq* has to travel to get contact with the spirits and the souls of the dead. The descriptions of the séances show, however, that he just as often summons spirits to his abode and deals with them in the séance as such, where the attentive audience in the darkness can hear their presence. Travelling is important when dealing with major problems but the summoning of spirits is equally so. The interesting aspect of the travelling is that it shows the power of the *angakkoq* over angry or evil forces and the strength of his helping spirits in assisting him.

Healing

Disease may be interpreted as being caused by the soul leaving the body or something alien penetrating the patient. The soul can either be stolen by an *angakkoq*, or simply go astray, or it can be in the land of the dead. If the latter is the case, a full séance is necessary as a journey has to take place. It is then the task of the *angakkoq* to restore the soul to the patient, or even change it, when the damage to the soul is beyond cure. They might use the healthy souls of animals or even those of young children (Crantz 1820: 185).

Hans Egede gives a detailed account of a healing event in 1723. He had arrived two years earlier in Greenland and was still not fully familiar with the language:

> The 'Hexen Mester', the witch-doctor, lay down on his back on the ill person's bed, as if he were dead and gone. Then the [*angakkoq's*] head was lifted by the woman of the ill person with a small stick; sometimes he let

his head be lifted easily, sometimes he made it heavy and stiff, so that she could not move it, and every time she lifted his head she asked him several questions with great sincerity, and as if in deep thought, which I could not understand, but when being spoken to he sometimes answered her with one word or two, sometimes not at all; in the end he began to mumble and sing and sometimes to scream and shout. (1925: 107 [my translation])

According to Hans Egede this procedure lasted about an hour and the sick person sat on the bench, his clothes placed on the floor. When he asked for an explanation, Hans Egede was informed that this was to heal the patient. He punished[82] the speaker and said, that they ought not to believe in this. This did not work, however, for the next evening they continued the procedure.

It does not always have to be a fully trained *angakkoq* who undertakes this healing procedure. Hans Egede is told by a man of a healing ceremony performed by a woman. She is curing a man's foot: 'She sat down and mumbled and witch-doctored over his leg, and sucked for a long time until she achieved a hole and out of the leg she took some pieces of fur and entrails, and no blood or matter came out, but the foot was instantly whole again as before, so that you could not see anything on it' (Ibid.: 205).

The man claims that this is the truth as he and others witnessed it. Such a cure is what their *angakkut* and wise men often perform. This naturally challenges Hans Egede, and he visits the woman and asks her to perform for him. At first she is not willing, scared of the consequences, but as Egede promises to pay her well, she comes to him with several neighbours: 'I let therefore the patient come forward, whom she ordered to sit on the floor, then she took hold of his leg, blew on it, mumbled and witch-doctored over it, and used strange movements, lay face down on the foot and sucked on it' (Ibid.: 206). Hans Egede keeps an eye on her and exposes her, as she is about to suck out the entrails. He beats her up and tells the others what she has done. They leave shamefacedly. Hans Egede has obviously no respect for their skills and comments: 'You can from this understand what sort of witchcraft the Greenlanders perform, it is pure imagination, without any result and effect, and all the same the stupid people are so gullible that they do not at all examine the deceitful art of their angakut, although nothing results from it' (Ibid.: 206).

Hans Egede later comments on the ceremony he describes here, by now wiser about the actual communication going on while the curing takes place. Describing the lifting of the head, the sick person is on the bed instead of the *angakkoq*:

> At times they use this way of curing the sick; they lay him upon his back, and tie a ribbon, or a string, round his head, having a stick fastened to the other end of the string, with which they lift up the sick person's head from the ground, and let it down again; and at every lift he communes with his Torgak, or familiar spirit, about the state of the patient, whether he shall recover or not; now, if his head is heavy in lifting it, it is with them a sign of death; if light, of recovery.[83] Notwithstanding all this, I am loth to believe, that, in these spells and conjurings, there is any real commerce with the devil; for to me it clearly appears, that there is nothing in it but mere fibs, juggling tricks, and impostures, made use of by these crafty fellows for the sake of filthy lucre, for they are well paid for their pains.(1818: 193-4)

The *angakkoq's* role in this healing ceremony is in this description that of a head-lifter, not as a substitute for the sick person lying on the bed. As the heavy head results in death, one would imagine that the patient would do his utmost to make the head light. The *angakkoq* therefore must perform the lift according to his expectation. As they are well paid the success rate in foretelling death or life must be convincing or the *angakkoq* would not be performing at all.

Lars Dalager observes how the healing process is performed on the west coast. If a Greenlander becomes ill he is carefully nursed and if not old the best *angakkoq* will be called for. If he, according to his experience, does not see the illness as severe, he will sit and talk to the patient about other people who had similar diseases and got well the next day. 'Such discussion often had an excellent impact on the patient, and one can say, that these angakut in this way imitate wise doctors, that are curing as much with talk as with pills and other kinds of medicine' (1752: 38 [my translation]). The *angakkoq* is often positive about the ill person's condition and gives the person hope; 'if he is reproached about this, he excuses himself that he did not understand his Torngak [helping-spirit] differently.' If the ill person is important, however, a séance will be established, which is different from the ordinary séance in that no lamps are extinguished, no window is covered and the *angakkoq* is not tied. He instead goes into a trance, the drum beating lightly. The conversation is then centred round happiness in the other world. 'Poor and people of low status and most women have to suffice with an ordinary witch-doctor 'Hexe-mester', or with the conjuring tricks of a witch' (Ibid.: 39).

When a father of an ill boy seeks help with a famous *angakkoq* and is told there is no hope, the father then asks the *angakkoq* whether he ought to seek the advice of the priest. The *angakkoq* answers: 'You can make up your own mind, as I think that the word of God and a sensible angakok has equal strength' (Ibid.: 40).

Hans Egede is obviously not convinced of the skills of the *angakkoq*, but neither is he prepared to ascribe it to the doings of the Devil. He sees them as exploiters of the credulity of the people; 'though they apply such remedies as have not virtue in them to cure, such as muttering of spells, and blowing upon the sick bodies;[84] wherein they resemble to a hair those conjurers of which the prophet Isaiah speaks, chapter viii, verse 19' (1818: 193). Hans Egede himself is seen as an *angakkoq*, and women who are barren will come to him to have him blow on their stomachs, as they risk losing their husband, if they cannot have children (1925: 293). The belief in the curing skills of *angakkut* is strong and Hans Egede faces defeat when one of the converts, a friend of his son, is persuaded to use an *angakkoq*, when he is very ill (Ibid.: 289). The sons of Hans Egede, Poul and Niels give, as mentioned earlier, several accounts of how the restoring or stealing of souls is attributed to the skills of the *angakkoq*. As soul and life are interconnected the power of life and death is, therefore, in the hands of the *angakkoq*.

Among the East Greenlanders, Holm describes the healing skills of the *angakkoq* in the following way:

> He does not function as a doctor as he does not know one single remedy nor can give any advice against illness or perform any operations, but during the performance he examines the soul of the ill person. All illnesses it is believed are due to the soul being damaged or stolen by a *Ilisitsok* or Angekok, or somehow disappeared. That is why it is the task of the Angekok to see where it is and to bring it back. His *Tartok* tells him the reason why a person is ill whether the soul is hurt or stolen. The Angekok then has to travel to the lower world or the horizon to get the soul back. Sometimes he only sends one of his *Tartoks* to retrieve it and in that case it can take several days, before the *Tartok* comes back. If the soul has been badly damaged, if it has been eaten by the *Tornarsuk* of a hostile Angekok then the person must die. (1888: 130 [my translation])

There is no description of head-lifting but instead the *angakkoq* or his *Tartok*, his helping spirit, is performing a journey.[85] The verdict is given after the travelling. In addition, the inability to catch seals or of women to have children is viewed as a disease. To cure the latter the *angakkoq* has to travel to the moon from where a child is thrown to the woman. After this performance, the *angakkoq* has the right to sleep with the woman. To be certain that the cure will work the *angakkoq* has to be paid handsomely, the payment being assessed according to the wealth of the giver. Holm mentions that Sanimuinak[86] has been paid a sledge, a dog, the point of a harpoon made of narwhale-tooth, a handful of pearls and so forth. According to Holm, Sanimuinak laughed at the gullibility of the people when he talked about it (Ibid.: 131).

From Thalbitzer's informant, Teemiartissaq,[87] in East Greenland, we know that, as a child, she wanted to learn the skills of a *qilaleq*, as she is very poor. The female healer is called a *qilaleq* and the *qila* is the subterranean assistant spirit. She therefore starts with head-lifting investigations. By the help of the spirit, she is able to tell whether a person is about to lose his soul. She then sends her assistant spirit for the soul or the part of the soul, which has been lost. The *qilaleq* can also blow on a sick person who suddenly begins to die (1923: 465).

As Teemiartissaq never became a fully educated *angakkoq* it shows that it is not only the *angakkoq* who can heal, but also skilled women (as is also seen in Hans Egede's description). As I have not discovered descriptions of séances performed by women, the healing skills might have been applied especially to women who were not functioning as *angakkut* but who could achieve healing by the assistance of a helping spirit. The term *qilaleq*[88] might cover just that skill. The reason given by Teemiartissaq for starting the curing procedure is that she is poor. The gifts connected with the skill are obviously attractive.

Rasmussen describes the healing role of the East Greenlandic *angakkoq*:

> When a person fell ill, the shaman could seek advice about it by creeping up on the platform and placing himself with his back to the room, covered with skins and with skins under him. There he sat silent and pondering, with no drum, sunk in deep thought, as if transported to the spirit world. In this state, or during this silent invocation of the spirits it was revealed to him that the sick person's soul had been stolen, and where it was, and who had stolen it. In most cases it was an ilisitsoq, a troll-woman, who had done it. At the request of the family the shaman would then promise to get the soul back again, but it could only be done if the family observed certain restrictions and held a diet. This diet might vary in the most

curious way. For example, one was not to eat *tajarneq*, the forearm of seals, another the *kujak*, the loin, a third the *kiasik*, the shoulder, and so on. If a sick person whom the shaman had promised to cure did not get better, it was not the shaman's fault; the family was to blame, for he would insist that they had not observed the conditions. (1938: 102)

The head-lifting is not mentioned here either, so it might be the case that this specific healing procedure was not done in the actual séance by the *angakkoq*. The mentioning of the *ilisiitsoq* as the stealer of souls has its parallel in West Greenland, as mentioned above. The imposing of injunctions on the family of the ill person can be seen as a safeguard on behalf of the *angakkoq* against failure. The death of a person can then be ascribed to transgression of these. As there has been no mention of this in the healing procedures previously described it might be connected with the séance.[89]

Severe illness is ascribed to soul loss. The soul might have gone astray or been stolen by an *angakkoq* or an *ilisiitsoq*. Illness can, however, also be self-induced. In *Ujuâts dagbog* a woman who is seriously ill confesses to having created a *tupilak* and the illness is therefore seen as a result of her evil intentions (Petersen 1957: 48).[90] As has been seen from the description of the healing procedure, the head-lifting and blood-sucking or blowing can be used outside the séance and by lay persons, often women, who have the skill of healing. The séance is used to invoke spirits who together with the *angakkoq* might travel and retrieve the soul of the sick person from the other-world. There might be a set of prescriptions that the patient or his family have to follow to achieve health. The whole healing procedure is aimed at restoring the health of the ill person by magic. Little is done in the nature of using remedies, except the injunctions in connection with food. The procedure is purely of a psychomental character.

The Concept of the 'Witch'

It is difficult to use the term 'witch' without conjuring up the entire gamut of European witchcraft connotations. The European version of the witch can be seen as mostly a reflection of Christianity, perhaps even as a construction of the Christian church. Although the witch in the Greenlandic understanding of the word has traits in common with the European witch, it is not sufficient to apply this concept without having scrutinised closely the function of the term within the Greenlandic belief system.

The Egede family constantly use the word 'Hexe Mester' for the *angakkoq* which obviously is directly related to the Christian concept of witchcraft, as Hans, Poul and Niels Egede functioned as missionaries in West Greenland. In their view the séance and the conjuring up of spirits is a deed of heresy and therefore has to be extinguished through a punishment system and that, as has been shown, can be of a severely corporal nature. They are literally trying to beat the *angakkut* into giving up their belief in spirits and adhering to the Christian belief system. Using the term 'Hexe Mester' will therefore indicate that the interaction between the *angakkoq* and the spirit is similar to the relationship between the witch and the Devil.[91] It is an understandable deduction, although Hans Egede is reluctant to condemn the Greenlanders as devil-worshippers, instead they are seen as victims of the work of the Devil: 'it cannot be denied, but that the evil spirit has a hand in all this, and is the chief actor upon this stage, to keep these poor wretches in their chains, and hinder them from coming to the true knowledge of God' (Hans Egede 1818: 194).

Among the Greenlanders themselves the *angakkoq* is obviously not seen as a 'witch' in the European sense as they do not have a concept of the Devil. They have on the other hand a name, *ilisiitsoq*, plur. *ilisiitsut*, for evil-minded people, often women, who bring misfortune and death on their fellow men. Birket-Smith gives a description of so-called witchcraft in Greenlandic society:

> Witchcraft was looked upon as an action directed against the community at large, and perhaps the most abominable practice imaginable, because people to a certain extent were defenceless against it. As a rule the lot of the offender was death, and the dead body was generally cut into small pieces, in order to prevent it from haunting the survivors. A 'lawful murder' of this kind, however, must not eo ipso be looked upon as a judicial act. This appears, for one thing, from the circumstances that the community was not organized as such, and for another from the fact that an actual crime was not always necessary in order to call forth such an act of the community, since it might also take action against a man with a fierce forbidding character, or against invalids and troublesome persons. (1924: 139)[92]

Hans Egede states that the *angakkut* are held in great honour, and are seen by the Greenlanders to serve the interests of society and are well rewarded for this:

> But, on the contrary, there is another sort of conjurers or sorcerers, especially some decrepit old women, which they call illiseersut, or witches, who persuade themselves and others, that by the virtue of their spells and witchcraft they can hurt people in their life and goods. These are not upon the same footing with the angekkuts; for as soon as any one incurs only suspicion of such demeanour, he or she is hated and detested by everybody, and at last made away with, without mercy, as a plague to mankind, and not deemed worthy to live. (1818: 192)[93]

Hans Egede Saabye, the grandson of Hans Egede, worked as a missionary in West Greenland and wrote the following account of his experiences with *ilisiitsut*. Among his flock Egede Saabye had an old widow, who had fled from the south because she was accused there of being a witch. According to Egede Saabye she was accused by a man, to whom she had given shelter and the use of her *konebåd*, the women's-boat, if he would repair it for her. The man kept this obligation in the beginning but later wished to become the owner of the boat. He then accused her of being a witch and she fled with an ill eight- to nine-year-old girl seeking shelter at a married merchant's house at Christianshåb. Egede Saabye heard about her situation and wished to baptise her. The merchant was against it as he was afraid of the problems it might cause with the people in the south. He pointed out that if she was killed as a baptised person it might create antagonism. Egede Saabye decided to baptise her all the same but was visited in his office by her enemies before this act. He was asked if he intended to baptise her and as he confirmed it, he was told 'She is no good, she is an Illiseetsok' (1942: 20 [my translation]).[94] Egede Saabye was not deterred but answered that the *angakkoq* was a liar and that he was prepared to defend the woman, as he did not believe she had committed any offence. After having baptised her he hid her in his office. Later travelling with her he was again challenged by her enemies in a boat, but as Egede Saabye explains: 'Here there was need for some courage, and I got it' (Ibid.: 21). They decided to withdraw.

Egede Saabye later experienced an old man coming to his office, happily hearing about Christmas, and a few hours later he was killed as an *ilisiitsoq*. His son came to the colony with his wife, because he would not live among the people who had killed his father. Egede Saabye talked in a severe way about this murder but he got the answer that in his country they also killed evil people. Although Egede Saabye answered that that did not happen until one was certain that they really were evil, the Greenlanders replied: 'You do kill the evil, and so do we; those that we kill, are evil, that we do understand better than you, priest' (Ibid.: 56).

Egede Saabye gives a description of the 'trial' of the *ilisiitsoq*. The accused was called out of his house or tent with a voice which proclaimed his death: 'Are you an Illiseetsok? Have you killed this person with your words and your evil?' (Ibid.: 56).[95] Regardless of whether the person answered 'yes' or 'no' out of mere fear of death, he was knifed and torn apart and each person ate a part of his heart so that he would not haunt them.

Egede Saabye seems to have experienced quite a fair share of 'witchcraft'. He describes how it was believed that if someone who was accused of being a witch died a natural death this person was incapable of resting peacefully in the grave. Next to Egede Saabye's dwelling was the grave of a woman thought to be an *ilisiitsoq*. The dogs got to the grave, dug her body out from under the stones, and tore off one leg. This was seen as a proof of her restlessness. Egede Saabye recovered the leg and buried it again. The people of the community concluded that he did not believe what they said (Ibid.: 59).

The missionaries must have seen these people condemned as *ilisiitsut* as the victims of aggression either caused by their own difficult personality or by the ill-will of fellow-men, greed being one reason for victimising a vulnerable member of society. It was often the old women or men who had difficulty in protecting themselves and were easily killed. Their murder brings a sense of power over evil forces or ill luck and is seen as an acceptable deed on behalf of society. As they, however, are seen as the creators of destruction they are inducing fear: 'The Ilisîsut-witches take clothes away from their fellow human beings and create a monster [probably a *tupilak*] that kills the owner that the witches hate; when the *angakkut* sees a witch that kills in this way they are afraid to say anything to that person fearing to be killed themselves' (Hanserâk 1933: 97 [my translation]).

In the séance the *angakkoq* might determine who is an *ilisiitsoq*. Crantz describes the work of the *ilisiitsut* as follows:

They will also cite the soul of a man, whom they wish to injure, to appear before them in the dark, and wound it with a spear, upon which their enemy must consume away by a slow disease. The company present will pretend to recognise the man by his voice. Such malevolent wizards as pride themselves most upon their power of doing mischief, are called *Illiseetsok*. Many old hags, who have no other chance of supporting themselves, likewise carry on this profession. They are particularly skillful in sucking out of a swelled leg, lumps of hair, and scraps of leather, with which they have previously filled their mouth. (1820: 198)

Old persons are tempted to improve on their miserable living by doctoring, but the failed treatments rebound upon them, and they are killed as evil-doers. The *angakkoq* revenges himself on a person by wounding him through magic, and thus causing him to die, but the *angakkoq* himself might be killed. The society has its system of retaliation for misfortune and death. The performer might be called an *ilisiitsoq,* he/she might be successful and his work prosperous. He might, on the other hand, cause harm and die. The term *ilisiitsoq* can be seen as covering the wise old woman and man, who deals with illness, receives the gifts and risks his or her life, because they become the focal point for the aggression of society. Dealing as they do with the healing of others, this undertaking can be compared with the concept in European witchcraft of the wise person who might be seen as being in contact with the Devil although he also practices healing.

According to Holm, an apprentice who, after the time the apprenticeship is over, does not declare himself as a full-blown *angakkoq*, will have to try to become an *ilisiitsoq*, who is feared and hated. The time of learning is about six years. Where the *angakkut* can learn by grinding the stone, the *ilisiitsoq* has to learn from an older *ilisiitsoq* and pay handsomely. The most important skill is the creation of the *tupilak* which kills the people against whom it is sent. The *tupilak* is made from parts of animals and part of the clothing of the man against whom it is going to be sent. It is brought to life through the chant of a magic song and, in order to grow, it sucks the *ilisiitsoq's* genitals. When this is happening the *ilisiitsoq* turns his anorak back to front and takes the hood up in front of his face. The *tupilak* is a manifestation of an evil will and is meant to kill the person it is sent against, when it is placed into a stream leading out into the sea. The *ilisiitsoq* has several means of killing and it is the task of the *angakkoq* to catch the *tupilak*.

Either the angakok's Tornarsuk eats them, or, if the angakok has a falcon
as his Tartok, it can catch them. When in the séance people hear the
Tupilek in the passage of the house walking up and down, they become
very scared because if it touches a human being, that person will die.
Normally the angakok stabs it in the entrance of the house and people
can next day see the blood stain. (Holm 1888: 136 [my translation])

The *ilisiitsoq* has several means of magic at his disposal. He
might create a snare out of a dead person's sinews, arrange it round
a knee-cap and stick a human rib on either side, pulling the snare.
He only has to mention the name of the man, and he will die. With
a capacity of killing by magic the *ilisiitsoq* obviously is a threat to
the community and has to be dealt with accordingly. The *angakkoq*
can be the remedy against the evil-doing of the *ilisiitsoq* but he can
also, according to Holm, be an *ilisiitsoq* himself.

He [the *angakkoq*] can be an Ilisitsok without performing the actions;
but if he does, he runs the danger of becoming mad, talking deliriously,
when he becomes ill. If this happens he is bound with his hands and feet
straight on the platform or the floor and gagged. He will get nothing to
eat or drink, and sometimes a big stone is placed on the chest of the ill
person. He will lie like this until he dies. This remedy is so incorporated
in the consciousness of the native that it is used without the presence of
an angakok. Often the torments are shortened as the ill person, after
having been tied up, is thrown into the sea. The only way that a patient
can be freed from this treatment is if he admits that he is an Ilisitsok and
mentions the crimes, either real or imagined, that he has on his
consciences, after which he cannot continue as a Ilisitsok. If he at the
same time is an angakok, he might continue this activity. (Ibid.: 137)

The delirious talk and the confessions might have a revealing
character so that the offences committed against the interest of the
society as a whole find their outlet. The patient being 'cleansed' by
his confessions is simultaneously deprived of his magic power and
neutralised. The society receives an explanation for misfortune and
ill luck and the *angakkoq* treating the sick person receives gifts and
power. If, on the other hand, the patient is not prepared to confess
and continues his delirious talk the remedy is death.

The *ilisiitsoq* is both a healer and a destroyer. In the healing
capacity he or she has traits in common with the European version
of the wise old woman/man, who through her healing might call the
reputation of being a witch upon herself, despite not having actually

performed any rites of a destructive character. In the destroying capacity the *ilisiitsoq* is a person who creates snares or *tupilaks* with the intention of killing and therefore poses a real threat to society; or the accusation of witchcraft might just be used as a means of ridding the society of unwanted members or to settle a personal score.

What is interesting is the closeness this concept of the witch has with other traditional societies. Among the Azande, death is never natural, it is always seen as a result of an act of witchcraft, the accused witch often being unaware of his or her magic powers (Evans-Pritchard 1937: 267). The same seems to be the case in Greenland. In a footnote (1888: 138) Holm adds that he agrees with Rink when he claims that 'when illness or death was unexpected, it was always seen as witchcraft and it is a question whether this has not been the initial explanation for death as such' (1982: 185 [my translation]).

Burial Customs

Death and taboo rules are in Greenland, as everywhere else, inseparable. When a relative dies strict taboo rules have to be observed, leading to complications in the life of the bereaved. Touching a dead body will result in several restrictions on one's behaviour, and to avoid these injunctions a person who is on the brink of dying, or is in grave danger, might not be helped, as the fear of death and the elaborated taboo rules prevent people from rendering assistance.

Holm describes a burial ceremony on the east coast:

> When a person is dead, the body is dressed in its best winter-clothing. The men are dressed in their kajak-fur coats, the hood is drawn over the face, and the fur is tied between the legs. A string of seal is tied around the legs and the body is dragged out through the house passage without any ceremony or if this is too difficult through the window. (1888: 105 [my translation])

This custom seems to be common all over Greenland. According to Holm, if one of the dead person's ancestors has died at sea, his body is thrown into the sea also. If not, it is bent up and placed under stones. The expression of grief consists of wailing, sighing and abstention from food and restrictions derived from taboo rules. The reason given for this is to avoid the anger of the dead person. The family and the other people sharing the house of the deceased have to carry their belongings outside, where they have to lie for three days. They also have to stop using their old clothes and new ones must be made as quickly as possible. Everything that the dead person has possessed except his knives and other valuables, which are kept by the relatives, are thrown away or put in stone-circles. The house dwellers have to mourn for three days; the mother and wife for a whole month, during which they may not work. The name of the deceased must not be mentioned and if two people have the same name the survivor has to change his. If the name is that of an animal this word has to be changed. This rule obviously has an impact on the language which undergoes changes constantly. The name of game and names of places might have to be changed: 'The people called themselves Angmagsalingmiut. The "angmasætter," the capelin, are plentiful in the area. The people do not call the place Angmagsalik any-more, as a man of that name died, but instead *Kersagkat*. The fjord is renamed *Kulusuk* and the inhabitants call themselves *Kulusumiutt*' (Ibid.: 55).

Death is a complication for the society as the dead person can revenge himself on the living if the protective rules are not followed. Among the Polar Eskimos this fear is expressed through taboo rules similar to those found on the east coast. After having buried the dead person, the Polar Eskimos involved in the burial have to stay silent in their houses and are not allowed to take their clothes off at night. When the five days have passed, they have to wash themselves to cleanse off the impurities. All this is performed to avoid the power of the dead person having an impact on the lives of the living:

> We are afraid of the big evil powers which strike down men with disease, and other misfortune. Men must do penitence because in the dead the sap is strong, and their power is without limit. We believe that, if we paid no attention to that over which we ourselves are not master, huge avalanches of stones would come down and crush us, that enormous snowstorms would spring up and destroy us, and that the ocean would rise in huge waves whilst we were in our kajaks far out at sea. (Rasmussen 1921a: 30)

As the body is seen as the abode of the soul and the body itself is mortal and therefore prone to misfortune and illness, 'all that is evil

remains in the body, wherefore one must observe the greatest care
in dealing with the corpse' (Ibid.: 31).

Fear of the evil inhabiting the body which is able to cause havoc
among the living is the reason for the elaborate burial rituals. When
the rituals are observed the living can feel protected against the evil
influence of the dead person.[96] According to Thalbitzer the corpse is
seen to send out corpse vapour: 'The *angakut* says that the surviving
relative of the diseased gets *pujoq* round his head and on his fingers
from the corpse. It is invisible to all others save the *angakut*' (1923:
265). As death is surrounded by fear the *angakkoq's* dealing with
the souls of the dead is of great importance to the society. He is the
mediator between the invisible world of the dead and that of the
living. He is able, with the assistance of his helping spirits, to
control the unpredictable consequences of the retaliation of the
dead, guide the behaviour of the people involved and keep society
from becoming the victim of evil forces. By his ritual death he has
overcome the fear of death and has thereby obtained the power of
handling what is fearsome, fearlessly.

Hans Egede describes the burial customs of the west coast
Eskimos as similar to those mentioned above among the east coast
and the Polar Eskimos. The reason given for the burial of utensils is
that they might remind the living of the dead person and renew their
grief (1818: 150).

The burial customs of the Iglulik Eskimos are described as
follows by John Frederick Dennett: a woman has been dead for
three days and her husband visits the grave site.

> Arriving at the grave, he anxiously walked up to it and carefully sought
> for foot-tracks on the snow but finding none, repeated to himself, 'No
> wolves, no dogs, no foxes, thank ye, thank ye.' He now began a
> conversation which he directed entirely to the grave, as if addressing his
> wife. He called her twice by name, and twice told her how the wind was
> blowing, looking at the same time in the direction from whence the drift
> was coming. He next broke forth into a low monotonous chant, and
> keeping his eyes fixed on the grave, walked slowly round in the direction
> of the sun four or five times, and at each circuit he stopped a few
> moments at the head. His song was, however, uninterrupted. (1837: 114)

The chant of the husband might be seen as a communication with
the dead person before the final departure of the soul, the burial
custom being carefully carried out. The belief that the soul is present

near the grave for five days seems to be a general concept among the Eskimos. The soul will then leave and continue its existence in the Land of the Dead and therefore need its tools and weapons. This interim period is dangerous as evil is believed to reside in the dead body and only the careful observance of taboo rules and the help of the *angakkoq* are the precautions that the living can take against the retaliation and the free force of evil inherent in the body.

Myths and Legends

Helge Larsen writes in his preface to H. Rink's *Eskimoiske Eventyr og Sagn*:

> Rink has been called the founder of the eskimological science, and it can be said that this scientific discipline started with his collection of tales. Although it was not well known or established at the time, Rink had a sense that the oral tradition of the Greenlanders would shed light on the customs of their forefathers, and he was not disappointed. In their tales he found a rich source of information about their social conditions, outlook on life, and their concept of the supernatural. (1982 vol. 1 [my translation]).

A culture can, Larsen claims, be understood through its oral tradition. The study of myth and legend throws light on the concept of the divine, the taboo rules of society, the customs connected with birth, marriage and death, but first and foremost it gives an insight as to how these important aspects of social life were perceived by the people themselves. This is where the strength of this material lies.

The way the *angakkoq* is presented by the missionaries, explorers and scientists and the way their skills and work are narrated in the tales differ in respect of one dramatic point: belief. The tales are told to confirm while the accounts of the outsiders are written to analyse. These two forms of presentation agree on several descriptive points, but the tales take us one step further because they are not sceptical about the reality of the work of the skilled *angakkut*. They might question the single *angakkoq's* credibility but not the power of the role of the *angakkoq* as such. He is the hero in the Eskimo tales and legends.

In his own preface to the collection, Rink comments on the role of the legends:

> The aim of the legend is to describe the strange and unusual and to depict ordinary human life by setting the imagination at work. They thus give in their totality a picture of the attitude to life of the people. When the legends exaggerate it shows what the people have especially held either as sublime and great or as awful and detestable in the nature of human beings, and when it calls the supernatural forward, it there by shows what is felt as a deeper religious truth in an allegorical form. (Ibid.: 5)

The collection made by Rink includes two different genres: myths and legends. Primarily, the myths narrated among the Greenlanders deal with the creation of human beings, of white men, the creation of the sun and the moon, the description of the Mother of the Sea, the Man in the Moon, and so on. The aim of this kind of myth is to create a concept of cosmos, to make human beings feel part of a whole, behind which a principle of order is ruling. This order is a combination of the knowledge of man and a metaphysical concept of the universe which arises out of the need to explain the unexplainable and thereby reduce man's sense of impotence vis-à-vis the forces of Nature.

In the myth of the Mother of the Sea the reason for a lack of game is established and human beings can take action by following the advice of the *angakkoq* and adhering to the taboo rules; the creation of the sun and the moon is connected with the human beings themselves, as the myth establishes the danger of transgressing the rule against incest. The moon and the sun were initially of human origin, the moon being the brother of the sun who, without her knowing his identity, had intercourse with her. The moon was therefore punished by forever following her round as she fled with a burning torch into the air. White men are perceived as products of the intercourse between a dog and an Eskimo woman.[97] All these myths are closely connected with transgression of taboo and therefore ultimately place the order of the cosmos in the hands of human beings and among those, first and foremost, of the *angakkoq*.

Most of the stories in the collection are legends, by which is meant narratives which are closely related either to a place or to a person, or both. Several have actors who actually have lived and therefore they are part of the ancestry of the narrator and his audience.[98] These persons are then ascribed supernatural abilities and skills of interaction with the supernatural forces, mostly malevolent spirits.

The reason for this interaction often stems from a dysfunction in the society itself caused by human emotions running out of control, which again displaces the equilibrium in the settlement as a whole. As Rink describes this, 'Ambition, but not covetousness, is the dominant passion in the mutual frictions' (Ibid.: 6).

Often the theme of a story is enmity and violent revenge. The supernatural forces are used to destroy the enemy and can be set to work by ordinary people. This is not the prerogative of the *angakkoq* alone. As mentioned earlier, the *tupilak* can be created by any member of society with the necessary insight and skills. There is a sliding scale between the work and skills of the *angakkoq* and those of the ordinary revengeful member of society. The first is working with the knowledge of and for the benefit of society as a whole, when he/she is seen as a good *angakkoq*; the second works in secrecy and is more to be compared with the *ilisiitsoq*.

The *angakkoq* can be seen as the hero of society. He is the typical mythical hero who leaves ordinary reality and goes to non-ordinary reality to fight on behalf of society with the malevolent forces there. Here the real battle takes place which makes it possible for the *angakkoq* to return with knowledge that will lead to the establishment of guilt and expiation by the guilty through adhering to the 'laws' dictated by the offended spirits through the *angakkoq* in the interest of his fellow human beings. The tales about his combats, his supernatural encounters and his magical skills all serve the purpose of supporting and sustaining belief in the power of the *angakkoq*. The stories of the *angakkut* of old times confirm the trust in the abilities of certain human beings' capacity for dealing with the interest of all by mastering the skills and insight in how to deal with spirits. The stories, therefore, ratify those skills and show themselves to be what Joseph Campbell (1972: 178) calls a living mythology, that is, a mythology which has the following characteristics:

1. To create and sustain a sense of awe in the individual in connection with the secret dimension of the universe, not so that human beings will live in fear of it, but so that they realise that they are part of it. The mystery of existence is as much the deep mystery of his own being.
2. To create a concept of the universe that agrees with the knowledge of the present time and the areas of life that the mythology is addressing.

3. To support the norms of a given moral code, that which rules in the society where the individual lives.
4. To support the individual step by step in connection with health, strength and harmony of spirit through a profitable life.

If the above are ascribed to the myths and legends themselves, it is easy to see how well these categories also can be ascribed to the upholder of the mythological world, the *angakkut*. Through his travels during the séance he carefully upholds, in the narration of his deeds, a cosmology that can be understood from the experience of the audience of the séance. The rules that he brings back from the Mother of the Sea or the Man in the Moon are easily understood as a valuable moral code. His healing of society or the individual therefore leads to harmony and a profitable life. The *angakkut* and the myths are, in that sense, interdependent.

In his preface, Rink gives a description of the *angakkut* and their role in society. He sees them as combining an ecclesiastical and secular power besides being healers.

> They must also have been seen as the carriers of their nation's scientific knowledge as those who preserved the knowledge of the rules of conduct inherited from the forefathers. In whatever dubious incident concerning the daily occupation, the avoidance of illness and other misfortunes, or the fighting of enemies, their advice was sought and unconditionally obeyed. Although they had the same occupation as the other natives, and led a life equally simple, they formed a special class that achieved its dignity through a certain schooling and had to observe special rules of conduct, as well as having a special language. When their worst enemies, the first missionaries, say about them, that among them the wisest and cleverest men could be found, one can with reason assume, that that was the common state of affairs and that they possessed a deeper insight into nature and the life of human beings than their fellow countrymen. (Ibid.: 15)

The stories, therefore, deal with the *angakkut* as the ultimate preserver of the cosmos. Human emotions out of control are the destroyers of balance. They set feuds in motion which break the peace of the society and involve the supernatural forces in a destructive battle. Several stories depict very severe retaliations without the narrator in any sense taking a stand in the ethical aspects of the story. *Kigdlinararsuk* told by Kristian from the Godthaab area gives an insight into the extent of the cruelty of revenge.

Kigdlinararsuk is orphaned but his sister takes care of him and he leads a happy life until one night when he is alone with the women, the men away on a hunting expedition, he has to go outside the house to relieve himself and he hears a boat arriving. In fear he hides and becomes the witness of a gruesome massacre. His sister is killed and her stomach cut open to reveal the foetus inside. From this time on, he is obsessed with the desire for revenge, seeks magical advice from an old woman and ultimately manages to encourage his fellow men to revenge themselves on the people of the south. The attack is successful, everybody including a pregnant woman having been killed. Kigdlinararsuk gets the chance to revenge his sister's death: 'Kigdlinararsuk ran up to [the woman], stabbed her and cut her stomach open, imitating the way his sister had been killed. This way he satisfied his need for revenge, and from that time he gradually put his sister out of his head' (Ibid.: 258).

Feuds are acceptable behaviour, an eye for an eye and a tooth for a tooth, part of a concept of controlling conduct. Where supernatural forces are at work the *angakkut* might be called in to establish who the perpetrators are. In the story *The Brothers*, a servant of the younger brother is out at night to relieve herself when a supernatural boat arrives and all the inhabitants of the house are killed. The servant runs to the elder brother who takes advice from an *angakkoq* as to who have committed the massacre. He travels inland and meets a one-eyed man who helps him to achieve his revenge by murder and thereby sets his mind at rest (Ibid.: 96ff).

There is a similarity of events in those two stories although the narrator of the latter comes from Holstensborg and of the former from Godthaab. In both stories a person of lower status, an orphan or a servant, is out at night to relieve him/herself and becomes a witness of the massacre and in both stories the end gives full satisfaction to the family member who is avenging the death of a sibling.

Rink uses a whole host of narrators and many stories have had several versions, some up to nine. It was, therefore, the task of Rink to decide how to organise this rich material and he states in his preface that he mostly uses the words of the narrator, but tries to avoid repetitions. 'Some expressions are left out as they will be in conflict with the European concept of decency' (Ibid.: 4). Initially, there were 350 legends which have been reduced to 170. 'The legends as told are almost literally identical although the narrators are living far apart and do not know each other' (Ibid.: 2).

Apart from the feuds and the murders in their wake, one of the dominant themes is the rehabilitation of the vulnerable in society, the orphaned, the bachelor, or the weak hunter who is ridiculed. The *angakkoq* often starts his life among them. He then proceeds to establish himself as a worthy member of society through his power over spirits and his séances. Some of the knowledge of the spirit world that he possesses might also be used by ordinary people. *Kagsagsuk* narrates the trials of a 'poor, orphaned boy, who lived among many merciless men', a sentence that could be found in almost any tradition of folk tales. As is the case in this genre, the boy receives magical assistance to become strong, here through an *Amarok*.[99] His meeting with this animal is identically described as that of the apprentice *angakkoq's* meeting his helping spirit for the first time. It is a frightening, violent encounter, where he has to overcome his own fear to achieve the strength necessary for rehabilitation in society.

There are several stories that deal with the use of magic by these outsiders in society. The concept of rehabilitation through achieving the necessary strength dominates the theme; whereas in many other traditions of folk tales the strength is achieved through the accumulation of wealth, this plays no major part in the way a person's dignity is assessed. It is honour and repute that are the main focus of the ambition of man and to further this ambition the *angakkut* can assist with his knowledge of the spirit world or the person can use magical means on his or her own.

It is easy to get the impression from reading the descriptions of the *angakkut* by missionaries and explorers that they monopolised the spirit world and that nobody else had access. The *angakkut* were the out-spoken, spectacular masters of spirits, and their fellow men might not have come forward with their less impressive use of the supernatural elements when the Europeans were present. The legends show a very different picture inasmuch as the relationship between the spirit world and people is very active. The concept of the place of the spirits is often located in unknown places inland or on the coast, invisible most of the time, but with the potential of becoming visible. It is a world highly loaded with the possibility of a supernatural encounter – also for ordinary people. The lower world and the upper world are the domains of the *angakkut* and their travels to major spirits, the middle world is the dwelling-place of humans and spirits and interaction between these two groups is common.

Marriage between a human and a spirit is the theme of several stories. A man loses his wife and gets a new one who turns out to be a fox in human form, which he then kills before committing suicide. A marriage between a woman and an *atliarusek*[100] functions to the happiness of all involved, even the in-laws. A woman marries a worm, but her brothers find her and kill her worm-child. They bring her back to her parents but she elopes back to her worm. The offspring of these marriages often produce beings of great height and strength (Ibid.: 61, 90, 120, 121).

The creation of a *tupilak*, the use of minor magical skills, and marriage with supernatural beings are all possible options for the ordinary member of society, but when it comes to the more ominous situations the skills of the *angakkoq* are called for. In the stories the *angakkut* deal with confessions, with the killing of an *angiak*,[101] who has become destructive and is murdering its relatives, the naming of enemies, the recovery of souls and the journeying to the inland dwellers.[102] The stories also describe the revealing of the work of "witches" (*ilisiitsut*) and the healing of an ill person by exposing an aunt as an *ilisiitsut*, influencing the weather, and so on (Ibid.: 54, 76, 97, 157, 161, 163, 213, 232, 308). There is a description of the *Ingnersuit*[103] that cut the *angakkoq's* nose off, but he then admonishes them, telling them that they should leave the stronger human beings alone and eventually his nose comes back and is restored to his face, 'but it has become a bit crooked' (Ibid.: 163).

The skills of the *angakkut* cover many of the life-threatening aspects facing Greenlanders and anybody who doubts those skills exposes himself to ridicule as is seen in the story *About Katigagse, the Doubter*, who always goes to séances to disturb the action. Once he experiences the skill of an *angakkoq*, which makes him forever give up attendance at séances. He sees a great flame coming over the house of the séance and as he is about to depart the flame hovers over the entrance and he becomes so scared that he hides under the platform among all the rotten boat skins and other kinds of dirt. When the fire has disappeared Katigagse reappears filthy and with his hair full of seal oil. 'Your stinking things I have relieved myself on' (Ibid.: 127): the narrator adds in brackets, that he was frightened. The Doubter has had his deserved humiliation.

Only one story, *Inugtujussok*, deals with an evil *angakkoq*, who is presented as the 'cruel angakok, a strong man and murderer' (Ibid.: 218). A young man marries a lovely girl and Inugtujussok decides to kill him. After the murder the brothers of the young man do not dare to attack the latter as he is very strong and a great *angakkoq*. He leaves the area as he has many enemies and later brings up a son, who is going to continue his work. When the son is strong enough, Inugtujussok decides to go back south. The brothers hear about his arrival and create a plan to kill him. They lure him into their home when his son is away hunting, ridicule him and kill him 'so that his head was smashed and the brain came out'.[104] When the son returns, he decides to stop the killing and the feud comes to an end.

There are few negative comments on the work of the *angakkut* and generally speaking they come across as caring for the community. The slyness and the greed described elsewhere do not seem to play a major part in the stories; instead, these emotions are ascribed to the *ilisiitsoq*.

The story *About a Widow* deals with a different use of magic or witchcraft. A man has lost his son and to forget his grief he travels to find his son's name-sake. Finally, he finds him and stays with the family. He obtains a fine knife for the name-sake, but it is stolen. Through the use of magic, 'hexeri', he makes the culprit, a young man who has suddenly become very ill, bring it back but he dies all the same. The other men then decide to kill the man and one day he returns so wounded and full of spears that he cannot roll round in his kayak. After his death, hunger results from a terrible snow storm, but his widow and children live in good conditions as he has hidden food for them. The snow is so overwhelming that even the widow is afraid of hunger and she sings a magic song to stop the snow. When she finally manages to crawl out all the other people have died and she then 'hexes' the ice away from the coast so seals again can be caught. 'But the widow died of her own sorcery and angakok art' (Ibid.: 131).

This story shows how 'hexeri', witchcraft, can be used for a destructive purpose, albeit for a justifiable reason and for the survival of the children and other house-dwellers of the widow. It clearly shows the use of magic for death and for survival and that the term 'witchcraft', therefore, is inappropriate when used for a European audience.

Magic on a smaller scale is available to many, but magic on behalf of all society is available only to the skilled *angakkoq*. Power and magic are clearly interlinked and magic in unskilled or destructive hands is dangerous. Some stories deal with precisely that aspect of magic. If the power falls into untrained hands it takes on a demonic character. The story *Kulange's Witchcraft* describes how the unskilled and kayak-less Kulange observes the way his only friend achieves magic by opening a fresh grave and cutting the bladder and a piece of flesh from the dead body. Kulange is then instructed that when placing the piece of flesh under the point of the harpoon, a good hunter will be reduced to a bad one. Kulange tries it out and realises that it works. The bladder he uses on his daughter-in-law when one day she tells him off. She becomes ill and her whole body swells up. Her husband gets hold of an *angakkoq* and the deeds of Kulange are revealed. He admits everything but also informs them that his friend has given him the flesh and bladder. 'As he had now explained all to them they sank the flesh and the bladder into the sea, but his friend they killed' (Ibid.: 212).

Anger and passion which get out of control, or just mere incompetence, are dangerous for the society as a whole. The control is performed by the good *angakkut*, they are the regulators of society and they are therefore often also the only people who can re-establish order. According to Rink and several other later observers the way the first European settlers behaved towards the *angakkut* was a great mistake.

> Concerning the Angakut, or the Greenlanders' only ecclesiastical and secular authorities, the Europeans acted not only with a high-handedness that superiority lends the right to, but in addition against the learning of Christianity and the rules of wisdom. Egede should presumably before all else have tried to win them over, and solely through them have influenced their fellow country men. Only narrow-minded racial arrogance could lead the Europeans to overlook the position of these men as secular authorities, when Christianity precisely commands people to render unto Caesar the things that are Caesar's. But this authority [the *angakkut*] could not be insulted more heavily than by the total overlooking of their existence. When Egede saw it as his first task to inspire the Greenlanders with contempt for Angakut it was similar to preaching rebellion in other countries, and he was no longer in the field of missionary-work but that of politics. But even from a political perspective it was unwise to destroy

all native authority. He had to recognize that the Europeans could not replace the Angakut. (Ibid.: 29)

In a society where the belief system and the social order are totally interlinked, the representatives of the system, the *angakkut*, have had tremendous influence. The attitude expressed in various stories is mostly favourable towards the role of the *angakkut*, and the negative use of magic is ascribed to ordinary members of society whose emotional equilibrium has gone out of balance. They are the users of magic in a destructive way. The term *angakkoq* occurs once in a negative sense in the story that deals with a great murderer. As murder and death are of a magical nature the bad *angakkoq* is an obvious murderer.

It is important to recognise that these stories were collected over a hundred years after Hans Egede's arrival in Godthaab in 1721. There had been a very active mission carried on both by the Egede family and by German missionaries called the Herrnhut, who arrived just after Egede. The purpose of the stories is to preserve and justify the life of the ancestors. As the *angakkoq*, no doubt, had a superior position in his society as the upholder of spiritual and social order, it would be undermining the society as a whole to tell stories that would diminish the institution. Evil *angakkut* were murderers, who were using their skills against the interests of society and were, therefore, ultimately killed.

> Because of a big chasm between the natives and the Europeans in the country, there reigns among the former a certain doubleness, as their behaviour towards the Europeans is restrained, constrained and partly feigned, whereas that which comprises the main part of their conversation during their own gatherings and mainly serves as entertainment during the long winter evenings is, as a rule, a closed book for the Europeans, even those who have spent most of their lives among them. Obviously, that which in old days occupied the thoughts and imagination of the people was not destroyed by the foreigners with the introduction of Christianity. As the more public entertainment hindered it, it is no wonder that the natives felt an even greater need to hear and preserve their old legends . . . that the Greenlanders had to preserve the knowledge of their old belief system and absorb it in a changed version into their present concept as they tried to reconcile it with Christianity. It is still through the legends that the natives from early childhood absorb these concepts, and it is the legends that serve as a guide for them. (1982 vol. 2: iii [my translation])

The legends, and thereby the narrators aim to preserve culture by telling the stories of ancestors and recounting the powers of the *angakkut*. Their purpose is to maintain the authority of the *angakkoq* inasmuch as the missionary tries to undermine it and the explorer tries to describe it from a scientific point of view.

Rasmussen, the other great collector of Greenlandic myths and legends, explored vast areas of Greenland, Canada and Alaska, ardently collecting the oral traditions of the people. In *Myter og Sagn I-III*, he describes the myths and legends of East Greenland, West Greenland, Kap York and North Greenland. He states that the *angakkut* were mostly well-intentioned people and he gives a detailed description of the apprenticeship of the famous East Greenlandic *angakkoq*, Missuarniánga. The first stages of his apprenticeship have several aspects in common with the descriptions earlier on initiation. The final experience of the initiation underlines the close relationship between madness and wisdom: 'One morning he woke with terrible pains in the head, his brain grew and swelled from the inside and the labour of tremendous thoughts were pressing to be released. He had to talk, to divine, to judge, if madness were not to overcome him' (Rasmussen 1921b vol. 1: 34 [my translation]). The result is that he performs a séance and becomes omniscient: 'a new angakok had arisen among human beings'.

The legends describe the deeds of another great East Greenlandic *angakkoq*, Avvgo, who is elsewhere mentioned as a notorious murderer. The legends, however, concentrate on his skills at journeying to the land of the dead in the sky and in the lower world, where a pleasant life is taking place and the dead seem quite content with their situation. On the way to the other world it takes about a year for a dead person to crawl under a skin so as to relieve himself of the juices of his dead body and the only limitation on enjoying life in the land of the dead is excessive mourning among the living (Ibid.: 72ff). Additionally, in these legends the relationship with the Man in the Moon and the Mother of the Sea is the focus of interest and the skilled *angakkut* the hero. He takes up the fight with awesome spirits and with the assistance of his own helping spirits overcomes their wrath, wins their approval and even their gratitude. The *angakkoq* depends on his own strength and that of his helping spirits. He has to confront and fight the spirits to create peace and harmony for his society. The preferable relationship between *angakkoq* and spirits is therefore that of mutual respect.

The West Greenlandic legends describe a character, the bachelor, who rises from being an object of ridicule to becoming a respected *angakkoq*. As is the case in folk tales worldwide, the ridiculed person is in closer contact with the supernatural due to his marginalisation by society. West Greenland was colonised in the early eighteenth century, but magic still has a role to play in the legends. Knud Rasmussen had collected such a wealth of myths and legends that he claimed that he had material for another collection. *Inuit fortæller. Grønlandske sagn og myter I-III* was published in 1981, edited by Regitze Margrethe Søby. Again the relationship between the bachelor and the spirit world is evident in West Greenland. Several legends tell of the fight of spiritual strength between the bachelor and *angakkut*, where the bachelor becomes the victor (1981 vol. 1: 66, 75, vol. 2: 13, 44, 58, 86).[105] The brutality and detailed descriptions of the destruction of people in these myths and legends are striking. The testicles are the object of dismemberment (Ibid. vol. 1: 50, vol. 3: 26),[106] but in general the cutting up of stomach, cutting off of limbs, and a total scattering of the body of a murderer to avoid the revenge of the dead, all point to a concept of a threatening environment where an eye for an eye and a tooth for a tooth is the predominant morality. Spirits and humans alike perform these destructive deeds and the justice that seems to rule is to allow the best man or woman to win using whatever tricks are necessary. Ultimately the role of the *angakkoq* differs from that of ordinary members of society in that his task is to re-establish a balance in society through his personal strength and that of his helping spirits. These are ultimately also a sign of the strength of the *angakkoq* as 'not everybody can become an angakok as it is not everybody that the spirits will serve' (1921b vol. 3: 28 [my translation]). In a society with no written laws, the judgements were in the hands of the spirits and ultimately of the *angakkoq* as their representative.

Angakkut in Oral Tradition on the East Coast

The *angakkut*, as described by explorers and missionaries, have been recounted with a sense of 'otherness', of curiosity or condemnation, of fascination or ridicule. The *angakkut* as they have been presented by the Greenlanders themselves in oral history, the accounts of the *angakkut* of old handed down, these masters of spirits have been described above. This section looks at the stories depicting the powers of *angakkut* who have lived recently and whom the narrator of the story has often known personally.

The people speaking of living *angakkut* mostly claim that in the past the *angakkut* were more powerful. The notion that the power of the ancestors was greater than that of the living is universal in oral traditions and one reason for telling stories about *angakkut* who died decades earlier is to keep alive their powerful influence over the spirits as an example to the new generation. Such dead *angakkut* are seen as powerful helping spirits. The stories also serve the purpose of preserving culture in the face of Christianity. Although several of the stories collected in this century are told by converts to Christianity the powerful image of the *angakkut* of old is still very much alive within the older generation who have either been related to an *angakkoq* or experienced their work.

What these stories keep alive is a detailed description of specialists trained to deal with and master the spirits. The *angakkut* represent the necessary mediators between the sacred and the divine that will appease the anger and influence of the ever-present indifferent or malevolent spirits. Although the Christian Church, when Christianity was introduced, employed the vicar to take care of this aspect, the fear of the supernatural interfering with the world of the living was still very much alive in the narrators themselves.

Ejnar Mikkelsen, inspector of East Greenland from 1933, describes how the Greenlanders remained afraid of the 'beings' which in the past did so much harm. The description of bacteria was seen as proof of the existence of 'invisible hostile beings that unseen could slip into a human being and kill it' (1960: 114 [my translation]). When a young man is fetching water he comes rushing home in panic and claims that he has seen an angel on the pathway. Attempts to calm him meet the logical reason for the profound fear: 'But where the good angels can tread the evil Devil can walk. And him I am very much afraid of' (Ibid.: 89).

The notion of dualism in every walk of life was prominent in the mind of the Greenlander. Evil might be just round the next corner. Ordinary human beings can try to protect themselves with magic songs and amulets, but when it comes to soul-stealing and soul-loss the specialist had to be called for: the *angakkoq*, trustworthy and terrifying, who, through encountering these malevolent spirits and through death and resurrection, would be able to turn these spirits into tools for healing or destruction. No wonder *angakkut* are presented as people with extraordinary power, to be admired and feared.

One of the important sources of information for the East Greenlandic *angakkut* is the work by Jens Rosing, *Sagn og Saga fra Angmagssalik,* which was published in 1963. Some of the material was collected in 1961 while other is from his father, Otto Rosing's collection 'Angákortaligsuit'. Several informants were given a heathen name before they had their Christian name as they were born at the beginning of the colonisation of Angmagssalik. Jens Rosing, a Greenlander himself, personally encountered a great female *angakkoq* when she was very old, and through that encounter experienced the powerful personality of the *angakkut.*

A major part of the material stems from one very important informant, Karl Andreassen, known as Kârale. His father, Mitsuarnianga, was a great *angakkoq* and Kârale has given a detailed personal description of his experience as a child through his father's abilities to contact the spirits. Kârale and his mother were among the first people to be baptised by pastor Rüttel and thereby given a Christian name, with the acceptance of the father. Kârale is therefore an interesting link between the last heathen and the first Christians whose account of childhood can throw light on the role of the *angakkut* as seen by an educated insider. The father remained heathen for many years after the son's baptism and Kârale experienced the presence of spirits through the father. In a period of misfortune in the family when Kârale was a boy, the father had a knee injury and the mother died in child-birth. The father was very depressed and became delirious. One evening when the father was very ill and had *angakkoq*-fits, the boy experienced 'a being, similar to a baby, disappearing between the bed and the wall' (1935: 107 [my translation]). The father later tells the boy that he saw the baby too. The 'baby', *Ungâq,* is a well-known helping spirit used by the *angakkoq* to frighten evil spirits. It often appears in séances and is very dangerous as everything it touches must die.

As mentioned previously, East Greenland was colonised late. When Holm went along the coast in 1883-84 few earlier visits had taken place. In the *Flóamannasaga* the East Greenlanders are described as troll-people and it was as late as 1752 that the first description of them as real people by Peder Olsen Walløe appears.

With Gustav Holm's 'Konebådsexpedition' in 1884 a more thorough ethnographic account of the people was written.

The reason for the many *angakkut* in Angmagssalik when Gustav Holm arrived was that the population was in decline and, therefore, there were a number of orphaned children. They were often in great need because nobody really took care of them, a theme that can be recognised in many of the accounts. An old man who had suffered the same way might then become their adviser in spiritual matters. He would encourage them to go and search for contact with the spirits and help them to get protection against the viciousness that they suffered from their fellow men. The spirits would, in a way, become the guardian of the child.

It might on the other hand also be the choice of the parents to make a child into an *angakkoq* to protect him against soul-loss or having his soul stolen by an enemy. The parents would search for insight into the way to 'create' a new *angakkoq*. They might seek knowledge from an *angakkoq* who through invocation would make the child appeal to the spirits. Then the child would begin training to become an *angakkoq* by going into the hills and following the pattern mentioned in the section on 'Initiation of the *Angakkoq*.'

It was important that the child should stay silent about his accumulation of helping spirits 'because only the person who can keep to himself what he has seen can become a great angakok' (Rosing 1963: 174). The apprentice could not commit many mistakes before he would lose the helping spirits that he had acquired and the spirits would turn their backs on him. It was clearly a delicate balance and according to this account few managed to get through to the final stage and become real *angakkut*. The child would start searching for helping spirits at the age of twelve and this search would last until he reached the age of eighteen to twenty. The actual apprenticeship taking place during the time of puberty is known in many cultures because this time of transformation makes the individual open to the contact with the spirits.[107]

Several of the stories about the legendary *angakkut* explain how they 'come forward', and admit their status as *angakkut*. They will then arrange a three-day séance. Beforehand they might have trained for this in remote caves in the mountains and used the stool of the kayak as a drum and the kayak skin as the curtain. The *angakkoq* might be very frightened of making a public profession and try to avoid this challenge. As the helping spirits can be kept at arm's length by grease, because they do not like dirt, he might try to hide from their demands and end up first becoming ill, then losing weight and finally dying. Such a person is called a *aquilitserdeq*, a person who has become tender (as with meat) (Ibid.: 176).

The sign for the fellow house inhabitants that something is happening with the young person and that he might be ready for 'coming forward' is seen by the bleeding from the mouth of the new *angakkoq*. Kârale tells the following story about Ajijak, one of the great *angakkut*. He had been chosen to become an *angakkoq* because his siblings had all died young. He went through the accumulation of helping spirits and when he was made to 'come forward' it happened during a song contest. Ajijak felt a sting in his side and stopped singing as he knew that *ôrtortoq*, the black guillemot, had come up from the deep and touched him. He first tried to avoid the calling but realised that he would let himself and the spirits down. He then went and sat behind his wife waiting for the events to progress. 'The wife of Ajijak had been so preoccupied looking at the dance of her father-in-law, that she did not notice her husband until he started shaking all over. She turned to him frightened and now saw that the blood was trickling out of his mouth' (Ibid.: 215).

The 'coming forward' then takes place over a period of three days. Ajijak runs round naked in the house and is covered in the blood that spurts out of his mouth. It is important that nobody is touched by the blood as they might lose their souls: 'The night was saturated with fear' (Ibid.: 216). On the last night he managed to roll off his face skin. The father then demanded that the lamps should be turned off, 'and people later said that they would have become frightened to death, if the lamps had not been turned off while Ajijak was running round with his face skin like that.' In the accounts of the redemption of the *angakkut* fear plays an important role. The final rites of passage for the *angakkoq* are dangerous to his fellow men.

Avko,[108] one of the most famous East Greenlandic *angakkut*, has the following 'coming forward', again narrated by Kârale (Ibid.: 241). One evening he feels there is something happening to him and as he has trained as an *angakkoq* apprentice he advises his wife to hide all sharp things. Later he goes mad and again his fellow co-habitees have to protect themselves against him either by having sharp weapons or by sitting on greasy places. This session lasts for about three days.

The pattern in the accounts by Kârale on the initiation process is that the apprentice goes mad and those surrounding him have to protect themselves against his violent behaviour. Avko does not bleed but instead swallows large objects; this behaviour is called *nîlerineq*, swallowing things whole. In the accounts the initiate behaves in an extraordinary way which is instantly recognised by the others as 'coming forward' as an *angakkoq*. The behaviour is interpreted as sound. In the case of madness which is not connected with 'coming forward' as an *angakkoq*, the treatment is more harsh. In Otto Sandgreen's family saga, *Øje for øje og tand for tand* a description of the treatment of madness shows that it can lead to the killing of the mad person (1987: 221ff). The District doctor in Umának, A. Berthelsen, writes that the treatment of madness was suffocation. 'Not even today can a person suffering from madness feel safe about his life' (1915: 48 [my translation]).

The interesting balance between interpreting behaviour as contact with the spirits or as soul-loss, and therefore an illness, is what I.M. Lewis points out when he claims that the patient and the shaman-to-be share the same starting point, an initial illness (1989: 111). For the shaman it leads to an insight into the spirit-world and later to controlled possession, for the patient it leads to healing or death.

> The signs of this 'Arctic hysteria', as it is usually known in the literature, are: hiding from the light, hysterically exaggerated crying and singing, sitting passively in a withdrawn state on the bed or on the ground, racing off hysterically (inviting pursuit), hiding in rocks, climbing up trees, etc. Unless there are contradictions, people who exhibit these symptoms of hysterical flight are likely to be regarded as possessed by a spirit and may, or may not, be encouraged to become shamans. (Ibid.: 47)

It is of crucial importance for these famous *angakkut* of the east coast of Greenland, therefore, that their fellow men recognise their behaviour as the initial stages of the calling to become *angakkoq*. If not, it can lead to death. The narrative however is dealing with the stories of those who became famous *angakkut*.

The expectations of the abilities of the *angakkoq* obviously include the capacity to use the achieved helping spirits for the benefit of the society, to travel on behalf of the society either to the underworld or the world in the sky, to travel through the sky like a meteor, something that seems to be of great importance because the *angakkoq*, according to the stories, travels and has competitions with other *angakkut*. Ordinary people might see the *angakkoq* when he is en route.

> At the settlements out near the mouth of Sermilik fjord people often witnessed Angákerduaq's air travels. Over the land you then saw a dark spot with a long tail of fire, and behind that several other dark spots, also sparkling from the backside: Angákerduaq, followed by his helping spirits. When that strange group was not too far away, one could make out the persons from the sparkles. (Rosing 1963: 196)

The story narrates how Angákerduaq travels over a group of people who discover him and run round gesticulating, driving what he determines to be small bear-like animals with thin legs in front of them. Kârale, who again is the narrator of this account, adds a personal touch to the story as he includes an experience he had in Ûmánaq as a student. He met an old man called Lûtivik who, when he spoke about Angákerduaq, got more and more exited. Finally Lûtivik describes a story from the west coast many years ago, when the missionary's servants were gathering sheep, and suddenly saw this glittering tail of fire. They were all petrified and when the ball of fire came closer they could see a man crouching with his hands tied. 'I who had started my story without expecting anything strange to derive from it sat seriously and wondered about the inexplicable. I was mute. But the old man said over and over again the words: "Oh, how strange – how astonishing it is"'(Ibid.: 198 [my translation]).

The story includes two aspects: a belief in the capacity of the *angakkoq* to travel where he wants, even to the west coast of Greenland, and the profound acceptance of the strangeness of the power of the *angakkoq*. For a Christian student and an old man who has lived on the west coast and therefore in a Christian environment, this apparent proof of the ancient powers must have been amazing.

In the stories the *angakkoq* travelling takes up a major part of the narrative. As journeys to the Mother of the Sea and to the lower world have been considered earlier, the travels I will look at here are the ones undertaken during the séance to other parts of the country. This might be a journey to challenge another *angakkoq* or it might be to visit the dwellings of helping spirits. The latter is important as it shows a concept of the helping spirits as living like human beings somewhere near the settlement. The *angakkoq*, however, needs his helping spirits to show him the way.

One of the great *angakkut*, Nauja, undertakes such a journey, with a host of helping spirits. They argue about the direction on the way and finally they wait for *tôrnârdik*, the great helping spirit to lead the way. He takes the group over two settlements and finally lands on the beach of a third.

> Nauja starts to examine the house. It is enormous with four gut skin windows. The house is swarming with people; there are as many platforms as pearls on a string. Over every second platform there is a dazzling gleam. The gleaming platforms are inhabited by *angakut* while the non-gleaming belong to laymen. In front of the *angakut* platforms rolled up sealskins are hanging on the house posts, curtain skins ready for use when the *angakut* have their séance. (Ibid.: 201)

People are going about their business not aware of the visitors and Nauja asks his helping spirits whether he is to scare them, but he is instead advised to creep under each *angakkoq*. When he has carefully done as he has been told, the last *angakkoq* jumps up and shouts: 'In old days it happened that human *angakut* recruited us as helping spirits; oh, I feel as I did then, oh, how wonderful – he reminds me of my old master during invocation' (Ibid.: 202). Then Nauja comes out of the floor when all the lamps have been extinguished. In this way Nauja has acquired more helping spirits.

This story provides an example of the human-like character of the helping spirits. The house is impressive and much larger than a normal house; the number of *angakkut* assembled there is also impressive. The light round their heads is a common feature in the interpretation of spirituality.[109]

> An *angakok* had confided in the people in his settlement that the souls were extremely attractive, as they were visible to an *angakok*. There was a radiance round them, a bluish gleam like a mountain crystal. But if you touched them, they were as airy ghosts. But when he was christened, the souls disappeared for him and the inner part of a human being became an inscrutable darkness. (Ibid.: 178)

Souls and people dealing with souls and spirits are connected with light for the Greenlanders. The spirits in the stories are generally speaking of non-human origin, as they are animals and insects in human form. The ancestors play a small part in the collection of helping spirits. In two stories a so-called ghost-spirit appears as a helping spirit. Ajijak is saved in a tight situation by such a ghost-spirit, 'which in life had been a big and strong woman, the mother of a man called Angîârneq' (Ibid.: 219). Also Maratse, another famous *angakkoq*, interacts with ghost spirits, but they are described as 'gruesome'. The relationship to the dead is problematic and even trained *angakkut* might be scared witless by the attachment of a ghost-spirit. Maratse, who had participated in the killing of another man, is haunted by his ghost and almost overcome. Finally he decides to counter-attack and during a séance the following exchange of words takes place:

> Maratse answered: 'I shall invoke my spirits.' The voice answered back: 'You can spare yourself the trouble I have seen you already. I will revenge myself on your children. When all – from your children to the rest of your family – are killed I will take you at last. I shall have revenge.' The ghost shouted and rubbed its palms against each other so that they squeaked. (Ibid.: 273ff)

Maratse overpowers the ghost and sends it back through the floor and thereby overcomes his own fright. 'And those, who had seen it, said: "He was fantastic".' Several stories mention the rubbing of palms as a way of invoking the spirits. The method can be compared to that of the *angîn*, the *angakkoq*-stone, mentioned in almost all accounts of initiation.

The daughter of the famous female *angakkoq* Kâkâq narrates a story about how her mother as a child helped a woman, the wife of a spirit called Paperqia, who had problems giving birth. Kâkâq is challenged by Paperqia to help as she is chosen later to become an *angakkoq* (Ibid.: 288ff). Kâkâq undressed and lay next to the woman. 'Paperqia now helped mother, as you normally do during an invocation, to "prepare" the road for the spirits by uttering long 'êq-êq-êq', and before she realized it mother was rubbing her hands against each other and blowing into them. Her cover started to flap, she was in the middle of possession, her breathing sunk into the depths.'

There are several well-known elements in this description of the condition of the *angakkoq* during possession: the rubbing of hands, the blowing, which is also used when healing is taking place on the body of the ill person, the state of breathing. Several stories mention that the breath disappears when the *angakkoq* goes into possession. Breath and soul are obviously interconnected and when the body of the *angakkoq* is taken over by the spirits he disappears and his diminished breathing is a sign of the travelling. The *angakkut* are using a breathing technique by which a sort of light trance is invoked; the stories clearly point to the fact that during possession the *angakkoq* is altering his breathing. Healing while under cover is called 'qilâqutserneq' and is performed lying next to the ill person, often in a state of possession. Maratse is described performing healing during which he lay down next to the patient, achieved assistance from his helping spirit and, changing slough, became a bear. He then stabbed the inflamed wound and licked the bluish-green materia (Ibid.: 276).

The breath also plays a part in activating the drum. The drum is believed to move on its own account during the séance and therefore has to be inspired. 'Símujôq blew life into the drum, and soon it hovered pounding over his shoulders. The curtain clattered, Símujôq was possessed. One window was only half covered, and through that the glimmer of the northern light shone through so that one could vaguely make out the drum and part of the back of the *angakok*' (Ibid.: 259).

In the battle between Maratse and the ghost mentioned earlier the drumming also plays an important part in the séance:

> The drum, which was lying a bit to the left of Maratse, moved, roaring, hopping on the handle towards him. It sprang up on his back and 'sparkled' for a long time against his naked shoulders. Then it jumped down and moved back to its starting point. A second time it moved rocking towards Maratse – and flew up on his back. His vision was blown into layers, and the knowledge of all the world gave his spirit-possessed vision wide horizons to contemplate. As the drum for the third time had been up on the back of Maratse and had jumped down again, the lamps were extinguished. – The drum roared and thundered, possessed by enormous forces. (Ibid.: 274)

As mentioned earlier, sound is an extremely important aspect of the séance. The audience participate actively to the extent that they might go up in the dark and touch the helping spirits which have arrived. In the first séance by Ajijak he is travelling under great drama. His drum is dragging him round and out of the house and he is replaced by his helping spirit, Ipak, who then communicates with the audience and tells them how Ajijak is getting on on the journey. During this conversation the drum hops about even up on the platform. Suddenly Ipak starts to shout that his master is bleeding from the wounds he has achieved in a battle with hostile spirits. Ajijak's father moans that now he will never escape.

> When the excitement was peaking the drum started to rock so violently that everybody expected it to be smashed. Then Ipak sprang up and shouted: 'He has escaped, he is out'. Ipak then rushed out of the entrance and everybody breathed a sigh of relief. But no sooner was Ipak out than he was replaced by another helping spirit. This way the helping spirits were changing while Ajijka was away. Every time a new spirit took a seat on the sitting skin people sprang up and touched it. Some were giant spirits some small but they were all in human shape. (Ibid.: 220)

The active participation of the audience is obviously an important part of the success of the séance. The audience see the *angakkoq* being tied, hear the drum getting excited, meet the different helping spirits, replace the journeying *angakkoq*, see his departure in a tail of light to the dwellings of helping or hostile spirits, or to the Mother of the Sea to sort out the transgression of taboo rules, and know the spirits entering one by one by their 'appearance' and their names and voices. Without this host of believers the séance would come to nothing.

The task of the *angakkut*, however, was seen as burdensome. A heavy responsibility lay on the shoulders of the skilled *angakkut* and often it was with hesitation and reluctance that the apprentice 'came forward' as the social role of the *angakkut* was a delicate one:

> The *angakok* has a heavy task, something which first really dawns on him when the period of training is over. Some *angakut* do not hide that they regret that they have become *angakut*. And the ones that did not complete their education and all the same survived this often express their happiness with the words: 'It was great that I did not become an *angakok*, because everything that happens I will be blamed for.' The *angakut* were often misunderstood, and their powers were queried. Often they were slandered. To maintain their position they had to perform séances. If they were asked to look into a matter, they ensured that they were well paid. (Ibid.: 178).

This attitude to the victimisation of the *angakkut* is not shared by the missionaries or by some of the Greenlanders themselves who have experienced *angakkut* who have robbed them of their belongings or claimed that they were *ilisiitsoq* or who believed that an *angakkoq* had sent a *tupilak* against them, and thereby tried to kill them. The picture painted in *Sagn og saga* generally shows the *angakkut* as well-meaning men or women who take upon themselves the dangerous and difficult task of dealing with and mastering spirits and thereby preserving the old traditions.

Sandgreen's *Øje for øje og tand for tand*, is a collection of narratives about two families on the east coast of Greenland. The description focuses on revenge, the concept of 'an eye for an eye and a tooth for a tooth', and points to the fact that family feuds were having a devastating impact on the population of East Greenland. The narrative has Naaja, a famous *angakkoq*, as its leading character. He lived at the beginning of the nineteenth century and his family had for four generations preserved the stories about him. According to the preface by Birgitte Sonne, the saga, as it is called, contains a wealth of information about the pre-Christian culture of the East Greenlanders although it sometimes can be difficult to establish 'its traditional validity' (1987: 8).

Sandgreen was a vicar in Ammassalik district from 1959 to 1963, and collected the material with the aim of spreading the knowledge of the customs of his forefathers. The work was published in 1967. Sandgreen had three main informants, and not all versions were identical, but the tapes used for recording the narrative do not exist any more, as the author used them for other purposes. The present material, therefore, represents information that has been edited by the author and there is no original available. Nevertheless, it gives some insight to an attempt at presenting cultural and historical insight to the pre-Christian era of the East Greenlanders.

The historical background confirms the serious impact of the feuds. When Gustav Holm arrived in 1884 he made a census which showed that approximately 500 people were living in the district. When colonisation happened in 1894, the number had been halved and nine murders and several attempted murders had been committed. Added to that were accusations of witchcraft. According to Birgitte Sonne, there was a general relief among the first candidates of baptism, that a prohibition against murder and witchcraft accusation was being established in the name of

Christianity. The population quickly expanded. There had been a fall in game animals, but the new weapons and help during periods of famine made the living so attractive that a group of people who had emigrated to the west coast returned. The murders had mostly been committed by two insane individuals who were themselves finally killed. The narrative does not deal with those but with another murder of the father of one of the informants.

The style of the narrative is coloured by the author's concept of nature. He describes the interrelatedness and the contradiction between the actions of man and the grandeur of the scenery. The narrative takes its starting point in a little nuclear family, two old people, their son and daughter-in-law and their twin sons. They live in apparent harmony 'and although they now and then felt a little uneasiness, insecurity and anxiety – towards nature and humans – there was up till now no apparent reason' (Ibid.: 35 [my translation]). The old man has an axe to grind and brings up his two grandsons to make them into strong men who can revenge a murder that he never managed to revenge. The two boys then die of a mysterious stomach ache. These deaths set the action moving. Mysterious death is always interpreted as soul-stealing and the father of the twins has no doubt about the reason for the loss of his two healthy sons. He sets out to gain knowledge about how to become an *angakkoq* so that he can make the next child an *angakkoq* and thereby prevent the son's death. This task proves difficult as knowledge of the art of the *angakkoq* is hard to come by.

The narrative then takes the reader on a journey of more than four hundred pages into the lives of the *angakkut* of the following generations. There is a wealth of information on rites connected with the *angakkoq* and only a few of the more interesting aspects not touched on earlier are considered here.

To make a child into an *angakkoq* the parents have to put a glowing piece of moss into the throat of the child 'so that he will become glowing' (Ibid.: 70). This appears to be identical with the concept of the glowing souls and the light connected with the *angakkoq* mentioned earlier. This glow makes the apprentice stand out from the group of fellow men in the eyes of the helping spirits and they will therefore be attracted to him and search out his company. It is interesting to note that in the narrative by the Greenlanders themselves about the relationship between the spirits and the *angakkoq*, there is an equality of interests present; the helping spirits are as eager to get a master as the apprentice is to acquire them. The apprentice is under pressure to 'come forward' as an *angakkoq* because the helping spirits want to act. If the apprentice is reluctant this might create a life-threatening fight between him and his spirits.

Naaja, who is the son born to become an *angakkoq*, loses his mother through soul stealing. This obviously continues the saga of feud but it also makes Naaja a typical apprentice: a child who is deprived of either of his parents. The description of his apprenticeship parallels that described above in the section on initiation, the emphasis being on the role of fear as the overcoming of anxiety. Fear is crucial. 'From now on Naaja tried to harden himself, and he was gradually made more and more thick-skinned by the outside invisible powers' (Ibid.: 90). Meeting a supernatural dog,[110] who eats him, his clothes act in the following way: 'and as they [the clothes] were contaminated by the fear of their owner, they fled' (Ibid.: 95). It is interesting to note that the clothes are described as having a mind of their own, their *inue*. The clothes return to Naaja and the whole incident can be compared with that of Sanimuinak.[111]

Sandgreen comments on the *angakkoq's* attitude to fear: 'And those who want to be angakkut have firstly to be afraid for a period of time to get started at all, because without fear one does not notice anything strange' (Ibid.: 103). The role of the apprentice is obviously to seek out and encounter the strange, first witless with fear, later mastering that fear. 'Now he trained to become an angakkoq without worrying whether he would die of it, and everywhere he searched for future helping spirits'... 'This way Naaja sought out the strongest – for although the murder he had committed was not discovered he had to be alert – he sought out the frightening and the dangerous to harden his life' (Ibid.: 131).

Naaja also is 'discovered' as an *angakkoq* apprentice when, during a party given by his father, he faints. 'They discovered that the blood trickled out from the corners of his mouth, the edge of his hair and the corners of his eyes and other soft parts' (Ibid.: 138). The séance itself is described as usual but the author comments on the role of the audience:

> But during the séance it was not only from the angakkoq, that something was demanded. The audience – guests and fellow residents – also had to behave according to certain rules and they were very demanding. No-one

was allowed to fall asleep, even the children had to stay awake during the séance, i.e. they were allowed to sleep if they were sitting on someone's lap, not when they were on the platform; if they fell asleep on the platform itself, it meant certain death. Besides no-one was allowed to perform any task, not even urinating – because the tub of urine was so frightening, that many spirits were afraid of it – and to avoid the need to pass water, one was not allowed to drink either. (Ibid.: 149)

The audience supports the *angakkoq's* change of place with his helping spirit by singing. Through the helping spirit the audience is informed about the strength and powers of their *angakkoq*, and, when in trouble 'that it was he that they had to address and necessarily fear' (Ibid.: 154).

The second part of the narrative deals with a female *angakkoq*, Kaakaaq. After experiencing her father's attack of madness, she becomes more aware of her own potentials as an *angakkoq*, helped by a grandmother. It is pointed out that she looks like a boy. Again the *angakkoq* apprentice is orphaned and therefore marginalised in society. 'She was humiliated like other orphans' (Ibid.: 251). Very few women are mentioned as *angakkut* and the fact that Kaakaaq is presented as boyish may be a statement of her closeness to the male sex.[112] This closeness takes on a different note later, when her attraction to men and men's attraction to her almost come in the way of her apprenticeship. 'An angakkoq must not let desires have the same free play as other human beings. Desire has to be kept under control' (Ibid.: 244). Kaakaaq never 'comes forward' as an *angakkoq* and has great problems with her helping spirits similar to those described in Jens Rosing's *Sagn og saga*. She instead becomes a skilled creator of *tupilaks*, so much so that she manages to kill her own husband and wound her son.

The last *angakkoq* to be described is Kukkujooq, the son of Kaakaaq and a member of the Naaja clan, who was murdered when Kukkujooq was very young. Kukkujooq is therefore fatherless and in the same situation as the previous two *angakkut*, short of one parent and left to unpleasant treatment by his stepfather. Both the mother and the son have experienced humiliation early in childhood and becoming an *angakkoq* makes it possible to retaliate against those who have maltreated them.

This attitude becomes very apparent in the description of Kukkujooq. He is clearly in search of power and trains himself for the purpose of being feared and finally he starts to steal souls. As the *angakkut* were the people one asked for help in connection with retrieval of souls, a trained *angakkoq* who was stealing them was obviously very much feared.

> The only people one would contact if somebody had the soul stolen were the *angakkut*. Because of their helping spirits they normally were able to find the soul that had been removed. Every time the *angakkoq* found the soul that had been taken away and hidden and brought it back he demanded an enormous payment. The crucial question was whether the soul had been easy or difficult to find; if the soul had been hidden for a long time it would have become destroyed and if it was very putrefied it could no longer heal its owner although the *angakkoq* actually found it and brought it back to its owner. (Ibid.: 316)

Kukkujooq is described as recklessly stealing souls. A chapter shortly after this account is called *God arrives* and deals with how the vicar introduces the concepts of God to the community in which this disturbed family lives. The arrival of Christianity is seen as the saviour of the intolerable condition of the people. The moral decline is total: mother kills husband and wounds son with *tupilak* and she is then described as having intercourse with her helping spirit – and enjoying it (Ibid.: 345). Finally she is even blinded by her helping spirit as she is not prepared to 'come forward' but her son Kukkujooq concentrates on stealing souls instead of helping his community. The whole moral condition is in decline and only the message of Christianity can save the people from the distress of destruction prevailing constantly in their lives.

Predictably the final chapters of the book deal with conversion and the introduction of peace. Kukkujooq encounters his dead father and thereby is rid of the wish to kill. As he confides in the vicar and receives teaching from him, the route to becoming a true Christian is clear and finally they are all baptised, having achieved separation from the helping spirits by refusing to perform more séances and leaving the area where the helping spirits are believed to be located.

The two versions presented here, Rosing's *Sagn og saga* and Sandgreen's *Øje for øje og tand for tand* both have the aim of preserving the knowledge of their forefathers in East Greenland. As the *angakkut* were often the carriers of tradition within society and the preservers of the old belief system, they have to take up a major part of the narrative dealing with the history of the Greenlanders before the

encounter with Christianity. Sandgreen clearly tries to make
Christianity the salvation of the people and therefore points to defects
in character among the *angakkut*, having the history of the survival of
the people of the east coast to show for it. What he does not have are
the original words of the three informants and it is therefore
impossible to establish whether what has come across as the 'voice of
the people' is more the voice of Sandgreen. Several descriptions
dealing with customs seem to be in accord with other accounts, but
the actual destructive behaviour of the later *angakkut* differs from
that presented in *Sagn og saga*. This work appeared simultaneously
with that of Sandgreen, but is not in the form of a saga. It deals with
the *angakkut* in separate accounts, especially focusing on their work
instead of their lives. The aim of this book was to present the accounts
more or less in the fashion of Rasmussen: the direct version as it was
narrated by the informant with some editing. There is therefore not a
moral bias to it, or a Christian message, in the end. The same
characters appear, both the work of Naaja and Kaakaaq is described,
their names spelled differently: Nauja and Kâkâq.

To show the difference in the presentation of Kâkâq, this chapter
will end by focusing on Rosing's own experience of her and that of
her daughter:

> One of the people who has made the deepest impression on me is the
> blind Kâkâq, a mysterious, dried-up old woman. She was, when I met
> her, approximately 75-76 years old and was in her dotage. But her
> whole behaviour burned itself into my 15-year-old mind so profoundly
> that neither time nor life's many experiences have been able to
> extinguish the memory of her. (1963: 281 [my translation])

The author has a sort of a supernatural experience being with
her. He had just gone to her small tent at the edge of the settlement
and given her tobacco which sent her into some sort of semi-ecstasy.

> She spoke magic words, she blew and hissed and rubbed her hands
> together. Now and then she called the spirits: 'Já, já, já, já, já – and then
> it happened: an enormous singing of whistling wings rushed over the
> tent, and old Kâkâq almost rattled: 'Já, já, já, já'. Shivers ran down my
> spine, and the blood was hammering in my temples, my nerves were
> bursting. Later a shrill raven's scream was heard, it was a pair of late
> ravens that had flown over the tent on their way to their resting rock on
> the other side of the sound. (Ibid.: 284-5)

Although presenting us with a logical explanation, the author gives a very clear picture of his state of mind while the incidents happened. This is also true for the description of Kâkâq presented by her daughter. She sees her mother as a skilled *angakkoq* although she never 'came forward'.

> Many things I have experienced by my mother's side, she was a strange person, permeated by all sorts of magic art. In the middle of the night I would be woken up by her suddenly screaming: 'Já, já, já', lying on her back she rubbed her hands together and was in the middle of a violent possession. The platform trembled, the skin curtains rattled. And I sensed her helping spirits, that inspired her. Then it was as if my mother was surrounded by something sparkling. And when her breath sank into the depth, she was lying as if dead. (Ibid.: 295).

The parallel in this description to that of Kârale with his father Mitsuarnianga is quite striking. The belief in the capacity of their *angakkut* parents to deal with the supernatural although they themselves are brought up as Christians makes the description all the more interesting. The aim of Rosing is clearly to show that for the people involved something was at work of a supernatural character that even the introduction of Christianity did not eliminate as pure superstition and trickery. Both authors leave the reader thinking that here is a group of people who truly had a contact with something incomprehensible and who formed their lives round that contact either to the benefit of those involved or to the destruction of their society, leading to immoral behaviour and murder. Rosing aims to represent the voice of the people, whereas Sandgreen, although having used informants, represents the voice of the vicar.

As has been shown in this chapter, the Greenlandic *angakkoq* is a master of spirits who interacts with the world of the spirits on behalf of his society. He might undertake 'mystical flight' using ecstasy to visit these spirits. He mostly uses his skills for the benefit of his fellow human beings but might also misuse his power over spirits and souls against his society to further self-interest.

In the following chapter traditional shamanism will be contrasted to the concepts of shamanism in the New Age and specifically in the courses in shamanism. The description of the *angakkoq* has mainly shown a form of shamanism before the impact of Christianity in Greenland. Neo-shamanism or core-shamanism is a creation of the end of the twentieth century based on the knowledge of traditional shamanism but adjusted to the lifestyle of a modern Western urban society. The next chapter will, therefore, compare neo-shamanism with the traditional shamanism presented above and especially focus on attitudes to the role of the spirits.

NOTES

1. Birgitte Sonne points to the possible influence of Christianity on this belief in evil (1988: 28) but it is equally possible that this Greenlander simply talks out of experience with the harshness of nature, an experience which may have been supported by the Christian approach to evil. The view does equal the general attitude expressed by other Eskimos on the conditions of life in the Arctic.
2. This concept exists in other parts of the Eskimo area: '"Everything lives!" said a Chuckee shaman. "The lamp wanders about; the walls of the tent have their voices, the urine tub has its special country and house. The skins which sleep in the bag talk every evening. The antlers lying on the graves get up in the night and wander about the burial grounds"' (Birket-Smith 1924: 432).
3. 'The Inue of the things are only mentioned insofar as they have influence on human beings' (Rink 1868: 201 [my translation]). 'The soul after death must be seen as an "owner" both of the dead body as long as there is anything left of it and of the belongings of the person' (Ibid.: 202). 'For a being to be free, self-possessed and powerful as a deity it has to be of inuk-root, related to the human' (Thalbitzer 1926: 11 [my translation]). Bogoras describes it as a human-like spirit that lives within the object (1904-1909: 279).
4. Sacrifices were, according to Rink, mostly used on travels, at certain locations where dangers were threatening. Food or tools were then thrown into the sea (1868: 227). Rasmussen describes how sacrifices could also be made to the dead by placing small pieces of meat at the grave, as the dead were then capable of enlarging these pieces to satisfy their needs (1921b vol. 1: 11).
5. 'According to their contents they are comprised in three groups. The largest group comprises those prayers which are intended to procure the man good luck with his hunting, and the next group includes those which are to secure, or restore, the individual's health. A third large group is concerned with the first breach of taboo after the time of mourning is over' (Thalbitzer 1923: 248). Kleivan and Sonne write, using the word formula for magic prayers comparing it with amulets: 'The formula was less a part of its owner. Nevertheless, the formula was only effective when owned by a single individual' (1985: 9). The magic song or formula could change hands and there are examples of quite substantial payments being made.
6. The amulet will be described in the section on 'The Paraphernalia of the *Angakkoq*'.
7. Rasmussen writes 'Simigaq, the oldest woman of the tribe, is also an angakoq of high repute, invoking helping spirits when fate is unkind to herself or her fellows;

moreover she is a well-informed story-teller, uncommonly versed in all the ancient traditions, magic spells and drum songs. When she dies, a great deal of interesting folklore will be lost to the world' (1928: 19). Or as Thalbitzer states:

> It is merely a question of time when the Eskimo culture on the isolated coast of Ammassalik will be levelled to the ground and the defenceless human flock up there will be just as denationalized and demoralized as many other primitive peoples have been by the complacent teaching of the Christian mission. Once more a beautiful and interesting culture, widely different from the European culture, will be blotted out of existence. It is a sad fact, and doubly sad when one considers that the idea of nationality has nowhere been so ardently preached and so readily accepted as in that quarter of the globe, which is the focus of the Christian mission. (1908: 464).

8. Although this comment is mostly praise of the good *angakkut*, Rasmussen was not oblivious to the fact that some turned murderers. Sonne describes Rasmussen's attempt to come to terms with this in his presentation of the Eskimos to the outside world: 'He resorted to divergent and mutually contradictory sets of explanation' (1988: 25).

9. Knud Rasmussen describes how the evil power of the shamans is prevented: 'If it is desired to render a boy invulnerable against animals and men, especially shamans and their attacks by means of witchcraft, if it is desired to prevent him from being bitten to death or otherwise killed by animals: walrus, bear, wolverine etc. and hinder shamans from causing him sickness of body by taking away his soul, then a shaman must be summoned as soon as the child is out of the womb' (1929: 172). The shaman takes the soul out of the boy's body and lays it under his mother's lamp. The soul must then remain there as long as the boy lives. A ritual is performed in connection with first seal: the flippers are put in a grave. 'Then, when the young man later becomes a great hunter, and some shaman or other grows envious, and endeavours to take away his catch by magic, i.e. steal the souls of the animals he gets, the attempt will prove fruitless. The shaman's helping spirits will be afraid of the outer part of the flippers placed in the grave, and will then protect the boy's catch against all evil' (1929: 178).

10. Hanserâk, a Greenlandic catechist, also mentions in his diary the fear of Maratsuk and Avgo, the latter being one of the most famous *angakkut* on the east coast (1885: 65).

11. Mads Lidegård describes how a woman has to leave her home district with her husband because an *angakkoq* had decided that her husband had to find another wife (1986: 172). The *angakkut* prerogative of sleeping with the wife of other men is known all over the Eskimo area.

12. Kirsten Bang uses Dekré as an informant about Maratse. He is related to Maratse and has undertaken several journeys with him: 'Maratse was a great angakok and his fellow men feared him very much, because he had powerful helping spirits and could steal souls' (1944: 18 [my translation]).

13. Steensby describes the fate of the evil-minded *angakkoq*:

> The angakok Kajorapaluk (Peary's Kyahpadu or Kyo) was a bad character and a bad comrade, who was always offending the other members of the tribe in various ways; but what was specially fatal was, that he was constantly lying and deceiving them with regard to the hunting. Sometimes he amused himself by warning them of bad hunting and consequent famine, in order to frighten them, sometimes he told them that he had

seen here or there, for example, the white whale or walrus; but it was always falsehood. At last it became too much for them; it gradually became the common feeling of the tribe, that it would be best to get rid of such a troublesome individual. He was killed by Uvdloriak and Masaitsiak, two of the best men of the tribe, and the latter married the dead man's wife, whom he lives with till this day. (1910: 366)

14. Mikkelsen mentions how the *angakkut* for some time after the introduction of Christianity still had an influence over the people when they hoped for recovery from painful illnesses (1960: 127).

15. Lars Dalager describes how the *angakkut* after a séance look totally disturbed and give confusing anwers. This, however, does not influence Dalager's view on the morality of the *angakkut*. A true *angakkoq* never does harm but only does good, but the fake *angakkut*, which are the majority, are doing both evil and good deeds (1752: 43).

16. Daniel Merkur states that the pathological/schizophrenic behaviour normally attributed to shamanism is not obvious in Greenland, where the intelligence of the *angakkut* is again and again emphasised (1985: 13, 40).

17. 'Konebaad' is the Danish for 'women's boat', the large skin boat used by Greenlandic women for transport purposes, known by them as an *umiak*. The spelling of the different names of the spirits in the following are according to Holm's way of spelling.

18. The *angakkoq* as the more intelligent and ingenious member of society is also mentioned by Niels Egede and David Crantz in the Chapter 2.

19. I have used Holm's own spelling of the name of the spirits.

20. One of the drawings by the East Greenlandic artist Kârale describes the arrival of such a spirit: 'The helping spirit âjumâq is floating into a house during a seance, it has black arms and legs, and everything it touches must die' (Geertsen 1990: no. 108 [my translation]). The spirit is stretching its arms out and the audience is fleeing the touch by hiding on the benches.

21. Several *angakkut* mention social humiliation as the impetus for becoming an *angakkoq*.

22. Thalbitzer also mentions the turning of the stone in the instruction of the future *angakkoq*. He adds, however, that the older *angakkoq* first teaches him 'how he is to go in perfect secrecy and fetch a special kind of sea-weed from the beach when the tide is low, and wash himself all over his whole body.' The apprentice is at that stage according to Thalbitzer about seven to eight years old (1910: 452).

23. A footnote explains that Sanimuinak showed that those which are in the sea are the size of a large hand, perhaps a crab.

24. The *Tornarksuk* is described by Hans Egede as the great spirit. Kruuse tries to establish 'whether Tornarsuk was one single personal spirit, but got the impression that at least Dakoda and some others (Akernilik, Misuarnianga and more) thought that there were more tornarsuks. Finally I asked whether there was one Tonarsuk, which was more powerful than the other spirits of all Inuit; but nobody seemed to know of such a being, a Tornarsuak. Alltogether it is probably not possible that a belief in one Divine Being should have developed among a people under their spiritual conditions' (1912: 44 [my translation]). The role of this spirit will be discussed in the section on 'The Pantheon of the *Angakkoq*'.

25. Thalbitzer mentions that in order to summon a spirit or soul one merely needs to know its name and utter it. 'Thus it is clear that the angakok novice cannot

summon the spirits that are to be his attendant genii, on the first occasion; they come of their own accord, or else he lights upon them unexpectedly when he is out rambling alone. But when he has once spoken with them and learnt their names he will henceforward be able to summon them again' (1910: 454).

26. As will be illustrated later from an account by Rasmussen.

27. To give the *tupilak* its power to kill the intended victim the *angakkoq* has to rub it against his genitals after having created the *tupilak* out of different animal and plant materials. The *tupilak* will be described in detail in the section on 'The Pantheon of the *Angakkoq*'.

28. The commentary points out that this kind of knowledge is normally granted to the *iliseeneq* (in modern West Greenlandic spelled *ilisiitsoq*, sing., *ilisiitsut*, plur.) which is mostly translated as 'the witch' (1923: 457). As childbearing can be a terminating factor for the apprenticeship of a female *angakkoq*, getting a husband might put an end to Teemiartissaq's attempts to become an *angakkoq*. M.A. Czaplicka writes that 'women may lose their gift of shamanizing after child birth' (1914: 245). Bogoras writes that, 'The gift of inspiration is thought to be bestowed more frequently upon women, but it is reputed to be of a rather inferior kind, and the higher grades belong rather to men. The reason for this is, that the bearing of children is generally adverse to shamanic inspiration, so that a young woman with considerable shamanistic power may lose the greater part of it after the birth of her first child' (1904-1909: 415).

29. The *Taarajuätsiaqs* are described as 'nature spirits which live under the earth near to the dwelling of human beings, and from which the angakut partly get their guardian spirit' (Thalbitzer 1923: 457). These spirits are obviously identical with those that Sanimuinak encounters.

30. In the commentary the last sentence is translated literally as 'you shall cease to be powerless'.

31. Other narrations of the experiences of the apprentice point to the role that fear plays as an incentive for becoming an *angakkoq*. Qúpersimân makes fear the motivation for his wish to become an *angakkoq* (1982: 41). He even achieves a former *angakkoq* as his helping spirit against fear (1982: 64ff), and concludes that 'to try and search for these helping spirits is first possible when one is scared. All spirits are horrifying the first time you encounter them, but you get used to them' (1982: 134 [my translation]). The vicar Christian Rosing, who writes in 1906, explains the visions and experiences of the *angakkut* by their fear. 'All Angâkut say, that they have been very scared, so scared "that they almost died of fear"' (1946: 44 [my translation]).

32. According to a footnote, the bear of the inland ice has no hair on its head and is enormous and overgrown with ice.

33. Among the Iglulik, Rasmussen describes how secrecy is a threat to the community. After a member of the society has seen spirits he comments 'One must never keep the matter secret when one has seen spirits' (1929: 49). Or, when visiting the Moon Spirit, 'Any human being who visits the Moon Man must never make a secret of the fact: to keep it secret would mean death' (1929: 75). This might indicate how precarious the situation of the apprentice is as secrecy is a necessity until the actual coming out as a fully educated *angakkoq*. Such an attitude to secrecy is easily understood in a social context where the secret transgression of taboo rules by an individual can lead to major disasters

for the society as a whole. The séance of the *angakkoq* therefore often takes the form of pure interrogation (1929: 133ff).

34. The translator has apparently decided to use the word shaman instead of *angakkoq* and, therefore, references to this text apply the word shaman.

35. Sanimuinak also experiences an encounter with a spirit which cries like a baby, but there is no mention of having to encounter this spirit three times before including it as a helping spirit, neither is the running away described by him.

36. This was a very important skill in connection with disclosing transgressions committed by members of the society.

37. Among the Azande, witchcraft substance is believed to be positioned in the body: 'It is attached to the edge of the liver. When people cut open the belly they have only to pierce it and witchcraft-substance bursts through with a pop' (Evans Pritchard 1965: 22). V. Diószegi also mentions the 'excess bone' which is found during the initiation process when the initiate is boiled by his ancestors (1960: 62).

38. No doubt the Greenlander is talking about a Greenlandic spirit, probably *Toornaarsuk*, but for Poul Egede, this spirit represents the Devil.

39. M.A. Czaplicka claims that a shaman will not show all his power in front of strangers (1914: 174) and refers to Bogoras who writes: 'A shaman of great power will refuse to show his skill when among strangers, and will yield only after much solicitation; even then, as a rule, he will not show all of his power' (1904-1909: 416).

40. Sonne mentions the special status of the *angakkoq puullit* among the *angakkut* (1986: 143ff).

41. The term 'wizard' is here used instead of shaman.

42. The description is similar to that found in *Intellectual Culture of the Iglulik Eskimos*, p. 111ff. Kaj Birket-Smith describes how the initiate among the Chugach Eskimos experience the encounter with the spirits: 'As soon as a spirit spoke to the novice he would faint, and immediately the spirit carried him up into the mountains or to the depth of the sea in order to teach him the secrets of his art, in the first instance his shaman's song. Finally the novice would wake up on top of a mountain or lying in water, but when the spirit was convinced of his abilities, it would take him home' (1953: 126). Rasmussen describes how a novice who aspires to become a magician also enters the mountains to achieve helping spirits. He meets two spirits but dares not speak to them. 'The day after I went home; and then I was a little of a magician, only a very little of a magician' (1908: 147). Then after more encounters outside the settlement the spirits finally come to him and he becomes a great magician. The use of magician instead of shaman may be due to lack of knowledge of the term by Rasmussen as this is an early text.

43. A footnote indicates that they follow the commands given by the *angakkoq*.

44. Holm adds in a footnote that from this description he believes that it is an octopus.

45. Rink claims that *toornaarsuk* is placed in the lower world and that it takes courage to meet him as he is frightful (1868: 204). He states that *toornaarsuk* now represents the devil for the Christian Greenlanders (1868: 209), a deduction which is obvious, taking the concept of the character and position of *toornaarsuk* from the missionaries into account. In the dairies of H.C. Glahn from 1767, however, *toornaarsuk* is described as the foremost deity of the Greenlanders as they see him as keeper of their existence giving support to the *angakkoq* on his travels (1921:

186ff). There is a strong ambiguity in the interpretation of this spirit on the west coast of Greenland, probably due to the influence of Christianity. Thalbitzer calls *toornaarsuk* a non-human being, a super-human nature spirit, perhaps representing the magical forces in nature. He appears under different forms. He might represent the intelligent aspect of life, but not its highest forces (1926: 15, 27).

46. The tooth of the narwhale was believed to be that of the unicorn by early explorers.

47. In a footnote Egede points out that others say that a huge dog is watching the entry, trying to keep the *angakkoq* outside. A myth stating the origin of the Mother of the Sea makes the dog her husband when she was still a young human girl.

48. Poul Egede mentions the same object but spelled *aglerrutut*, which is a piece of material on which a woman has aborted and which is not to be used anymore (1939: 36).

49. Thalbitzer mentions the name Nivikkaa as the name of the girl in the myth about the Mother of the Sea in South Greenland (1926: 41). The Mother of the Sea, is according to Rasmussen, called *Nuliajuk* among the Netsilik Eskimos, *Takánakapsâluk* among the Iglulik.

50. Rasmussen describes the attitude to the Moon Spirit among the Iglulik Eskimos as follows. Contrary to the East Greenlandic concept the Moon Spirit is here seen as 'the good and well-intentioned spirit, and when he does intervene, it is often more for guidance than for punishment' (1929: 74). If a woman is barren the Moon Spirit will keep her with him until she is with child. He is well-intentioned and the provider of game as the sea-woman is holding game back.

51. On East Greenland, Holm gives a description of the various spirits:

Timerseks	These look like human beings but are larger. Their souls alone are as big as a human being. They hunt animals and sometimes have fights with human beings whom they might steal.
Erkiliks	Their upper part looks like a human being, the lower like a dog. They have a hostile relationship to humans and live on the inland ice. *Timerseks*, *Erkiliks* and *Kavdlunaks* (Europeans) all have the same origin, they are offspring of a girl and a dog.
Gobajaks	These are women with round bellies and iron nails.
Tarajuatsiaks (1888: 115ff).	These are shadows, which are helping the *angakkut*.

52. Birket-Smith stresses that among the Chugach Eskimos 'once the connection with the spirits was established, it was founded upon co-operation on so to speak equal terms and not upon a state of dependance of the shaman and superiority of his assistant spirits. A shaman was simply called kala•lik, i.e., one who has spirit(s)' (1953: 126). Among the Iglulik Rasmussen describes an interview with a shaman: 'Otherwise he could tell me nothing more definite about these spirits. He merely said that their power lay in their own unfathomable mysteriousness. They had appeared to him in the first instance without his asking, he had touched them, and they had thereby become his property or his servants once and for all, coming to help him whenever he called' (1929: 38).

53. Eliade describes this lack of costume:

> The shaman bares his torso and (among the Eskimo, for example) retains a belt as his only garment. This quasi-nudity probably has a religious meaning, even if the warmth prevalent in Arctic dwellings would apparently suffice by itself to explain the custom. In any case, whether there is ritual nudity (as in the case of the Eskimo shamans) or a

particular dress for the shamanic experience, the important point is that the experience does not take place with the shaman wearing his profane, everyday dress. (1989: 146)

54. Thalbitzer gives a description of another instrument, a *makkortaa*: 'it consists of a round, flat piece of black skin from five to five and a half centimetres in diameter, which is held tightly in the hollow of the hand, while it is struck or rapped-on with a carved wooden stick with the other hand. By aid of this little instrument the angakok produces a loud rhythmic knocking as a preliminary to his meeting with the spirits below the ground' (1908: 458).

55. Therkel Mathiassen describes one of these stones:

an oval gneiss pebble, one side of which has been rubbed smooth through friction against something hard without actually forming facets: Thus it has scarcely been used as a whetstone, and it has no bruises as the hammer stone has. More probably it is one of those stones which the shamans employ in their séance, rubbing it against another stone with a rotating movement in order to conjure up their helping spirits. A stone of this appearance, found at Kûngmiut near Angmagsalik, was identified by Karl Andreassen, the Greenland artist and story-teller, as one of these angakoq stones. (1934: 113)

56. Christian Leden describes in a diary from 1909 the singing and dancing involved in the *angakkoq's* séance. The old *angakkoq* Massaitsiak is facing a younger man, Ajorsilak who is carrying a piece of driftwood between his teeth. Ajorsilak stares at the old *angakkoq* as if to hypnotise him. Suddenly Massaitsiak starts to sing and dance swinging the upper part of his body and soon everybody follows suit. The *angakkoq* utters wild wails with a loud voice. At the end of the séance, Ajorsilak holds the driftwood under the nose of Massaitsiak and screams and thereby wakens the old man from his trance. 'After some time another angakok took the drum and began to dance and perform some of the old songs, that he had learnt from shamans long dead. The old songs floated mournfully in his deep soft voice, telling about the suffering, an expression of the fear of the long polar night' (1952: 25ff [my translation]).

57. Thalbitzer gives an example of the use of pieces of dead people.

Ajukutooq told me that the nail of a dead man's great toe might be used as amulet for a child; it had to be sewn round the great toe of the child, when even the slightest kick by the foot would cause the assaulted enemy to be swollen on a part of his body, or make an approaching tupilak take to his heels. The nail on the fourth finger of a dead man might also be used as an amulet if placed on the breast or back; on the approach of a disease during sleep, i.e. the attack of an evil thought or spirit, the nail grows unseen and on account of its hardness and sharpness prevents the disease from penetrating within. (1914: 627)

58. Berthelsen describes how as a medical doctor he has only seen a few traditional amulets and that Christian symbols are now used instead, such as a piece of the psalm-book or the Bible or as a remedy against illness. The cutting up of Our Lord's Prayer can be put into the patient's food. Berthelsen questions if the latter can be seen as the use of an amulet and continues to give examples of other remedies that resemble those found all over the world in folk medicine (1914: 37ff).

59. Thalbitzer describes a wooden model of a *tupilak* by Mitsuarnianga, the great East Greenlandic *angakkoq*. He had seen it moving or creeping later across the water in the Ammassalik Fjord. 'The real tupilak which in his capacity of

angakoq he had created and made living the usual way was a sandpiper (Tringa maritima), on which he had placed the head of a dead child.' Thalbitzer comments that it is not unusual to use parts from dead children (1914: 643).

60. The translation uses the word magician instead of the Greenlandic term.

61. It might point to the fact that the *angakkoq* is dealing with death and the dead and therefore can be seen as a parallel to the skeleton symbolism used on the Mongolian and Siberian shamans' dresses.

62. This understatement of skills is also described by the Egede family but is taken by them at face value and, therefore, seen as the *angakkoq* admitting his jugglery to be false. Holm also says that the *angakkoq* Sanimuinak describes his skills as all pretence. It is necessary to have the custom of not offending the spirits by bragging of one's capacity in mind when one assesses the true message of such a statement.

63. Daniel Merkur applies the term 'demonstrative shamanism' to cases in which the shaman is indeed in a trance. By contrast, 'imitative shamanism' describes non-ecstatic rites that are modelled on shamanic séances. 'It must be immediately admitted that there is often no necessary evidence by which to establish the presence of trance; but, because the simulation of a trance is itself a technique that induces trances, I see no reason for inordinate scepticism' (1985: 93). 'Demonstrative shamanism is not a mere show of ventriloquism and sleight-of-hand, intended to impress the gullible. It is always a physical demonstration of something that the shamans regard as genuine in a metaphysical manner. However, a shaman performing an elaborate demonstration in light trance cannot simultaneously be experiencing his free-soul's journey in deep trance' (Ibid.: 210).

64. There are, however, varied interpretations of the number of souls that a human being possesses.

65. Whereas soul and life are totally interconnected, so that the soul leaving the dead body still represents the person, the spirits are described by Shirokogoroff as immaterial, they cannot be seen unless they take special form. They do, however, possess all the human characteristics and should therefore be treated in the same way as human beings (1935: 55).

66. Chr. Rosing mentions (1946: 13) that some believe that a human being only has one soul whereas others believe that each joint has a soul that looks like a tiny human being. Illness in a part of the body is caused by the stealing of that specific soul.

67. The helping spirit of the *angakkoq*.

68. These may, however, be the *angakkut puullit* and therefore of high status.

69. This metaphor for the sound is also used in the description of *Sagdloq* by Rasmussen.

70. The word used for Europeans, who are believed to be derived from the mating of a woman and a dog.

71. In *Hansarâks Dagbog* there is a description of this séance (1933: 78ff). He also gives a description of another séance through the performer himself:

> He said that when he performed witchcraft, *heksede,* with his troll spirit and took a round piece of bearded seal skin in his hand and hit it with the drum stick and then, when it rattled, he would move over to the drum next to him, the drum would start to hop of its own accord, to move into the air and dance round his head; then his head

became as if open, and he could see the spirits. When he was behaving like that, he was able to get all his wishes fulfilled, for example to make a bear appear, to see the reason for some illness, or whether the ill person had maybe lost his soul, how he could find his way on an impassable road. (Ibid.: 51 [my translation])

Kirsten Bang writes about the famous *angakkoq* Maratse that his

violent temperament and the swelling power of his mind involved everybody and bent them under his will. One could fear Maratse, and one could hate him, but everybody that got in contact with him had to accept his power. When Maratse sang, all his audience had to follow him in his increasing ecstasy to the culmination, when he abruptly stopped the drum beats and in the utmost sensual pleasure and pain gargled and howled and twisted, rolling his eyes, the big mouth distended – until he suddenly relaxed and smiled, and everybody was released of the spell. (1944: 35 [my translation])

72. As a comparison to the séance of the Eskimos of Greenland, Rasmussen describes the Canadian Eskimos' séance (1927: 29ff), which has much in common with those of Greenland:

The wizard preparing to set out on such a journey [to the People of Day] is placed at the back of the bench in his hut, with a curtain of skin to hide him from view. His hands must be tied behind his back, and his head lashed fast to his knees; he wears breeches, but nothing more, the upper part of his body being bare. When he is thus tied up, the men who have tied him take the fire from the lamp on the point of a knife and pass it over his head, drawing rings in the air, and saying at the same time: 'Niorruarniartoq aifale' (Let him who is going on a visit now be carried away). Then the lamps are extinguished, and all those present close their eyes. So they sit for a long while in deep silence. But after a time strange sounds are heard about the place; throbbing and whispering sounds; and then suddenly comes the voice of the wizard himself crying loudly: 'Halala–halalale halala –halalale!' And those present then must answer 'ale–ale–ale.' Then there is a rushing sound, and all know that an opening has been made, like the blowhole of a seal, through which the soul of the wizard can fly up to heaven, aided by all the stars that once were men. Often the wizard will remain away for some time, and in that case, the guests will entertain themselves meanwhile by singing old songs, but keeping their eyes closed all the time. It is said that there is great rejoicing in the Land of Day when a wizard comes on a visit. The people there come rushing out of their houses all at once; but the houses have no doors for going in or out, the souls just pass through the walls where they please, or through the roof, coming out without even making a hole. And though they can be seen they are as if made of nothing. They hurry towards the newcomer, glad to greet him and make him welcome, thinking that it is the soul of a dead man that comes, and one of themselves. But when he says 'Putdlailiuvunga' (I am still a creature of flesh and blood) they turn sorrowfully away. He stays there awhile, and then returns to earth, where his fellows are awaiting him, and tells of all he has seen.

As to be expected, there are several parallels between the séance of the Eskimos of North America and those of Greenland.

73. Mikkelsen writes about Missiorianga's (Mitsuarnianga's) conversion: 'Missiorianga was the Angmagssalik area's famous, ruthless and feared Angakoq, when the Danes arrived in the country. Karl Andreassen [his son] was the first male child, who was baptised in Angmagssalik, even with his Angakoq-father's approval, as the sly heathen probably realised that perhaps it would be a good idea for himself as the former leader in the area to show some interest in the dawning new age' (1960: 168

[my translation]). Mikkelsen participates in the christening party in the hut of Missiorianga, 'where there were drum song and drum dance with invocation of all his helping spirits whom he asked to take care of his son in the dangerous world that he was now to enter'. Missiorianga is later christened himself, 'but that was when he had realised that his power as Angakoq had been broken by church and priest'.

74. Rüttel describes how Ajukutok performs his séance. The preparations are similar to the known pattern: the covering up of windows, the dry skin in front of the entrance, the moistening of the drum. Then the lamps are extinguished and men and women call the spirits. The *angakkoq* utters several sounds rising to a roar, then sighs. At this point the drumming starts, slow at first and then very fast. Suddenly the audience stop their shouting and a voice is heard from the deep, the words cannot be understood, but according to Rüttel as the voice of the spirit gets clearer it has the voice of Ajukutok himself. The spirit leaves and the rattling and shouting start up again but no spirit arrives and Ajukutok gives up (1917: 84).

75. This challenge has a parallel in the Siberian shaman's trials: 'His soul is taken to the shaman-ancestors and there they show him a kettle full of boiling tar. There are people in it. There are some who are known to the shaman. A single rope is fastened across the kettle and they order him to walk over it. If he succeeds he will live long. If he falls into the kettle, he still might become a kam, but usually they do not survive' (Diózegi 1968: 58). In both descriptions it is the courage of the shaman or *angakkoq* which is challenged by this rope trial.

76. Poul Egede gives a similar account of the *angakkoq's* journey to and the encounter with The Mother of the Sea (1939: 36ff). His vocabulary is more out-spoken, The Mother of the Sea is called 'the Devil's Grandmother and The Goddess of Hell'.

77. In *Across Arctic America. Narrative of the Fifth Thule Expedition* Rasmussen gives an account of the journey of the *angakkoq* to *Takanalukarnaluk*, the Mistress of the Sea:

> [T]he wizard sits, if winter, on the bare snow, in summer, on the bare earth. He remains in meditation for a while, and then invokes his helping spirits, crying again and again: 'Tagfa arqutinilerpoq–tagfa neruvtulerpoq!'(The way is made ready for me; the way is opening before me). Whereupon all those present answer in chorus: 'Taimalilerdle' (let it be so). Then when the helping spirits have arrived, the earth opens beneath the wizard where he sits; often, however only to close again; and he may have to strive along with hidden forces before he can finally cry that the way is open. When this is announced, those present cry together: 'Let the way be open, let there be way for him!' Then comes a voice close under the ground: 'halala–he–he–he' and again farther off under the passage, and again still farther and ever farther away until at last it is no longer heard; and then all know that the wizard is on his way to the Mistress of the Sea. Meantime those in the house sing spirit songs in chorus to pass the time. It may happen that the clothes which the wizard has taken off come to life of themselves, and fly about over the heads of the singers, who must keep their eyes closed all the time. And one can hear the sighing and breathing of souls long dead. All lamps have been put out, and the sighing and breathing of the departed souls is as the voice of spirits moving deep in the sea; like the breathing of sea-beasts far below. (1927: 31ff)

The description of the visit to the Mistress of the Sea is similar to that in Greenland. When the *angakkoq* returns the people participating in the séance are asked to confess the breaches of taboo that they have committed. According to Knud Rasmussen they are very eager to confess lest they might be the cause of famine and disaster to all. The famous *angakkoq* Aua explains that all is well because in the confession lies the forgiveness and all rejoice in the averting of disaster. Aua adds that there is even something like a feeling of gratitude towards the 'sinners'. Rasmussen decribes the Netsilik Eskimos' concept of the Mother of the Sea. She resides in a house at the bottom of the sea which is similar to those in which humans live. She is called *Nuliajuk* and according to a myth is a girl who has been punished by her father and thrown overboard from a boat. He cut off her fingers which were then transformed into seals. Becoming mistress over everything that man hunts she obtains great power over mankind. She becomes the most feared of all the spirits, controlling the destinies of men. Therefore, almost all taboo is directed towards her:

> In her house Nuliajuk lives remote from all, hasty in her anger and terrible in her might when she wishes to punish mankind. She notices every little breach of taboo, for she knows everything. Whenever people have been indifferent towards her by not observing taboo, she hides the animals; the seal she shuts up in her in•aut: a drip basin that she has under her lamp. As long as they are inside it, there are no animals to hunt in the sea, and mankind has to starve; the shamans then have to summon their helping spirits and conjure her to be kind again. Some shamans are content to let their helping spirits work for mankind, they themselves remaining in their houses summoning and conjuring in trance, whereas others rush down to her themselves to fight her, to overcome her and appease her. But there are also some who draw Nuliajuk herself up to the surface of the land. They do it in this way: they make a hook fast to the end of a long seal thong and throw it out of the entrance passage; the spirits set the hooks fast in her, and the shaman hauls her up into the passage. There everybody can hear her speaking. But the entrance from the passage into the living room must be closed with a block of snow, and this block, uvkuaq, Nuliajuk keeps on trying to break into pieces in order to get into the house to frighten everybody to death. And there is great fear in the house. But the shaman watches the uvkuaq and so Nuliajuk never gets into the house. Only when she has promised the shaman to release all the seals into the sea again does he take her off the hook and allow her to go into the depths again. In that way a shaman, who is only a human being, can subdue Nuliajuk and save people from hunger and misery by means of words and his helping spirits. (1931a: 226)

The *angakkoq* clearly shows great strength in summoning *Nuliajuk* to his séance and keeping her from doing any harm to the audience. Fear is created, as everybody can hear the voice of the greatest of all spirits. The *angakkoq* is the only one who can deal with her and is, therefore, the upholder of the cosmos, of the life and death of the settlement. The interesting part of this description is that the Mother of the Sea is dragged out of her dwelling and actually is seen to enter in direct contact with the settlement. Instead of letting the battle between the *angakkoq* and the spirit take place in the remote area of the sea it is literally performed on the doorstep. As the Mother of the Sea is in control of all game and watches the transgression of taboo rules carefully, anyone who has committed an offence must be very meek in the face of the anger of the spirit and his own fear and therefore very grateful for the power of the *angakkoq*.

78. In a study by Sonne on the myths relating to the Mother of the Sea, she concludes that 'early attempts by the first missionaries to relate *toornaarsuk* to Sea Woman, whom they assumed to be the daughter (or great grandmother) of the Devil, left no traces in the Greenland stories' (1990: 30).

79. Thalbitzer mentions this person as *Irdlirvirisissong* in East Greenland, *Erhaveerisoq* in South Greenland (1926: 58). In most descriptions this person is a woman and it is possible that Rüttel has got the gender wrong. Rasmussen describes her as follows: 'The Moon Man does all he can to keep her out of his house, but nevertheless it happens sometimes that she finds an opportunity of throwing down her dish on the floor; a dish quite white at the bottom from the fat of entrails. And then she herself comes leaping in after it, dancing and hopping and twisting her body in all manner of ludicrous and sensual gestures and movements, ready to fall on any who smile, in a moment, and use her knife' (1929: 76). The concept of the Moon Man among the Iglulik is that of adviser.

80. This description is similar to that of David Crantz (1820: 186ff) and there is no doubt a mutual source in Hans Egede's description of the passage of the dead: 'As the souls of the dead, in their travel to this happy country, they meet with a sharp pointed stone, upon which the angekkuts tell them they must slide or glide down upon their breech, as there is no other passage to get through, and this stone is besmeared with blood; perhaps, by this mystical or hieroglyphical image, they thereby signify the adversities and tribulations those have to struggle with, who desire to attain happiness' (1818: 205). The concept of the dead both going to the sky and under ground is similar to that among the Iglulik, where 'The people of the day' reside in the sky and 'The Dwellers in the Narrow Land' below the sea. 'The dead suffer no hardship, wherever they may go, but most prefer nevertheless to dwell in the Land of the Day, where the pleasures appear to be without limit' (Rasmussen 1929: 95). Rasmussen ascribes this concept to the fact that there seems to be no fear of death among old people. The Aurora Borealis is one sign of the fun going on; the dead play with the skull of a walrus.

81. 'Himmel' in Danish and Swedish covers both the concept of 'sky' and 'Heaven'; I prefer to use the translation 'sky' when it refers to the Greenlandic concept.

82. According to the usual procedure of the Egede family, this was, probably, corporal. All this punishment obviously led to the Greenlanders being reluctant to share their ceremonies with the missionaries.

83. In a footnote Hans Egede adds that while *angakkut* are conjuring, nobody must scratch his head, nor sleep, nor break wind; for they say, that such a dart can kill the enchanters, nay the devil himself. After a conjuration has been performed, there is a vacation from work for three or four days.

84. Birket-Smith describes healing through blowing on the west coast: 'The conjurer rubbed the patient, who happened to be his own son, in fish glue, turned him round so that he lay on his stomach and breathed along his back. By this treatment the sufferer recovered' (1924: 424). As the breath is understood as life, therefore the breath of an *angakkoq* must have healing potential. Hanserâk describes in his diary how healing can also take place by rubbing the drum against the floor while whispering and muttering like an *angakkoq* (1933: 111).

85. Rüttel describes how in the year 1904 he came across a strange treatment: 'A man, who suffered from difficulty in breathing was helped by a woman tying a string round the forehead of a child and who thereby heaved and lowered the child lying on the ground. It does not seem to matter whether it is a child or a grown up, a man or a woman, who is lifted or bound, but if the bound person is heavy to lift, it is a bad sign, as the soul has then left, if on the other hand it is easy, it is a good sign, as the soul is still present' (1917: 216 [my translation]).

86. Sanimuinak is Holm's informant; he is mentioned in the section on 'The
    Initiation of the *Angakkoq*'.
87. The initiation of Teemiartissaq is described in detail in the section 'The
    Initiation of the *Angakkoq*'.
88. Rasmussen refers to the term *qilaneq* (1908: 155) as a binding of a string round
    the head or a leg of a person. When the head or leg is heavy, the spirits are present.
89. Among the Netsilik Eskimos in Northern Canada Rasmussen describes the healing
    procedure carried out by two shamans. A woman narrates the story of her
    husband's illness. He had been ill for a long time without knowing why, when one
    day he sees himself standing outside his own body. He realises that it is his soul and,
    trembling all over, he tries to get it back. But the soul does not return to the body.

    > Then a man came up, a man named Oqortoq. He came with his wife, they
    > were both shamans and when they heard what had happened, they insisted
    > that I [the wife] should go into a corner of the tent, right over behind the
    > fireplace; there I had to lie with my head hidden in a heap of caribou bones.
    > While I remained concealed there, the two shamans conjured and summoned
    > their helping spirits. They held a great séance in order to call the soul back to
    > Qaorssuaq's body. And it was not long before he again saw his soul. The two
    > shamans, to whom nothing was impossible, could see it too. They uttered
    > magic words and spoke with their helping spirits' own tongue until the soul
    > came quite close to Qaorssuaq; then they suddenly sprang to him and began
    > to beat him here and there on his body, the consequence being that the soul
    > was frightened and became so scared that it slipped into Qaorssuaq's body
    > once more. At the very same moment he was well again and I could hear him
    > shouting and singing with joy. Only then did I venture to rise from the heap
    > of animal bones where I had hidden my head till then, and we all sang with
    > happiness. In that way Qaorssuaq got his soul back. (1931a: 216)

    In this séance the two shamans obviously create an atmosphere whereby the ill
    person is treated with vigour and is convinced of his having been healed by soul
    retrieval. There is no audience, only the wife hidden in the corner. The two
    shamans do not use head-lifting but instead conjure the reluctant soul back into the
    body. The ill person sees his soul and feels the treatment by which it is frightened
    into obedience. All are convinced of the success of the healing procedure.
90. Ujuât or Johan Petersen participated in Holm's expedition as interpreter.
91. Hansen Resen describes in 1688 how Jens Munk found traces of devil worship
    in Greenland as he came across a figure which was in the shape of 'half a devil',
    with horns and claws. Hansen Resen comments: 'Whatever they are
    worshipping it is clear that it is not God. For the Greenlanders that Dannel
    brought with him were not worshipping God, they were not praying before or
    after meals nor at evening or morning prayers. On the contrary, they were
    laughing at the Danish way of praying. When in Holsten they were shown an
    idol, which was among the rarities in the duke's collection and originated from
    some American islands, they recognised it at once and said: *Nalygivisangum* –
    this is how they pronounced it – They said futhermore, that their children used
    to dance round the image' (1987: 124 [my translation]). *Nalygivisangum* may
    be translated as 'we know that'.
92. Rasmussen decribes in detail the cutting up of the body to prevent retaliation
    (1921b vol. 1: 51ff). This applies to any murder.

93. Lars Dalager describes how an old *angakkoq*, when he hears about the burning of witches, is annoyed that the same law does not apply in Greenland, as he would happily be the first to carry wood to that fire (1752: 41). Dalager states that these 'Hexe-Mestere', witch-doctors and old witches, only create misfortune and that is the reason for the *angakkoq* being so hateful towards them. On the other hand the *angakkut* are seen by Dalager: 'What makes an Angekok study both to do evil and good is that he thereby becomes more feared and admired, but definitely also because he thereby can improve his economic state' (Ibid.: 43 [my translation]). There seems to be a concept of evil and good deeds of the *angakkoq* and the purely evil deeds of the witch. Dalager expresses a certain respect for the old *angakkoq*: 'He likes to hear about God and his divine deeds, which he admires, but for the rest he keeps strictly to his own principles. His way of living is exemplary and I have to admit that my knowledge about Greenland I have mostly achieved from this great man' (Ibid.: 41).

94. Rüttel describes how a woman is lying at the water's edge ready to throw herself in the water for being accused as a witch. She is saved but dies next day (1917: 77). Another women is killed by her sister, as she is seen as a witch. The community applaud the murder (Ibid.: 93). Rüttel adds in a footnote to the confession of witchcraft by a woman that 'she can only be saved by confessing all her sins or she will be killed' (Ibid.: 113 [my translation]).

95. Here is a clear comparison with witchcraft as it is seen in other indigenous cultures. It is the result of an evil will, produced by a human being, and by the use of magic imposed on an innocent victim.

96. Rink mentions similar precautions taken on the west coast (1868: 249). The concept of retaliation of the dead person on the living is also known in other cultures. Robert Hertz's study among the Olo Ngaju of Indonesia and the Dayak of Borneo, points to the fact that the soul is believed to keep an eye on the behaviour of the living and will inflict disease if the duties are not fulfilled. Even the bones are 'warm with spiritual power' (1907: 72).

97. Rasmussen describes these kinds of myths as *Oqalugtuat*, old myths which are common for all Eskimos (1921b vol. 1: 67).

98. These legends, according to Rasmussen, are called *Oqalualât*. He divides these into four categories: the epic, the religious, the humorous and the soporific. The legends that I focus on are the religious as they describe the deeds of the *angakkut*.

99. *Amarok* originally meant wolf, but as they are only known in legends in Greenland, it covers the concept of a fantastic and enormous animal (note by Rink).

100. An *atliarusek* is a supernatural being who lives among the rocks on the shore line.

101. *Angiak* is the foetus or child born secretly and killed. It becomes an evil spirit.

102. The origin of the inland dwellers is described in a note by Rink: 'This expression includes different fabulous people by which the Greenlanders imagined the inner part of the country to be inhabited and of which some are called *Inorusek* (giant), *Erkilik* and *Igalilik*. Originally *Tunnek* must have meant Indian in the inner part of North America' (1982 vol. 1: 372 [my translation]).

103. *Ingnersuït* are supernatural beings who live in the rocks on the shore line and among whom the *angakkut* often have their helping spirits (1982 vol. 1: 373).

104. If this description is adjusted linguistically, it is still typical of the rather colourful descriptions when it comes to describing the killing of people.

105. It seems, however, as if the stories about the bachelor mostly stem from the West Greenlandic area. It might be due to the fact that Christianity introduced monogamy and thereby created a group of unmarried sexually marginalised individuals, as equally pitiful as the orphan and the old unmarried woman.
106. The strength of a man is also connected with his testicles in the creation of the *tupilak*.
107. Van Gennep suggests a division of the rites of passage into three main areas: 1. rites of separation, 2. rites of transition, 3. rites of incorporation (1960: 11). This schema can easily be applied to the initiation of an individual becoming an *angakkoq*. The calling is often connected with behaviour that sets him apart from other members of his society – severe illness, orphanage, solitude and so on – and can therefore be described as rite of separation. The period of apprenticeship and the achieving of knowledge of the spirit-world and the rituals involved in shamanizing is that of transition, and finally the initiation to the mastery of spirits that of incorporation.
108. Spelled Avvgo by Knud Rasmussen.
109. Light as the sign of spiritual power is mentioned by Qúpersimân (1972: 95ff, 134) as one of the ways that spirits recognise the *angakkoq*. The same explanation is offered to Rasmussen by the Copper Eskimos: 'The spirits of the air, they said, saw the shamans in the form of shining bodies that attracted and drew them and made them wish to go and live in them and give them their own strength, sight and knowledge' (1932: 28).
110. The dog has taken the place of the bear in the lake in the narrative of another apprentice, Qúpersimân (1972: 58ff).
111. Sanimuinak describes to Holm how he is eaten by a bear and the clothes afterwards come running for him (Holm 1914: 298ff).
112. Czaplicka describes the Siberian shaman as not belonging 'either to the class of males or that of females, but to a third class, that of shamans. Sexually, he may be sexless, or ascetic, or have inclinations of homosexualistic character, but he may also be quite normal' (1914: 253). In Greenland I have found no source mentioning possible homosexual aspects of the *angakkoq*, only that women through childbirth might be excluded from continuing the work of the *angakkoq*.

Chapter 4

NEO-SHAMANISM
AND THE NEW AGE

Search for the meaning of life and commitment to a higher order that interacts with human existence is hardly specific to the New Age. The cave paintings of 'shamans', the *angakkoq* Aua's explanation to Knud Rasmussen about the reason for taboo rules, the New Age courses in shamanic healing, all reveal human beings perceiving themselves as relating to divine forces or energies that make sense of suffering, death and the general conditions under which they live. The search for meaning and the attempt to understand spiritual experiences are not new; what is new is the way that this search is conducted, the social conditions within which it unfolds and the highly individualised interpretation of spirituality that it encompasses.

In spite of scientific developments which in principle should lead to more and more satisfactory explanations of the unexplained, there seems to be a constant search for spiritual fulfillment among a large section of people in the modern Western world that transgresses the rules of science. Human beings may be perceived not as analysts of causality but as receivers of divine messages and interactors with those forces hidden behind what it is possible to grasp in 'ordinary reality'.

Friedrich Nietzsche describes the role of modern man vis-à-vis this search and writes in the frame of mind of a true modernist:

The most characteristic quality of modern man: the remarkable antithesis between an interior which fails to correspond to any exterior and an exterior which fails to correspond to any interior – an antithesis unknown to peoples of other times. Knowledge ... now no longer acts as an agent for transforming the outside world but remains concealed within a chaotic world which modern man describes with a curious pride as his uniquely characteristic 'subjectivity'... for we moderns have nothing whatsoever of our own; only by replenishing and cramming ourselves with the ages, customs, arts, philosophies, religions, discoveries of others do we become anything worthy of notice. (1983: 78)

The New Age is 'modern man's' attempt to bring this antithesis to an end; to create a synthesis between the exterior, the body, the earth and the interior, the soul, the divine. It might be achieved through 'cramming ourselves with the discoveries of others' but the ultimate goal is to find a new way into the soul and to the spirits which can make sense of the experiences of modern man at the end of the twentieth century. 'Subjectivity' is more than ever the approach. Although the search is in origin as old as man, the experience of the material world is constantly changing for Western civilisation and demands yet another approach to the quest for soul and spirits.

This quest can be seen as personified in the following description of a 'modern shaman': she is dressed in a long black skirt and a black top. Round her neck several necklaces are hanging with different objects: stones in different shapes, a little leather bag with herbs, and so on. Round her forehead is a band of beads and in several places are feathers hanging or sticking out. She is in her late forties or early fifties and her 'face paint' is so thick that it gives her a mask-like appearance. In front of her are placed different crystals and other magical objects and the stacks of cards which are used to determine the destiny of her clients. She is from Birmingham and she is sitting in Oxford Town Hall on a grey day in October 1995. She offers several ways of telling the destiny of the clients. The price is between £15 to £25 depending on how much information the client seeks. On a photocopy she states her credentials:

She Wolf Lodge.
Native American and Celtic Shamanic Teachings.
Being a teacher native American & Celtic esoteric traditions. I am a seer of Celtic descent. My grandmother was a Scottish Irish seer & Shaman taught me the art of being a seer, healer & psychic in the Celtic traditional way. I can trace my ancestry back to almost the legendary Firb Olgs: the people of the bogs, also known as the people of the Goddess Domnu. I have used my psychic abilities to help many people for many years. I read the native American sacred path cards and I am

a colour healer, dream analyst. Earth astologer [sic] & rebirther which I was taught by native American people. I am a member of the Seneca Indian Historical Society, Brant Reservation Irving New York U.S.A. I am able to show you your pathway in life. I can guide you on your way to reach the pathway you wish to walk.[1]

She has many customers, probably due to her 'authentic shamanic appearance', more than any other stall in the two large rooms which the 'Age of Aquarius Fair' has hired. In her self-description she includes a lot of skills that are typical of the New Age: seer, healer, psychic, colour healer, dream analyst, astrologer, rebirther and, most impressive of all, with roots in two famous shamanic traditions: the Celtic and the North American Indian. She represents a synthesis of the spiritual search and covers a large part of what a potential client needs to consult if he or she wants to know about his or her life. She is fully booked.

In the bookstall, 'Greensleeves. Books for a new world', tapes and books can help the uncertain to get wiser or the converted to get support. The other stalls offer herbalism, natural healing, iridology, reflexology, massage, biorhythms, crystals, astrology, tarot and jewellery. It is a typical New Age fair. These fairs takes place all over England and I have attended several. They are identical in nature, the stalls being mostly run by middle-aged men and women. The experiences can sometimes be eerie, such as when a total stranger manages to describe a lot of one's life correctly, to a sense of waste of money when a self-proclaimed shaman interprets medicine cards superficially. Why then, does a modern, apparently enlightened, Western person engage in such an activity?

Lowell D. Streiker, an American pastor of Ladera Community Church in California, describes the users of the New Age in the following way:

New Age may be a hodgepodge, but it is scarcely novel. It was not born yesterday. Under the New Age umbrella, one finds a plethora of groups with histories, traditions, liturgies, literatures, and distinctive ways of life. It may be a jumble, but it is a vital and living jumble, and like all such tumultuous muddles it attracts the sincere as well as the unsavory, the wise as well as the imbecilic, the well-intentioned as well as the self-serving. It is not a spiritual blight, a fungus among us that flourishes when the divine light is eclipsed. It is not a kind of disease that surfaces now and then when orthodox faith in God has gone into decline. New Age has been around for a long, long time, and it will continue to be around as long as it serves the real needs of real human beings. (1990: 47)

According to Streiker, the New Age attracts and encompasses many different types of people. There is something for everybody; there is no sense of exclusion or of an esoteric society. There is not even a threat to the established church. The New Age is not to be feared as it has for a long time existed side by side with Christianity. It apparently is not going to go away either as it 'serves the needs of real human beings'. The question on the tip of one's tongue is, 'Why should not Christianity provide for that need?' This is an important question in connection with the relationship between the Church and the New Age. Is it the shortcomings of the Church and its relationship to mystical experiences that creates a vacuum in which the New Age concept of spirituality can find its *raison d'être*? Streiker's concept of the reason for people's preparedness to participate in New Age fairs, buy New Age products, and so forth. is a sense of helplessness in their own lives:

All the New Age rhetoric about making one's own reality masks the experience of many New Agers, who feel that they are helpless to resist forces that rule their lives – forces of economics, prejudice, racism, ageism, and sexism, over which they exercise no control. The strident insistence that each of us creates his or her own world gives utterance to the desperation of the marginal and the powerless – particularly of women, who today comprise 70 to 90 percent of the New Age market. (Ibid.: 49)

This description of the New Ager as predominantly female, to the extent described above, is not, however, my experience from the fairs or my visits to New Age bookshops. Neither is it my impression that it is a confused disillusioned group with a sense of impotence. Several of the people I have encountered in courses, in conferences and in other New Age activities are highly articulate and very well informed. For the people I interviewed it was often an unexpected spiritual experience that made them search outside the church and look into other traditions. The experience was of a supernatural character with no relationship to their understanding of Christianity in its institutionalised form. On one hand, such experience either created joy because of a sense of contact with something divine, pouring meaning into life, or, on the other hand, a fear of going mad, and a sense of alienation from other members of society.

The need to overcome the sense of a social and spiritual void as the drive for people to seek among the multitude of spiritual approaches on offer in the New Age fair, the New Age bookshop, or New Age courses is shared by one of the most famous writers on this movement, Marilyn Ferguson. In her popular but highly regarded work, *The Aquarian Conspiracy. Personal and Social Transformation in the 1980s*, she determines the relationship between the individual and the society as follows:

> The paradigm of the Aquarian Conspiracy sees humankind embedded in nature. It promotes the autonomous individual in a decentralized society. It sees us as stewards of all our resources, inner and outer. It says that we are not victims, not pawns, not limited by conditions or conditioning. Heirs to evolutionary riches, we are capable of imagination, invention, and experiences we have only glimpsed. (1989: 30)

The New Ager is often a person who acknowledges a sense of crisis. This sense might stem from a personal sense of stress or failure, from an experience of something supernatural or it might stem from a fear of the development of a political and environmental disaster on a worldwide basis. This sense of crisis might lead to action and participation in a network of people, in Marilyn Ferguson's terminology: a conspiracy, members of which 'Whatever their station or sophistication, the conspirators are linked, made kindred by their inner discoveries and earthquakes' (1989: 24), and who are prepared for 'deep inner shifts' (Ibid.: 32).

> At first glance, social transformation seems a foolhardy, even perilous ambition for any group to undertake. There is a necessary and critical chain of events. First, profound change in individuals who care deeply about social change, who find each other, and who acquaint themselves with the psychology of change, with insights into our universal fear of the unknown. They must then devise ways to foster paradigm shifts in others; they must perturb, awaken, and recruit. This aligned minority, knowing that changes of heart and not rational argument alone sway people, must find ways of relating to others at the most human and immediate level. (Ibid.: 223)

Trying to define the movement that these seekers are joining is very difficult because of its highly individualised character. There is no institution in which New Agers gather, there is no single leader who can be the overall organiser and creator of rituals, there is no umbrella organisation. The need of the single New Ager is determined and satisfied by 'shopping around' in the courses, fairs, and bookshops. The New Age bookshop plays a very important role as the intermediary 'between the sacred and the profane'. As several of the publications on offer are manuals purporting to show how to become a shaman, how to become a healer, how to meditate, how to massage, how to improve your diet and so on, one can be a New Ager without having had any other contact with the movement than through the New Age Bookshop. On the other hand one might also through that bookshop find and create links with like-minded people and join courses or participate in, for example, established drumming groups, meditation groups, ley line outings.[2]

A definition of the Aquarian Age, as it was called in the 1960s and 1970s, and the New Age, which is the term more frequently used today, is therefore rather diverse and diffuse. David Hess attempts the following definition. He finds that it is difficult,

> to accommodate the New Age movement to conventional analytical categories such as religion. An interest in modern science is one of the key 'elements' of New Age discourse and practice, along with an interest in Eastern philosophies and the psychology of human potential. To these three elements I would add four others: Native American religion, goddess religion and primitive matriarchy, therapies that integrate body and mind (and 'spirit' when it is a separate category from mind) and all things understood to be 'natural' (e.g. organic food, natural healing, and ecology). Together these elements locate New Age discourse and practice in an arena of debate and dialogue that takes place with reference to science, religion, feminism, biomedicine, psychotherapy, environmentalism, and non-Western philosophies. (1993: 4)

It is almost impossible to imagine a broader definition of a movement. But precisely this broadness is also its strength. It is very difficult to pin-point the New Ager. They might be characterised as 'greying baby-boomers', and there is no doubt that a large part of the New Age users are middle-aged and come from the middle classes. It is a middle of the road movement both in terms of age and politics. As New Age cannot be described as a cult, i.e. a religious belief with the worship of a person or idea, it appeals to those who do not want to be trapped inside an institution but at the same time want to feel a certain sense of belonging to a spiritual movement. The sense of a spiritual urge is predominant.

Transformation is a key word in the New Age terminology. Streiker describes the awakening in the following way: 'At the heart of the New Age are ecstatic experiences, encounters with mystery, brooding intuitions and strange imaginings. First come the powerful feeling states, penetrating one's soul like an unexpected, but impenetrable, fog. These states have no name and no content, but soon they attach themselves to symbol-pictures, images of the world as meaningfully related to the individual' (1990: 143).

This experience sets the search in motion for the individual concerned. It becomes important to incorporate this transcendental experience into a concept of life. 'Making a life, not just a living, is essential to one seeking wholeness. Our hunger turns out to be something different, not something more. Buying, selling, owning, saving, sharing, keeping, investing, giving – these are outward expressions of inward needs. When those needs change, as in personal transformation, economic patterns change' (Ferguson 1989: 355).

Buying and selling is a very important aspect of the New Age lifestyle. As mentioned earlier the bookshop is at the centre of this exchange. Often the bookshop sells candles, incense, crystals, jewellery, pentacles and other paraphernalia for the private spiritual space. It is consumerism, in many ways similar to other kinds of consumerism in our society. The difference lies in the attitude: 'Part of the appeal of the New Age commodities must be that unlike the culture industry, which turns cultural productions into commodity production, New Agers view themselves as turning commodity production into cultural production: they produce goods with a heart' (Hess 1993: 38ff).

When people have reached an understanding of this aspect of consumerism their whole attitude to their work might change. They have become: 'autonomous, their values become *internal*. Their purchases and their choice of work begin to reflect their own authentic needs and desires rather than the values imposed by advertisers, family, peers, media' (Ferguson 1989: 359).

The sense of upheaval, of isolation and loneliness is part of this transformation and, interestingly, not that different from the isolation of the apprentice *angakkoq* when he approaches the spirits in secrecy, but where the *angakkoq* has the understanding of the society towards his secret behaviour it can be more difficult to accept that one's wife, husband, parent or child suddenly talks of a power-animal or helping spirits as part of their reality. 'A mystical experience, however brief, is validating for those attracted to the spiritual search. The mind now knows what the heart had only hoped for. But the same experience can be deeply distressing to one unprepared for it, who must then try to fit it into an inadequate belief system' (Ibid.: 398).

According to writers on New Age, the individual might have a mystical experience, a sudden transformation and upheaval of the values and attitudes held by the surroundings, and the way forward is then to seek consolation within the New Age movement as the Church does not provide an understanding. Seen from the perspective of the surrounding society, belief in the paranormal might be seen as representing 'a new irrationalism that may even pose a danger to society' (Hess 1993: 13) and as an anti-Christian attack on the Church.

> As they pursue their idiosyncratic light, New Agers – men as well as women – are surprised to find themselves regarded as crazy, confused, misguided, or charlatans by those who, in their eyes, have never known anything but darkness. To the seeker and to the seeker's critics, the seeker's values, attitudes, and pattern of behaviour seem novel, but the newness is usually in the eye of the beholder. (Streiker 1990: 50)

When a person has reached this crucial spiritual awakening point the New Age bookshop might be the next step. Here he or she risks becoming more confused than enlightened and naturally there are books available to counteract just that. In the introduction to the *New Age Primer. Spiritual Tools for Awakening.* Glenn Phillips writes:

> The idea for this book came to me while I was browsing through a bookstore in Sedona, Arizona. It was my third or fourth New Age bookstore in as many days, and my mind was starting to go into overload at the many subjects and authors available. I was baffled by the task of trying to keep my selection down to what I could afford, to say nothing of what I had room to carry home. I had been on the road to self-awareness for a number of years, but I began to wonder how anyone just starting to take that first tentative step toward enlightenment and the New Age could ever possibly make a selection from among this smorgasbord of delicacies laid out before me. (1993: introduction)

A smorgasbord, or rather a smörgåsbord, of spiritual enlightenment. The phrase smörgåsbord is apparently a very popular way of describing the multitude of spiritual routes on offer. To help the perplexed, Glenn Phillips has compiled a set of articles covering the more important key areas of New Age such as reincarnation, rebirth, crystals, tarot, creative visualisation. This is a perfect example of the way the spread of the New Age movement takes place: the search is highly individualised and should be to the seeker's own taste. The New Age movement presents a publishing niche where there is ample opportunity for the production of literary works. The Oxford-based couple John and Caitlin Mathews can serve as an example. Between them they have produced more than 40 books on the theme of Celtic shamanism and the Grail myth.

The New Age movement is able to encompass a variety of experiences and spiritual needs, making the seeker a 'heroic crusader', carrying a two-edged sword of egalitarianism and individualism.

> As underdogs, these heroes are located 'beyond' or 'alongside' society: they are paraheroes. In their struggle for the lofty goal or a better knowledge and society, they sometimes violate the very rules of the knowledge and society they seek to preserve. ... By making a journey outside of society the heroes undergo a trajectory that begins to look like a rite of passage: the ordinary citizen is transformed into a hero by passing through a 'liminal' or marginal social position toward reinstatement into a better and reformed society. (Hess 1993: 90)

There is little doubt that the New Age offers a paraculture where it is possible to circumvent the traditional social stratas and rise in a spiritual context to high authority. Some of the well-known personalities in the movement started from a relatively low traditional social position to attain sudden fame and great influence in the lives of many. One of the exceptions to this is Sir George Trevelyan, who wrote in his vision of the New Age in 1977:

> The veils separating the levels of consciousness are growing very thin. The truth is that, in a most profound sense, the New Age is already here, waiting for us to bring it into manifestation by lifting and opening our awareness and allowing the timeless to be earthed. It is thus dependent on us when and where the New Age manifests. But the moment we learn how to open ourselves and invoke them, the New Age energies begin to flow. Thus man's understanding, acceptance and creative channelling is an essential factor. Just as we have noted that the higher worlds are to be

found wherever we can direct our attention to them, we must also recognise that the New Age already exists. It only remains for us to determine how and where it shall assume concrete form. (1977: 65)

The New Age energies are flowing, the concrete form is being shaped but it is a highly diffused and individualised mould with no formal worship. 'New Age is a network of people, books, periodicals, clichés, conferences, psychic faires, and inchoate feelings' (Streiker 1990: 69). Whilst there is a need for sceptics there is also a need for an understanding of the role the spiritual elements of the New Age movement play for many members of society.

> Without a doubt, sceptics have performed a useful social function by exposing the numerous cases of charlatanism and fraud associated with the paranormal beliefs. Like ten thousands of other people, I read with interest the *Skeptical Inquirer*, however, the world of paranormal beliefs and practices cannot be reduced to cranks, crackpots, and charlatans. A large number of sincere people are exploring alternative approaches to questions of personal meaning, spirituality, healing and paranormal experiences in general. (Hess 1993: 158)

Ferguson talks about a paradigm shift with a distinctly new way of thinking of old problems. There is a belief in the existence of a power which the individual can make use of if he or she finds the right way of connecting to it. The ways are many and they are believed to lead from individual transformation to transformation of society through a network of people who have understood the connection between body, mind and spirit and how these relate to the Earth and the Universe and ultimately thereby to create a holistic approach to life.

The attitude to the body has changed and interest in folk-medicine arisen as an alternative to the scientised and secularised medicine. The placebo effect is recognised scientifically and it is accepted that the role of trust and belief on the part of the patient in the healer has huge implications for the success of the treatment. Healing therefore plays an important part in the New Age. People who claim to have tuned in to the energies and the power of the Universe are believed to be able to use that 'attunement' for the benefit of their fellow human beings. Massage, aromatherapy, acupuncture, homeopathy, Reiki healing, psychotherapy, Bach flower remedies, are all seen as an alternative to the GP and the hospitals. The sums of money changing hands in this alternative system of curing are enormous. It is not cheap to have a treatment. £30–50 is not an unusual hourly rate. But there is a preparedness to pay on the part of the sufferer for a sense of being cured by a mediator between the sacred and the profane: the true healer.

It is not difficult to see how neo-shamanism fits this whole scenario: there is a communication with spirits, there is an awareness of the soul and the well-being of the soul, there is healing and there is an established cosmology from which one can build one's own, whether it is of South American, North American, Circumpolar, Asian, African or European origin. And last, but not least, the individual can develop his or her shamanic skills alone, with just a drumming tape for assistance.

In the literature on neo-shamanism the North American Indian plays the leading role but also the role of the Mexican *brujo* is important through the writings of Carlos Castaneda. The contribution of Carlos Castaneda in the concept of the shaman among New Agers cannot be overestimated. His six books, *The Teaching of Don Juan, A Separate Reality, Journey to Ixtlan, Tales of Power, The Second Ring of Power* and *The Eagle's Gift* are descriptions of the personal journey of Castaneda from being an apprentice to becoming a Nagual, a teacher and leader. Starting out as a young anthropologist he meets don Juan and gets involved in an apprenticeship which takes him through terrifying and sublime spiritual experiences helped by the use of hallucinogenics, especially peyote. The use of euphoric plants is characteristic of the first of the six books written in the 1960s whereas the use of the dreaming body, the 'other' which is a perfect replica of the dreamer's body, is characteristic of the 1980s. 'It is inherently the energy of a luminous being, a whitish, phantomlike emanation, which is projected by a fixation of the second attention into a three-dimensional image of the body' (1992: 25). There has been a movement away from the drug-induced realisations of the spirit world in the 1960s to the use of the inherent potentials of the body to call forward and interact with special energies that creates the same experiences through what is called 'dreaming' in the 1980s.

It has been claimed that the whole work of Castaneda is a construction of his own imagination. Reading the books it is very tempting to believe that this is the case as Castaneda, challenged by the academic establishment, apparently failed to produce field-notes. But in the context of looking at the books and their influence on the New Age concept of the shaman, it is fair to say that Castaneda has had a considerable influence. There is no doubt that his writings have created an interest in shamanism as such. Together with the courses in shamanism created by another anthropologist, Michael Harner, the work of Castaneda has brought the knowledge of shamanism to Western urban areas. The United States has been in the forefront of neo-shamanism but, as will be shown later, it has now settled on the shores of England and Denmark, two countries less susceptible to manic spirituality.

Old Traditions Moulded to the Needs of Westerners in Search of Spirituality

In *The Aquarian Guide to the New Age*, an 'introductory guide which has been compiled to demonstrate the range of ideas and activities that go to make up the New Age' (Campbell and Brennan 1990: 10), the shaman is described as follows:

> The Shaman is a follower of a visionary tradition reaching back into the dawn of prehistory and based on animistic ideas about the world. (S)he will typically make use of rhythmic drumming, dance, chanting, fasting, drugs, sweat lodges, and vision quests to induce trance states which allow the shaman's soul to enter the spirit worlds and there enlist the aid of certain allies for healing, divination and magic. There are similarities in techniques whether used by indigenous people in Australia, the Amazon or Eastern Europe.[3]
>
> Long looked on as a primitive precursor to religion, the dawning of the New Age has seen the emergence of a new breed of urban shaman, sometimes with impeccable credentials in anthropology, bent on adapting the ancient system to modern needs. (Ibid.: 275)

The emphasis here is on trance as the most important tool for the shaman in his work. This mentions the aid rather than the mastery of spirits and refers to academically trained practitioners as part of 'the new breed of urban shamans'. This may not relate directly to the definition of a shaman but it adds a sort of credibility to the new concept of 'an urban shaman'. And, interestingly, it is correct in pointing out that several academically trained people are involved in neo-shamanism. Carlos Castaneda and Michael Harner, to whom this guide refers in bracket, are the obvious anthropologists, but also Serge Kahili King, who has a doctorate in psychology and has published *Urban Shaman*, and Fred Alan Wolf, a former professor of physics and author of *The Eagle's Quest*, a description of his experiences among the *Ayahuasqueros* (shamans using ayahuasca) in South America, to mention two who, while not anthropologists, have received an academic training. There is no doubt that, among the people involved in New Age phenomena, the number of those with an academic background who are interested in shamanism is relatively high.

Carlos Castaneda and Michael Harner are at present probably the most famous among the writers on neo-shamanism as they pioneered the idea of introducing shamanism into the life of Westerners. Carlos Castaneda claimed to present the traditional method used by the Mexican *brujos* whereas Michael Harner in his work *The Way of the Shaman* first published in 1980 introduced the concept of urban shamanism or core-shamanism, i.e. the kind of shamanism available to Westerners with no background in traditional shamanism. In the preface to the third edition Michael Harner writes:

> During the last decade, however, shamanism has returned to human life with startling strength, even to urban strongholds of Western 'civilization' such as New York and Vienna. This resurgence has come so subtly that most of the public is probably unaware that there is such a thing as shamanism, let alone conscious of its return. There is another public, however, rapidly-growing and now numbering in the thousands in the United States and abroad, that has taken up shamanism and made it a part of personal daily life. (1990: xi)

It is with this 'other public' that the second part of this book will be concerned. Michael Harner and the organiser of courses in shamanism in England and Denmark, also an anthropologist,[4] on whose courses I have concentrated my research, belonged to the same organisation: The Foundation for Shamanic Studies. This organiser has recently left the organisation.

Harner, a former professor and chair-person of the department of Anthropology at the Graduate Faculty of the New School for Social Research in New York, has also taught at the universities of

California, Berkeley, Columbia and Yale. He did his fieldwork in the Upper Amazon, Mexico, western North America, the Canadian Arctic, and Samiland (Lapland). *The Way of the Shaman* mostly refers to his work among the Jívaro Indians in Ecuador in 1956-57 and the Conibo Indians in the Peruvian Amazon in 1960-61. It is an introduction to traditional shamanism at the same time as it is a manual introducing methods of shamanism derived from different traditional cultures into the Western culture.

> Shamanic methods require a relaxed discipline, with concentration and purpose. Contemporary shamanism, like that in most tribal cultures, typically utilizes monotonous percussion sound to enter an altered state of consciousness. This classic drug-free method is remarkably safe. If practitioners do not maintain focus and discipline, they simply return to the ordinary state of consciousness. There is no preordained period of altered state of consciousness that would tend to occur with a psychedelic drug.
>
> At the same time, the classic shamanic methods work surprisingly quickly, with the result that most persons can achieve in a few hours experiences that might otherwise take them years of silent meditation, prayer, or chanting. For this reason alone, shamanism is ideally suited for contemporary life of busy people, just as it was suited, for example, to the Eskimo (Inuit) people whose daily hours were filled with tasks of struggle for survival, but whose evenings could be used for shamanism. (Ibid.: xii)

As the dark dominates a large part of the Arctic year, there must have been a lot of shamanism going on. The idea that a busy Eskimo sits down at night and gets on with his spiritual work is, I am afraid, rather a simplification of the spiritual experience of the Arctic people. On the East Coast of Greenland it took an apprentice several years to arrive at the level of communication with the spirit world which was necessary for a practising *angakkoq* to accumulate the sufficient number of helping spirits, to work through his fear of the supernatural, to travel to the frightful Mother of the Sea, and to achieve the insight that would make him a human set apart, a person who was no longer just an ordinary member of society.

But Harner points to an important question that rightly can be put to neo-shamanism. How can it be that a Western person living in a secular society can achieve a spiritual experience in a few hours which took the large part of a life in traditional societies to reach? I shall return to this question in depth in the actual analysis of the shamanic courses in which I participated in England and Denmark.

What is also worth noticing is the attitude to the use of drugs. Both Castaneda and Harner seem to have made a clear break away from the use of hallucinogenics to achieve shamanic altered states of consciousness, although their insight to traditional shamanism comes from a culture in which hallucinogenics are totally interlinked with the practice of shamanism. In arranging organised courses in Western cultures it might not be wise to use drug-induced states of consciousness as the law forbids it and the experience of drug use in the Western world has shown itself to be more destructive than enlightening. In the 1980s both Harner and Castaneda had enough bogeys not to be associated with drug use. Michael Harner writes in his instruction to the beginner in shamanism: 'Wait until you are calm and relaxed before undertaking this or any other shamanic exercise. Avoid psychedelic or alcoholic substances during the preceding twenty-four hours, so that your centeredness and power of concentration will be good, and your mind clear of confusing imagery' (Ibid.: 31).

It is the relationship to spirits that is important in the Harner method. *The Way of the Shaman* starts with an account of Harner's own experience with spirits among the Jívaro Indians. It is the achievement of *tsensaks* (magical darts) that is essential to Jívaro shamanism. 'These *tsensaks* or spirit helpers are the main powers believed to cause and cure illness in daily life. To the nonshaman they are normally invisible, and even shamans can perceive them only in an altered state of consciousness' (Ibid.: 16).

The shaman collects all kinds of objects that represent his spirit helpers and thereby become his *tsensaks*. As long as they are small enough for the shaman to swallow, insects, worms and plants can become helpers. The drinking of *ayahuasca* then reveals the hidden form of the *tsentsaks*. These spirit helpers are then used in healing by the shaman. But as every person has, or has had, a guardian spirit, often a *power-animal*, what is specific for the shaman is that he uses these spirits actively: 'The main difference between an ordinary person and a shaman with regard to their guardian spirits is that the shaman uses his guardian spirit actively when in an altered state of consciousness' (Ibid.: 43).[5]

Harner stresses the fact that, although he has been inspired by the Conibo and Jívaro Indians, the North American Indians, such as the Winton, Poma Coast Salish and Lakota Sioux have taught him how to practise without the use of drugs. 'Finally I learned from the worldwide ethnographic literature on shamanism, where lie buried many gems of information that supplement and reaffirm what I had been taught firsthand' (Ibid.: 19).

The Harner method of urban shamanism or core-shamanism is a conglomerate of different cultural forms of shamanism and is therefore peculiar to Western man. In that sense it is a new form of shamanism adapted to the cultural reality of Western society. One of the major differences between traditional shamanism and neo-shamanism is the length of time the apprenticeship lasts. It is up to the individual to assess his own development through his/her experiences of the journeying between realities. In the traditional Eskimo society the end of the apprenticeship was determined by the spirits. The *angakkoq* apprentice was often very reluctant 'to come forward' and be a fully fledged *angakkoq*. The accounts of how apprenticeship turned into initiation demonstrate that it was often a very dramatic situation where the initiate was bleeding from the nose and undergoing fear and mental agony, trying in some cases to hide from the demanding spirits who, according to the informants, were tired of not being openly recognised. The initiation was not only an experience of the *angakkoq* but shared and participated in by the whole community.

The neo-shamans on the other hand are mostly urban practitioners and therefore not part of a close community of expectant people waiting for their skills to develop. They might be members of a drumming group but they are not surrounded in their daily life by a knowledgeable and supportive society. It is a highly individualised process. The Eskimo apprentice is also on a lonely path until his/her initiation but everybody he interacts with respects and understands the reality of an apprentice even though he/she might not have confessed to this condition as it should remain secret until initiation. The urban shaman apprentice does not necessarily have that underlying recognition in his immediate environment. His initiation therefore takes on a different character:

> In its essence, shamanic initiation is experiential and often gradual, consisting of learning successfully how to achieve the shamanic state of consciousness, and how to see and journey in that state; acquiring personal certainty and knowledge of one's own guardian spirit, and

enlisting its assistance while in the shamanic state of consciousness; and learning successfully to help others as a shaman. A characteristic phase of more advanced shamanism is having personal certainty and knowledge of one's own spirit helpers. There are even more advanced phases, as well as some important kinds of shamanic experiences, that are not dealt with in this book. If you succeed in experiencing the first three phases listed above, however, you can probably call yourself a shaman. But shamanic initiation is a never-ending process of struggle and joy, and the definitive decisions about your status as a shaman will be made by those you try to help. (Ibid.: 44-5)

The urban apprentice is left firstly to assess his own progress and then finally to let others judge the outcome. This is essentially not different from the Eskimo *angakkoq* as his society also assessed his skills. What is different is the frame in which this process takes place and the concept of the role of the spirits. The *angakkoq* is not assessing himself, he is forced to 'come forward' by the ever-present spirits. The urban shaman might feel equally forced by the spirits but it is not necessary according to the above description; that process belongs to more advanced stages of shamanism. There is apparently a hierarchy of shamanism which differs from the concept of the *angakkoq*, some *angakkut* being more skilled than others, but the requirement for 'coming forward' is the same for all *angakkut*: the acquisition of an appropriate number of helping spirits that, until the initiation, are more or less in command of, and, after the initiation, mastered by the *angakkoq*.

Through the courses and reading *The Way of the Shaman*, it is possible to become an apprentice. There is no prior demand such as special birth, inheritance of supernatural skills, special behaviour verging on insanity, illness, near death experience or any other spiritual insight, although it is likely that the people commencing a course in shamanism have had just that and do not know how to relate such experiences, to their 'normal' role in society as teachers, architects, nurses, psychotherapists, and so on.

The participants in courses or the readers of the book then have to test their own skills against other people's perception of them. That might lead to a slight confusion as the experiences of the participants in the courses are highly individual and although the journeying starts off with the same method, going through a tunnel to the Lower World to find a power-animal, the individual journeys might not have anything in common. How is this assessment going to take place when there is little common ground for the urban shamans? They do not have a mythology or the knowledge of a specific set of spirits in common. There is no group of inland or coastal spirits, no Mother of the Sea, no *Ingersuit* or *Toornaarsuk*, that everybody can relate to and encounter on their travels but there is a whole flourishing variety of spiritual encounters highly individualised and partly depending on the concepts of other cultures' spiritual encounters. Who can claim the right to be the assessor of these journeys and state whether a person has reached the initiation state? According to Harner, the answer is nobody: 'A true master shaman does not challenge the validity of anybody else's experiences, although less capable and less humble shamans may. The master shaman will try to integrate even the most unusual experiences into his total cosmology, a cosmology based primarily on his own journeys...The master shaman never says that what you experienced is a fantasy' (Ibid.: 45).

This way of avoiding anybody monopolising the urban shamanic experience by claiming that such behaviour only reflects on the assessor, not the assessed, is an important element of neo-shamanism. If a specific cosmology were introduced the highly individualised concepts of spirits would be discarded and an institutionalisation and eventually a cult might be formed which by its nature would limit the number of apprenticeships and thus initiates. As neo-shamanism is a universal movement for people living in the common conditions of urban life but coming from cultures of a very diverse stock, a restriction on the cosmology would create havoc in the whole system. The decision of whether a person is a shaman or not seems more to rest on the attitude of the person vis-à-vis his/her individual experience than on the character of the experience. Is the attitude of the person to his skills in accord with a shamanic attitude, i.e. not challenging the validity of others, not dogmatic, is his/her guidance of other people non-intrusive, are his/her healing skills apparent, is his/her overall attitude one of humility?

Compared with the traditional Eskimo society most of the above mentioned 'virtues' were not always applicable to the skilled *angakkoq*. There was no doubt that a sort of rivalry existed among the *angakkut*; some admitting doubt about their own skills, might fear those of others or might ridicule other *angakkut*. Although some *angakkut* were only trying to help their fellow human beings others definitely used their skills to manipulate and create fear. An *angakkoq* had to convince his audience of his special gifts by creating an impressive séance. There were among the *angakkut* both 'white' and 'black' personalities. Harner seems to be aiming at avoiding the development of the 'black urban shaman' by stating that a true master shaman never monopolises the shamanic experience.

> Shamans are people of action as well as knowledge. They serve the community by moving into and out of hidden reality when asked for help. But only a few shamans become true masters of knowledge, power and healing. There is typically a great deal of critical evaluation by the people in their communities as to how proficient particular shamans are, how successful they are in healing people. Shamans' 'track records' are well known, and people decide which shamans to go to in matters of life and death. So, although many people can become shamans, only a few are recognized as outstanding. (Ibid.: 46)

The shamanic skills, the time for initiation, the credibility of the healing power of the shaman is all between him/her and the community. In that respect the urban shaman is subjugated to the same conditions as the traditional *angakkoq*.

The urban shaman must be able to move between two realities. Harner uses the terminology 'Ordinary state of Consciousness' (OSC) and 'Shamanic state of Consciousness' (SSC), Carlos Castaneda uses the terms 'ordinary reality' and 'non-ordinary reality'. In this moving in and out of altered states of consciousness the urban shaman receives the information that is beneficial to his fellow human beings. This skill is essential to any shamanic behaviour. The aim of the courses is, therefore, to teach the participants how to make that transition. The courses I have been studying have used the methods introduced by Harner in *The Way of the Shaman*, as the course organiser was originally an apprentice of Harner.

Courses in Neo-shamanism

The courses in shamanism offered by the course organiser and his partner form the basis of my fieldwork. Based in Copenhagen, they run a series of courses all over Europe with the main focus on Denmark, the other Scandinavian countries and England. The centre provides basic and advanced workshops in shamanism.

The basic courses all have the same heading explaining the shaman's journey:

> Shamanism is humanity's oldest tradition for healing, problem solving, and maintaining balance in the individual, as well as in society and Nature. During this basic course, participants will be introduced to some of the core ideas and methods used by shamans around the world, including Northern Europe, for thousands of years. The main emphasis of the course will be on the shamanic journey to the other, non-ordinary reality to gain power and knowledge for oneself and others.
>
> By using the traditional methods of singing, dancing, and drumming, participants will learn how to experience shamanic consciousness, explore the spirit world, rediscover connections with Nature, meet their Spirit-helpers and non-ordinary Teachers, and learn one of the most important shamanic healing techniques. While part of the course time will be used in sharing the discoveries made on shamanic journeys, attention will also be put on how to apply this information and how shamanism can be used in the modern society we live in today.

This heading shows how core-shamanism fits the whole New Age concept. The emphasis on healing, and the balance in the individual as well as that of Nature are principal issues in New Age thinking. The course does not use a specific traditional method, as seen in the North American Indian inspired courses, but includes concepts drawn from the origin of the cultures that the participants represent, i.e. Northern Europe. This is very important as there is a great interest in part of the New Age to re-establish a contact for Western man with his severed roots. The courses in and books about Celtic shamanism are one aspect of this interest. The Centre provides an advanced course that deals with Nordic shamanism, which will be described in detail later.

The emphasis of the basic course is on the journeying, the connection with Nature, the acquisition of spirit-helpers and teachers and the knowledge of how to apply this method to life in modern society. The Advanced Courses for which the Basic Course is necessary include different themes of shamanism such as Spiritual Ecology, Soul Retrieval, Death and Dying, Nordic Shamanism, Spirit Voices, Moon Cycles in Shamanism (for women only), and Shamanic Counselling. There is beside these courses an 'on-going core Shamanic group' which began meeting in 1994 and continues to this day. This group consists of the same participants and is lead by the course organiser. The group meets about three times a year.

After having participated in a Basic Course it may be possible to join a drumming group to continue the training and to interact with like-minded people. These groups are run by people locally and meet with variable frequency. They are important as support for the newcomer in his/her attempt to preserve contact with the shamanic frame of mind.

A Description of the People Participating in Courses

The age span in the courses is large; at the courses I studied it ranged from 22 to over 60 years of age. The average age is about 40. The groups in Denmark included several nationalities – Finnish, Norwegian, Irish, Greenlandic, and Swiss with the majority being Danish. In England the nationalities represented were Irish, Iranian (having lived in England for most of her life), Danish and German, the majority being British.

The educational background of the participants shows a high representation from the caring professions: nurses, social workers, psychotherapists and analysts. Teachers can also be seen as belonging to that group.[6] It appeals to people who are quite highly educated, dealing with members of society in need of care and healing. In that respect the parallel to the role of the shaman in traditional society is clear. These professions, to a large extent, cover the same areas as those of the shaman: the diseased in either body or mind, albeit from a secular point of view.

Several of the interviewees voiced a need for a spiritual dimension in their work and saw shamanism as the way to achieve that. As one informant, formerly working as a nurse in the National Health system in Denmark, answered when asked why she changed from being a nurse to a psychotherapist:

> There had to be a reason why people are feeling so bad. There has to be a germ somewhere and that germ I wanted to find. Through working as a psychotherapist I have found a root. I started with older people but am working my way downwards age-wise and am at the point where egg and sperm meet. From there I have gone further to the idea of re-incarnation and our past as such and that is where shamanism comes in. I have immersed myself in the spiritual part which has followed me as

knowledge from my childhood. I was not really aware whether it was shamanism or spirituality as such. But that it is shamanism, that has always been with me, I know now.

The re-establishing of the spiritual connection in people's lives that the courses in shamanism offer seems to be one of the major reasons for members of the caring profession signing up for the course. When the link with the spirit world has been established it can support the carer in his/her work with clients:

> I sat together with a young man I had had in therapy for quite a while and I had a strong sense that we never reached the essence. Suddenly I got the message: ask him if he wished to be a girl instead. At that stage I did not even know what he was talking about. It became uninteresting. I instead asked him whether he had always been treated like a girl. He stopped completely and said: You are the only one who has found out that this is what really is my problem. It was not me that this came from. We then worked with his gender identity, and he got back his power as a man.

The psychotherapist's statement that it is not from her that the break-through question comes but something outside herself shows a concept of a helping-spirit or teacher supporting the carer in her work. There is help to be received from the spirits when dealing with difficult cases. The use of the spirit world in her work as psychotherapist for this informant is very clear and she stated that she told her clients that she was using helpers if the client asked her how she could raise such a question.

> I tell them that I have my helpers. I tell them without mentioning the word shamanism because some might get frightened. I work shamanically with my clients who have been through a sequence where they say: you can also do something else. Then I perform soul-retrievals or teach some of them to travel or I travel to get a power-animal.

Social workers and teachers might not have the same direct way of using shamanic insight but might still receive guidance from the spirit world regarding their own behaviour which ultimately is seen to help everybody with whom they are involved. The courses provide access to a concept of reality and non-ordinary reality where the latter is an inexhaustible source of help and advice for people employed in trying to sort out the diseases of fellow human beings. With the secularisation of these professions the carer has been left to carry the burden of knowledge unaided by spiritual support. The shamanic concept of the universe offers precisely that, and the holistic view of the relationship between human beings, Nature and the Universe incorporates individuals in a meaningful connection with each other and Nature, and excludes them from the senseless isolation of modernity. There is always someone there, the individual helper or teacher who has been found in the carer's own non-ordinary reality, independent of institutions of any kind, be it church or state or even other people.

Some of the participants in courses do not come, however, to obtain support in their work with other people but to have their own lives supported. One of the participants that I interviewed was a drug addict. She was 43 years old and had been using both drugs and alcohol for several years. At the time of the interview she was trying to stop her abuse and get her life back on track. She came from an affluent background but her parents' divorce and her mother's suicide when the informant was sixteen had upset her life. She had never had a conventional education but worked in temporary jobs. At the present she was unemployed and living with a family in the countryside. She had more or less tumbled into one of the courses and after a week felt that she had so much energy and strength to cope with lots of problems and that feeling had lasted ever since:

> The best thing is that you get strength and energy. A spiritual and social fellowship, you feel welcomed and loved. Although it is difficult for someone like me to have confidence in it. You can really feel that this is right. It gives me a lot. It gives me strength [to lower the use of metadon]. I do not know how many people use it [the course] in the same way as I do. It is fantastic for me. It is like a loving family. I have not felt anything bad between people [on the course]. Nature and the trees and the circle[7] you can always contact. The trees mean a lot to me. They are old, can tell many tales and have a lot of knowledge. I think it is so good that you can sing as you like and not have it received badly. That is fantastic for me. Thinking in the same way gives a sense of fellowship, and the people here were relaxed and well-balanced. On most other courses there are people who try to drag others down, but I don't think that this has happened here.

Because of the spiritual dimension in the courses the participants seem to relate to each other in a very caring way. For a person in need of fellowship and love this is very important and as the shamanic approach to Nature in the courses also involves the participants in a loving and caring relationship to the plants, trees and animals in the immediate surroundings, the sense of belonging to people and place becomes very strong. It takes the sense of loneliness away and replaces it with a sense of community. This informant does not mention the spirit world directly but her statement about the trees shows the animistic approach.

The third major group that the courses might appeal to is people within creative work such as play writing, sculpture, graphic design. Some of these, who had already felt a contact with a spiritual dimension in their work, might use the courses as inspiration or confirmation.

One informant had a conventional academic training, a BA in Religion and Psychology. He had been offered a postgraduate place at Oxford but turned it down to try to live the life of the Renaissance man. 'I had moved intellectually but I did not know any other part of my body.' He pursued organic farming for some years but then set up his own business in management courses. At the time of the interview and at the age of thirty-five his life was again to change as he was planning to go to New Zealand 'to look at sustainable economy out there'. He had an unconventional childhood: 'I had a religious upbringing. We have all been raised by my mother really. We have different fathers. A matriarchal family. In the sixties my mother took LSD and we had monks round the house all the time. We always related well, my mother being a spiritual Buddhist.' He had always had a perception of the world as magic:

> Because I have been steeped in the world of myth and religion I have been attracted to the transformation that religious systems provide. We talk in an intellectual way. I remembered at university a vision: it suddenly dawned on me my whole life would be devoted to unfold that one vision, that vision being: we are journeying. This earth is like a descent into hell and that it really looks like hell but hell is a part of the shamanic dismemberment process which is only one phase. My life is about creating some type of communication channel that people can understand is a journey and the dismemberment is just one phase.

The informant had incorporated that view into his present management course, where he tries to examine how the academic approach can interact with the practical use of shamanism:

I construct rituals. We go into ritual caves, where business managers have the experience of being reborn when they come through holes. It is in the outdoors in a very transformative way. I have used my education in terms of religious studies and looked at transformation and am bringing these structures into the work I do. I am really grateful for it. Recently in the last year I have started to acknowledge and value my intellect. Because after university my life was a mess I had to work on myself. There was a big period of time where I had to do the outdoor stuff just as a physical experience rather than bring a discriminating mind to it.

Another informant also worked on organising courses such as 'Management and Uncertainty'. 'I like doing team work courses but a lot of what I do is to create a container for people to have their negative feelings in, so they can re-connect with their positive feelings and go forward.' She was 53 and had her roots in the hippie movement. She had had children early but split up from her husband and later got an MA in American Studies at Sussex University. She was now a psychotherapist and combined this with her group-work for business people. She had just started on the courses in shamanism:

When the shamanic stuff finally came up I had been looking for it for a couple of years. There is a woman doing workshops close to me [in Wales] but I did not want to see her. Then a friend sent me a leaflet on a workshop and I was very impressed by the gentleness and the humility of it. It was the right place. I also felt very apprehensive because I knew if I came I would not be able to reverse. I still feel a bit nervous about this course [Soul Retrieval]. They knock on your door.

The 'they' that knock on the door seem to be one of the major reasons for many of the participants' search for courses in the first place. It was very significant to realise that many of the people I either interviewed or just talked to on the courses had actually had supernatural experiences. These experiences had been both frightening and awe-inspiring and seemed in most cases to stimulate life-transforming actions, from attempted suicide to change of lifestyle, job or acceptance of the spiritual side of their lives. In this respect they had undergone some kind of first-hand experience with the spirit world quite similar to that of the *angakkoq* apprentice and often just as fear-provoking. The difference was that they did not have a cultural context to fit this experience into and the fear could therefore not always be transformed to positive action.

One informant talked about her psychic experiences as a child:

I never had any conventional kind of religious discipline. I had a conventional home, my father was an atheist. I went to church and got confirmed, I had a strong spiritual sense, but not anchored. I had psychic experiences as a child. That made me feel a bit odd. Some people have labelled it pathology and that makes me very angry. People think that those things happen because something else is happening in my life. That is not my experience and I don't want to reduce it in that way. Just a very powerful connection with nature and experience of ecstasy, when I was outdoors. A therapist once said to me, because I said that where I live now I found very nurturing, 'Is that a pattern in your life, turning to nature when relationships are in trouble?' I just felt so alienated with that because my relationship with nature is as powerful as my relationship with any person. That is what I am part of. I feel a bit defensive about that.

Later in life the same informant, under the influence of drugs, saw the face of her friend turn into that of the friend's dead mother. The informant felt she had to rescue the friend:

She was talking about her mother and this happened: I had a dream, I was not really sleeping. There was an altered state in the room and there was a dog howling outside. Shutters banging and everything started happening. This is very relevant to today [for being at the course]. I knew that she was becoming possessed by her dead mother. And her face began to change into her mother's face. I was very frightened, I was very cold and sweating and terrified. And suddenly I felt golden light shoot through me and I went warm all over and just touched her, stopped her and said: 'You have to come back. Back to me now.' Neither of us knew what happened and she was okay. We were totally blown away by it next morning and we could not talk about it because we did not know what we were talking about. When I flew back to England next day I was so blown away by this experience, that I just babbled to the person who came and picked me up. And we were driving down the road and as I was talking about it there was a huge black presence in the back of the car, just bang. We pulled into a lay by and we both jumped out of the car and looked at each other and said: 'What was that'? It went on for months. I started hyper-ventilating, I did not know what that was either and went to the doctor. He said you are hyper-ventilating but I don't know why you are doing it. I then went for some spiritual healing, all of this happened about fifteen years ago. The black shadow I understand to be my own ego. I was describing it as though I had done it [the rescue of her friend in the States]. It had happened through me but I was not equipped to actually do it. And so I think when I talked about it, it was my ego. Really bad news. Had to stop talking about it because I realized that I was contaminating people. For fifteen years I did not do anything. I would not touch any psychic kind of thing. I thought it was bad news for me. I would just hurt people.

What is interesting about this account is the sense of impotence by the informant in the face of the supernatural experience. She did not find any understanding of these events either with the doctor or with the therapist and finally decided to exclude them from her life, frightened that the knowledge of and contact with the supernatural might contaminate other people. There is no institution in modern society – except perhaps a mental hospital – that might take her seriously. For this informant it led to silence for fifteen years, for another it led to suicide attempts.

Before this 29-year-old woman started on the courses she had some experiences of a supernatural character. She was walking in the woods with a friend when she suddenly saw a spirit in front of her with raised arms. She cried out loud but her friend had seen nothing. She felt that her body moved through the spirit and later saw the spirit come running after her with elf maidens. She said nothing to her friend; 'But I think that I thought of that experience every day for many years.' She also experienced a female shape with no face coming to her at night. A shining shape entered her room at night, a mixture of steam and blue, yellow and white light. The shape lay down next to her and melted into her body. 'Although the situation was frightening, it was not unpleasant, and the next day I felt as if I was flying in the clouds.'

Later she experienced a flat-mate with whom she had a strained relationship coming in the night to try to strangle her, her dead grandfather also visited her but the main feeling after such experiences, although frightening, was a sense of energy. It is the experience of being 'torn' by these supernatural events that ultimately led her to sign up for shamanic courses although she was frightened and for a while cancelled the bookings.

> The main reason for me to start the courses was personal, because I was so torn by the experiences I had, and that I did not understand the meaning of, which I kept at arm's length. I think they are the main reason for me having a lot of suicidal thoughts last spring. During that

period I worked a lot with death. On the courses there is a lot of support and respect for the things that you tell about, there is nothing that is strange or wrong.

This informant had also been disappointed in the attitude of a psychologist, who had asked her, when she told about the spirit in the wood, whether she had taken LSD. She quickly stopped seeing the psychologist.

It seems to be the 'senselessness' of the supernatural experiences that makes these people react so strongly. Had they been under the influence of drugs in every interaction with the supernatural, there would be no reason to be surprised. It is the unexpected events that have the transforming influence. In its nature these events are not very different from that of the initial 'calling' of the shaman's apprentice in traditional societies. The borders between ordinary and non-ordinary realities become fluid. Where the shaman can move between those worlds at will the apprentice is often very much at the mercy of the spirits. They decide when and if he is going to interact with them. The *angakkoq* apprentice might seek loneliness in the wilderness and turn his *angakkoq* stone to attract spirits but he has no power over the experience. Only the initiated *angakkoq* is the true master of spirits.

Another informant had a supernatural experience in connection with a journey to Ireland and a life-threatening illness:

Life was spinning happily along but then I got to the time in life where you reach a turning point. I got there a few years ago about the age of fifty. I went to Ireland, felt a great bird going over my back, an eagle. It was a numinous experience. [In her drive at home a few months later she saw a buzzard stabbing the breast of a starling. Shortly after she was ill and almost died of pneumonia.] I wanted to die. I had a vision of my cat filling the room, then the fever broke and I got better. After that everything went dead and I was searching for something. I was recommended a Sioux Indian workshop, a dance workshop, where I met a Nicaraguan man and then he turned round and looked straight at me and said that his grandmother was a famous witch. I was stunned, it was as if an explosion took place. He later sent me on my first shamanic journey. I did not know what I was doing.

This informant told that she had always been a spiritual seeker. She had a degree in English Literature, had started on a Ph.D. on Jung and Blake but stopped because of having children. At the time of the interview she was teaching and working as a sculptor:

> I have always been a spiritual seeker. My parents forbade me to go to church when I was nine years old, because they thought that I would have religious mania. My father was an atheist and my mother was religious. I did not go to church until I was fifteen and by the time I got there I was quite disenchanted by it; it was a brief interlude. I gave it up and went to university, met a religious man and was persuaded to marry in church. Moved to London and met a woman there who sent me and my husband to a retreat. We loved it so much and I became a member of the convent.

There seems to be a general pattern among the informants of one or several experiences with the supernatural that cannot be understood within the framework of the Christian Church. There is no institution of a spiritual nature that can be consulted in connection with the kind of supernatural encounters described by these informants. They clearly do not go to the local vicar. Instead some go and try to get help either from a psychologist or a psychotherapist, none of whom really is equipped to understand the awe that the experience has produced. For these informants it becomes an insult to their integrity that a psychological explanation is sought. Having to deal with the experience on some level the informant ultimately searches for companionship with people who respect supernatural occurrences in their lives. There are plenty of possible ways to do that within the New Age movement. Shamanism is one, the Wicca movement another.

One of the informants had started her spiritual search within the Wicca movement,[8] and had felt she had to leave because of a relationship going wrong. At the time of the interview she was fifty, her interest in spirituality had started at the age of forty. Before then she had never had a religion.

> I never gave up the craft, I became ostracized... I do not identify with the craft anymore. My tools are in a cupboard, my wand and pentacles are in a cupboard. I virtually had a break-down. I don't think that it is so uncommon. I have heard of people in the Salvation Army who have been thrown out. It was my whole life. I dedicated my life to it.

Whereas the members of cult-like groups have to interact with each other, core-shamanism offers a choice. A participant can go home after a basic course and continue forever searching for advice from the helpers on his/her own. There is no need for further communication with other people. You are no less of a shaman because you are working on your own. You can still apply your shamanic skills in daily work for other people by seeking help from the non-ordinary reality. On the other hand it is also possible to continue in a group either within courses or in drumming groups. This informant pointed to this difference: 'One of the things that attracted me about shamanism funnily enough was that it was something I could do on my own, I can journey on my own.'

Core-shamanism, because of its highly individualised character, does not demand continuous contact with specific people who might take over your life. You are not threatened with a sense of being ostracised. This is important in a time where there is so much awareness of the dangers of cults or Christian movements that trap their members into personal dependency. The way the courses present shamanism, the destructive sides of shamanic behaviour are eliminated and almost excluded. There is no 'black' shamanism presented in the courses. 'It is a very different way of using energy to witchcraft, which may be unhealthy. In some ways I was addicted to it.'

Addiction and the use of drugs had been a reality of some of the informants years earlier but I had no impression of drugs playing a part in their lives now. As the course organiser did not want alcohol to be consumed just before or during the courses, drugs were not even an issue. One of the informants had been taking drugs from the age of fifteen to twenty-one:

> I used to take them with an intent to sort something out. The last time I took fly agaric I did it to sort things out about my parents. I was thrown out at the age of eighteen, on my birthday. My family is very strange. The mushroom grows wild and I was very experimental about taking drugs. Smoked cannabis quite a lot. I took LSD three or four times. The whole subculture of Windsor is drugs. LSD was a positive experience. I never had a bad experience. I was unemployed, an assistant butcher, I was a vegetarian at the time but I don't have a moral conflict with meat eating. I became psychologically addicted to drugs, mostly cannabis... I then met my partner and I stopped smoking. I suddenly started to realize what happened to close friends and the ones who survived, left. The others were bringing their smaller sisters and brothers into contact with the drug world, with older men and catching venereal diseases.

In general, the impression of the people participating in the courses is that the experience with drugs of this 31-year-old man is rare. His interest in shamanism started through reading literature about it and trying to create journeys on his own by using Michael Harner's *The Way of the Shaman*. Although he had no experiences on the first attempts of journeying he had the following happen to him:

> I came home from work one evening and I looked up at the sky and this huge winged horse walks across it. This was Pegasus, yea, yea, it was not shocking, it did not shock me, I was so ungrounded. I continued with the tape but it did not work, I tried to sit out. I did not have an intent. I was devouring these books.

The shamanic courses and drumming groups functioned as a way of focusing these experiences and to help his journeying, as he found this difficult. He is now using his shamanic knowledge to create role-plays with a shamanic content.

> I am building my shamanic experience into my role-playing and people are getting really inspired by it. If I step into a bigger culture picture; Campbell says we are going in circles after the fall of Western Religion, we are back into the void again and neo-shamanism is coming around and established religions falling into anarchy. I think we are in the beginning of a new circle.

No doubt among many people there is a feeling of the fall of traditional religions, that this is the time for the emergence of a new spirituality that enhances the social, cultural and spiritual reality of modern Western people. Neo-shamanism with its highly individualised method of using spirit-helpers and healing, its non-cult character, its openness of mind to the supernatural experiences of the participants and its link with an archaic past of all cultures and thereby the sense of universality and fellowship between present cultures, its holistic approach to Nature and man; all appeal to the members of a society which is seen as highly fragmented and diffuse, secular in its approach to healing, education and social interaction.

Several of the informants mentioned the doubt that sometimes could arise from the interaction with the spirit world, the question being, 'Am I making it all up?'

I have asked myself whether shamanism is my imagination or something that really exists. As it was said today by the organiser, it took some time before she gave in and accepted that it was not her imagination, but something that really is. That is what I constantly return to, a belief that this is not my imagination. I do not pose this question any more but I sometimes think, is this my imagination or what? If I then ask for advice and reach a deeper level then it functions again.

The concept of non-ordinary reality is closely intertwined with the relationship to nature. The Lower World is often either a wood, a plain, a mountain area, and so on, the helper is of either of plant or animal origin. There is a belief in human beings and nature communicating on a spiritual level where Nature is the wiser. The search for roots is closely connected with the search for a relationship to the land, to ancestors who are believed to have lived in closer contact with their environment with a respectful attitude to all living beings, including sacred places. The shamanic courses appeal to many different people from that point of view. With the sense that human beings are guilty of the destruction of Mother Earth, the re-establishment of respect for Nature from a shamanic viewpoint satisfies a need to make up for the present state of affairs. One of the informants, the owner of a factory making colours from plants, had started his interest in shamanism in the North American Indian philosophy 'because it connects human beings with all of the Earth and the Universe' and continued to explain why he participated in a course on Nordic Shamanism:

> Shamanism is new for me. I have been interested in many spiritual matters. In connection with the production of plant colours one is concerned with the basic processes. This a natural approach for me towards a part of our world which we have forgotten to relate to: Nature. ...We also have some roots. They are more or less destroyed after the introduction of Christianity. I am not a member of the church anymore.[9] Are these roots here still? For they must be a part of me.

The search for roots that are earlier in human history than Christianity is important to many participants in the courses. The whole relationship to the Christian Church is either non-existent or of a strained nature. The Lutheran and the Anglican Churches do not leave space for the experience of elves and spirits in the wood. The attitude to Nature is of major importance. The need to respect the immediate environment, to be part of it on its own terms, the whole holistic approach to Nature is not new and has many romantic aspects to it. What is new is the sense of daily environmental disaster and a growing alienation and isolation of human beings by their own actions. The courses attempt to re-establish a contact between the participants and their immediate environment which is seen to be beneficial to both.

Many men participate in the shamanic courses. One of the female participants gave the following explanation: 'I have thought that there are many men, who really are men, I do not know, but I think it is because the courses have a lot of action, the drumming, the rattling. I think that is more attractive to men and introduces a new aspect in this spiritual work so it is not so brooding and theoretical.'

A male participant, on the other hand, responded to the question about men's participation in the following way: 'There has been a great movement among women claiming that they have something to contribute to re-establish balance. The Christian religion is in reality very male-orientated and hostile to Nature. The side we have to develop as men is the female side. The male side is analytical and theoretical, not aimed at experiences.'

Although the explanations of the two informants are contradictory, it shows possible major reasons for the courses' appeal to men: the respect for a female, caring side to their personality and the action orientated dance, rattling, exploration in Nature, a movement from 'head' to 'body'. The traditional shamans were often men but also many woman became shamans, as has been shown in the work of Shirokogoroff among the Tungus, Haslund Christensen among the Mongolian shamans, Kendall in her recent work about the Korean *mansin*. For women among the Greenlanders becoming an *angakkoq* took so many years that they would reach the age of child-bearing and, therefore, often not finish their education. The initial calling was for both sexes. Neo-shamanism is, in its nature, not gender specific.

Another important part in connection with the appeal of the shamanic courses is that it is not necessary to be prepared. For the basic course there is some recommended reading but it is not an essential prerequisite. There is no fixed concept of spirits, no need for an understanding of the traditional spirit world. Some participants are very well read in Castaneda, Harner and Campbell, some come with no knowledge at all. The outcome for either group of people might be the same, because success in travelling and achieving helpers is not connected with prior information but with an openness of mind. It is a very egalitarian system, embracing all cultures.

One informant was a Greenlandic woman who had been raised in Denmark. She was 33 years old and worked as a social worker. She joined the courses because she had felt that she was searching for something:

> Although you live in a materialistic world with a job from 8 am to 5 pm there is still a sense of respect for those things [the spirit world]. I experienced that from my mother [who is Greenlandic]. I am searching at the moment, I am in a phase of my life where I have a husband and two children. Now I can look around and think of myself again. I can feel some kind of restlessness, I am searching for something. I think that I can feel that there is something I am waiting for.

She felt that she was more inspired by the North American Indian philosophy than the traditional Greenlandic spirituality and when she did a course in shamanism a couple of years ago she had fantastic experiences but there was no Greenlandic element in them. It was more a contact to indigenous peoples throughout the world. This is not surprising as there is no active shamanism left in Greenland and therefore no point of direct contemporary reference, whereas the North American Indian culture dominates a major part of the New Age literature. When I asked whether she felt a different starting point from the rest of the participants on the course, she replied, 'I probably have too great expectations of myself and my connections back to my roots. It will come in due time and I may want too much.'

The universal form of shamanism that these courses try to create, with many participants sharing the mutual experience of city life with its fragmented structure, opens up the possible meeting point for many cultures and therefore does not adhere to a specific cosmology. The Greenlandic informant could have used traditional Greenlandic concepts of different spirits in the courses but as she had been brought up in Denmark and only had a little knowledge of the traditional beliefs system in Greenland, she found it more appropriate to connect her experience with North American Indians. This posed no problem for her.

One aspect which is not dealt with in the courses in a direct way is possible fear-provoking experiences in the process of journeying. Fear is not of major concern in the running of the courses. As overcoming fear is of such importance in the transformation from apprentice to *angakkoq* in the traditional Greenlandic society, I asked some of the informants whether they had experienced anything fearful during the courses. Some of the advanced courses encourage the participant to sit out during a whole night and that in itself is a challenge which might create a sense of fear. Most of the people experienced slight fear but several were surprised how little they were afraid of being on their own in the 'wilderness'. Some had frightening experiences meeting hostile spirits and one informant had a typical shamanic death experience during her sitting out. In the beginning she was surprised how little fear she felt then she heard a tiny female voice speaking very penetratingly in a foreign language and then:

Death was standing in front of me and showed me his skeleton... It was as if there were two deaths, if you can talk about that, a light and a dark that were fighting. I could feel the old need to take my own life and I felt like going out of the circle and disappearing into the black shadow, and then I said: 'What is it you want? Shall I say I will include you or shall I ask you to disappear?' I sat rattling [as protection]. I cannot remember in details what we talked about. The light death, that in a way represented life, took over and the shape of an S was created which was flowing. ... This was a crisis point. I was afraid. With the female voice I thought: now I will go home, but with death I thought, if I leave the circle I will die.

The process of death and transformation is totally interlinked in the shamanic traditions worldwide. Overcoming fear of death, suffering symbolic death and rebirth all are important factors of the necessary transformation of the apprentice to a shaman. The Greenlandic *angakkoq* apprentice experiences being devoured by what later becomes his helping spirit. He wakes up after this frightening experience and finds that he is naked. He is then approached by his own animated clothing and dressed. What this woman experienced in the wood during her sitting out is closely connected with the transformative experience of traditional shamans. During the interview it was clear that she was not one of the more widely read participants and was, therefore, not aware of the obvious link.

Another participant had a very frightening soul retrieval journey for a course partner and had to be helped by the course organiser to cope with the situation. She said that she was not afraid although she claimed that the organiser had said that it was one of the most disgusting things he had heard. 'It was a strong experience but I was not afraid. I knew that the person I was travelling for was feeling so bad. When you travel for other people it is definitely not a "piece of cake".' But the normal experience for most participants is not fear-provoking and core-shamanism rarely seems to call forward the kind of challenge by spirits that is so characteristic of traditional shamanism. This will be discussed later in detail.

The last point about the course participants which is rather striking is their preparedness to pay from £90 for a basic course of two days to more than £400 for a week's course in advanced shamanism. One of the courses was £255 for three days, people staying in a Youth Hostel, sleeping in bunk beds and eating institutional food. Not one, however, mentioned anything about the course price. When asked about their financial situation some participants had taken bank loans, some had even sold belongings. The attitude has generally been that the price is acceptable. In some ways this is not surprising. Alternative healing can be very expensive, an hour's consultation costing £40–50, so a course of three days with food and accommodation, albeit basic, can in this context be seen as reasonable. If people participate in more than one course, they can easily spend as much as £500–1000 in a year. The cost does not seem to be important for many of the participants and would probably be seen as an inappropriate concern. The benefit of the courses outweighs the financial strain.

The Basic Course in Shamanism

As a large part of the methods of journeying and healing introduced in the basic course are repeated in the advanced courses these are examined in detail in connection with the description of the basic course. This course lasts two and a half days and costs Dkr. 1200; approximately £130 when residential or £90 if not.

The conditions under which the courses are conducted are, like many of the New Age courses, mostly very rudimentary. Some courses take place in a scouts' hut in Jutland in Denmark. The participants either stay in two large rooms, men and women together, or in tents. The hut is surrounded by a wood but some of it is privately owned so that the participants cannot use it as it is closed for hunting. The accessible wood stretches down to a large lake with a meadow nearby.

The Paraphernalia

The courses take place in a large room with an open fire. A circle of mattresses surrounds the centre where a deer-hide with stones, a candle, a feather and incense, made from Danish herbs and sage, is placed. The participants have been asked to bring their own blankets and scarves, rattles and drums. There is no other paraphernalia.

Introduction to the Concept of Shamanism

All courses start with an introduction whereby the participants first have to memorise the names of everybody else, then the rules of conduct during sessions are laid down. They include having no cups in the room, keeping to set times for visits to the lavatory, and so on. In a basic course the course organiser then proceeds to introduce himself. He is an anthropologist, who came to Denmark in 1972, then 30 years old. He had had six years of university education and the Vietnam war behind him. At that stage he started to ask himself how shamanism works. 'It is not me who is working but the spirits.' Never, in any of the courses I have attended, does he refer to himself as a shaman.

The main points that the course organiser stresses at the beginning of a course are the relationship between the shaman and his spirits and the shaman's use of an altered state of consciousness: 'The shaman changes his consciousness for a reason and contacts the spirit world to bring something back. He travels to the world of the spirits to bring power back to this world. A sorcerer seeks personal power, a shaman gives non-personal power.' There is an impression of the contact being sought with benevolent spirits, which makes the interaction less frightening.

From the beginning it is underlined that the purpose of shamanism is to cure, to help and *not* to achieve power for one's own end, which verges on the concept of black magic. The education that the course provides is a knowledge of how to work with a change of consciousness to achieve contact with non-ordinary reality, 'an invisible universe'. The terminology 'non-ordinary reality' is used as a description of the three main areas that the participants will travel to in their journeys: the lower world, the middle world, and the upper world.

The existence of a non-ordinary reality is easily accepted by several of the participants as they have already had supernatural experiences and this might be one of the reasons for participation. It is, therefore, of importance that the course organiser proceeds to point out how some people experience dead relatives turning up at their bedsides or have 'near-death-experiences' and that some people even experience a spontaneous shamanic initiation, which in modern society they cannot share with other people. They might even be thought of as mad and be treated with drugs. This, however, is not the case in a traditional society where the initiate learns how to use the power with the assistance of a powerful person in his or her society.

Mentioning the limited acceptance and understanding in modern society of the kind of impact a vision or the experience of other supernatural phenomena can have on a person's life is important at the beginning of the course. This acknowledgement of spiritual encounters and the understanding of this experience in traditional society leads to an acceptance of the concept and experience of non-ordinary reality that will take place later in the course. The course organiser explains that in the history of ethnography shamanism has been seen as some sort of schizophrenic behaviour. But for the initiate of shamanism it does not happen involuntarily. One controls it, chooses when the experience will happen.

Control, and thereby mastery, of behaviour which is comparable to a mental disease but which serves other individuals and the community as a whole is a worldwide characteristic of the shaman. The involuntary, uncontrolled primary phase (Lewis 1989: 111) is what some of the course participants have already experienced, the voluntary and controlled secondary phase is what the courses offer. For those who have not been through the primary phase there seems to be no problem in going straight to the secondary phase and establishing the initial contact with the spirits in a controlled manner. Aware that some might be expecting to become shamans overnight, the course organiser points to the fact that 'this is a week-end course. Everybody here has a high level of awareness and there is a pleasant atmosphere. Although it only takes 45 seconds to have a shamanic experience you will not get proof of your being a shaman on this course.'

Among the Greenlanders it takes a great deal of exposing oneself to the spirits to become a shaman. A person might become a shaman within seconds but might have prepared himself for years as an apprentice. Without stressing that preparation, it sounds as if there is a possible chance that any participant might suddenly be so transformed. This leads to one of the major questions about the courses and neo-shamanism: time. Modern people cannot invest all the time that the apprentice *angakkoq* had to spend. There has to be a short-cut. This is mainly created by making what was hidden available to everyone. The knowledge that the apprentice accumulated through hardship and encounters with his own fear is to be revealed in a few days. The secret teachings of the traditional shaman are presented in a week-end course.

The course organiser explains that the shaman travels in non-ordinary reality not only to the upper and lower world but that some shamans also travel in the middle world. The goal is to achieve a knowledge of the geography of non-ordinary reality. Shamanic work is not only done by shamans but there is something that links shamanic work all over the world. 'I am not concerned with a special culture during this week-end.' Like Michael Harner, the course organiser underlines that his courses in shamanism are not culture-specific. That is of importance to the understanding of the content of the course. It is a new inter-cultural method created especially for modern Western people. The concept of the different worlds are traditional shamanic concepts, the drum and the rattle as tools of inducing an altered state of consciousness are equally so, but the course participants are offered a knowledge of the 'geography of non-ordinary reality' that they might use to become shamans or just take home as assistance in their everyday lives.

The Instruction in Journeying

The start of the journey to non-ordinary reality has to be from a place in ordinary reality, for example a hole, a cave, a well, so that the participants return to this area when the journey ends. The concept of the two realities has to be clear. The participants, like the shamans, have to know the difference and master the transformation from one reality to the other. It is control over this transformation that the drum supports by different kinds of beats. The intention of the journey has to be clear. The course organiser pointed out that 'there might be issues in your life that you would like to deal with. On the first journey that you will undertake your intention is to ask for help, not to ask for meaning. That is the key issue: the shaman asks for help from the spirits – he does not use his own power.'

The awareness of the temptation to use personal power in connection with dealing with spirits is underlined several times. The participant in core-shamanism seems to be dealing mostly with benevolent spirits where he/she does not have to put up a fight. The universe of spirits for the Greenlandic *angakkoq*, on the other hand, mostly consisted of at best indifferent spirits and at worst malevolent spirits and, therefore, called for several violent encounters between shaman and spirit world on behalf of his fellow human beings. The course participant is not made aware of this possibility and generally expects a pleasant and benevolent exchange with the spirit world.

According to the course organiser,

> the spirits can take many different forms. The definition of a spirit is that it is a part of the power of the universe that can co-operate with you, a bundle of universal energy. The more you work shamanically the more help you receive. It is your work here that makes it possible for you to help other people. The spirits are very curious towards the people who participate on the course. Most people in our culture think it is only something in their heads but, if you continue, it will lead to an understanding and realization of the autonomy of the spirits.

With a concept of the autonomy of the spirits the relationship between participant and spirits is very different from that of the Greenlandic *angakkoq*. The spirits depend on the *angakkoq* 'coming forward', i.e. admitting he is an apprentice and ready to be initiated. They, in some cases, force the *angakkoq* to reveal himself so that they themselves can enter 'ordinary reality'. The relationship is reciprocal. The shaman is a mediator between the two worlds and as much as he receives help from the spirits, the spirits also receive help from him to communicate with ordinary people. The relationship with the spirits as an apprentice is that of dependency, as newly initiated *angakkoq* that of equality, as a trained *angakkoq* that of mastery.

Respect between participant and spirit is of importance. The course organiser in answering a question about evil spirits said that the spirits are very neutral. 'You have to ask yourself what the intention is with shamanism. Do you want to establish your own power or do you want to be part of the power of the universe?' He then mentioned three key concepts: clarity of intention, trust in the universe, and love. 'One has to have love in one's heart when one works shamanically. The sense of contact with the spirits can be very strong, maybe the answers you get will be inappropriate; it is all about trust.'

The concepts of love and trust are important in many of the New Age undertakings. In a large society like an urban area, the relationship to other human beings might become impersonal and disinterested, but through these courses a kind of universal love can be re-established which the participants can take with them from the course and apply to their own community. In the relationship between spirits and participants there was a warning: 'Take care what you ask for. If you are searching for something you might find it.' To a question of the possible mis-use of spirits the course organiser replied that the spirits love to play but as they know the rules of the game better, he would not recommend it. To another question whether intentions could be too egotistical the course organiser replied that the spirits have their own teaching methods, that one should leave one's ego on the shelf and use humility. When one has experienced how strong the contact with the spirits can be, then one feels the confirmation and the humility.

Love, humility and care for one's fellow human beings, are concepts shared by most great religions, not least Christianity, and they are not necessarily typical of traditional shamanism. It is clear that the questions asked by the participants deal with the possible dangers in the interaction with spirits but the concern is silenced by the use of traditional concepts of love and humility.

Before the actual journeying can take place the group has to be 'rattled together'. The course organiser said, 'we all have a tendency to exaggerate the easy solution, i.e. hallucinogenics. The rattle is a power-antenna – it is both receptive and sending. When you rattle you might begin with the east, but it does not matter in which corner you start. We will give you some tools to work with, but you have to find your own helpers.' The course organiser instructed participants in the method of rattling: 'Rattle four times in each direction to call the helpers from the four corners, then also the spirits of the Earth and the Sky. Then rattle all the way round. They have to feel like helping. The Prairie Indians and the North West coast Indians have different ways. You have to find your own way, you are not a North American Indian. You have been brought up in a technical society. You have to find your own method.'

Finding one's own method of communicating with the spirits is clearly within a core-shamanic frame of mind, but it is, in a way, also what the traditional shaman did. The Greenlandic apprentice had to turn the *angakkoq* stone but the way the spirits arrived was not predictable although some forms of encounter, i.e. that of being devoured by a bear, occurs in several accounts. The difference does not lie so much in the individualised interaction with the spirits but in the fact that the traditional shamans had a cosmology in common with their community, while the neo-shaman might have information about the cosmology of other cultures or even of his own archaic culture but he is ultimately creating his own.

The rattling together of the group is commenced as mentioned above by the course organiser calling the spirits from the four corners, sometimes whistling, sometimes singing short tunes, or stamping his feet. This is followed by a rattling round each person. The participants have a whole range of reactions to this experience: feeling something around them, the room expanding, seeing a jungle and a tiger and being told to let the tiger loose, a sense of flying, of letting the air out so that all dirt disappears. The course organiser said that the rattle has a cleansing influence. One person experienced the appearance of a dead mother. The course organiser explained that shamanism works with unfinished business with dead people, and that one could have a dead person as helping spirit. Another participant explained how she had felt a pain in the jaw, a whistling and then silence, calmness of mind, a feeling of a need to cleanse herself in the incense.

The variation of experiences on this initial shamanic experience in the basic course makes it abundantly clear that there is a very strong sense of being in touch with another reality but at the same time there is a great variety in the character of the events. This underlines the fact that the lack of a common cosmology creates a range of experiences, valuable for the individual but not necessarily shared by the group.

Power-Song and Journeying

The next stage of a basic course is to create a 'power-song'. A dance in a circle takes place to the beat of the drum and the rattling of the participants . 'Open your mouth and let the song come to you. The idea is that you get power from the song. The spirits are attracted by the song.' During singing, participants experienced dizziness, tears, meeting a gorilla, wolf, donkey, etc. The course organiser commented: 'for the journey one can start to sing power-songs in non-ordinary reality, this is also as a way to get down into the other world.'

For the actual journeying a special pattern of beating the drum is necessary. The course organiser describes how the shaman in other cultures used the drum as a horse or reindeer or boat to the world of the spirits. 'Try to ride on the sound wave from the drum into the hole.' The calling back followed the same pattern: four beats four times meant good-bye then the quick beating was the journey home and the four times four beats in the end. 'One soul travels, the other soul stays at home. Christianity is one of the very few religions with a concept of only one soul.'

During all the shamanic work the participants take notes on their own journeys and as far as possible share their experience with the group. The first journey is to the lower world to ask for help and achieve the assistance of a *power-animal*. The members of the group lie down and cover their eyes. The drumming lasts about fifteen minutes in all.[10]

During reporting back to the circle, meetings with power-animals were presented–bear, fox, badger, wolf, and so on. The course organiser commented, 'those who find it difficult to travel have put the wrong questions. Some people also find it difficult to get down there because the lower world has got bad press.' The questions might be too big, such as what is one's task in life or what is one's aim with shamanism, the need for more clarity in one's emotional life. The course organiser added that it is very important to ask for help, to pose one clear question. To strengthen the relationship with the newly achieved power-animal the group danced. The dance lasted about twenty minutes and each participant danced in his/her own way, sometimes moving like the animal that they had encountered. As the number can be over twenty-five participants, the group might be divided in dancers and musicians alternately.

Journeying for a partner is the next step of the training. The same procedure is followed as for the first journey but the question is asked on behalf of another person. This obviously creates a sense of helping a person with an important question in his or her life and points to the caring role of the shaman for fellow human beings.

The journey to the upper world is then introduced. The course organiser explained: 'you go there for divination purposes. You pose a question to a knowledgeable helper. The way to get to the Upper World might be up a tree, or the rising on the smoke from a fire. In Lapland they climb a mountain and spring from it. The Chukchee travel through the polar star. In the folk tale tradition you have "Jack and the bean stalk".' There is a difference between the questions in the lower and the upper world. In the upper world the participant asks for advice. The same procedure with the participants lying on the mattresses with scarves over their eyes is then performed for the journey to the upper world.[11]

Compared with the character of the journey of the Greenlandic *angakkoq* these journeys become highly personal, dealing with the individual quest for knowledge. The *angakkut* travelled on behalf of society to the Mother of the Sea or in the middle world to the home of the different spirits, who somehow were interfering with the society of the *angakkut* or the Man in the Moon to help with fertility. Modern Western people cannot journey on behalf of their society, which is largely indifferent. They can, however, journey in the hope of an improvement in the conditions of that society.

Healing

The healing aspect of the basic course is of great significance. The participants here get an insight into one of the major tasks of shamans in traditional society. The course organiser explained that there are two reasons why people get ill:

(1) something has entered their body which should not be there; or
(2) they have lost something from their body.

In the shamanic 'first aid' it is almost impossible to do something wrong. Go out and find a power-animal for your partner and bring it back. If you are doing this at home get somebody to drum or get a tape with drumming on it. It is important that the ill person is resting well. Rattle first in all directions then rattle with your flat hand between the ill person's body and the rattle. Try to feel the energy-area, the change of temperature, the buzzing on the palm of the hand, one of the fingers starting to vibrate. Take care that you touch the partner while travelling for him or her with your shoulder and ankle. The person being helped does not travel and the other travels to find a power-animal. Rule of thumb for choosing which animal is the right one: the one that shows itself four times. Take that animal to your chest and try to be in both realities at the same time. Then move the animal over to your partner's chest. The hands have to be rounded with a hole to blow through. Blow and close up at the chest. Then go to the crown of the head and perform the same procedure. Close with the rattle. While doing this at home you can talk your experience into a tape recorder for the person being treated.

This rather simple but traditional procedure is performed in pairs created by the participants themselves. No reptiles or insects should be introduced to the other person's body as they can also be carriers of illness. Animals that show their teeth are also connected with disease. 'Sometimes you blow out the illness with the power-animal. You are protected by your own helping spirits.'

Before the healing in pairs the healing in the 'spirit boat' took place. One of the participants had been chosen by the course organiser to be the person who was going to receive help from the whole group. The arrangement in the centre of the room had feathers added to it. The course organiser dressed in a suede skin waistcoat with different objects of personal significance to him dangling from shoulder and chest. This was the only costume of ritualistic character that was used throughout the course and therefore showed the significance of the event. The change of costume changes the concept of the person and lends him a special power. The use of garments, head dress and paraphernalia to induce transformation not only in the shaman but also in the perception of him by his audience is known from most cultures. The course organiser dressed in front of the participants and explained the meaning of the objects on the waistcoat which created a familiarity with these objects which would otherwise have been of a highly personal character. In a traditional society the significance of most objects would already be known.

The boat was formed round two mattresses where the ill person and the course organiser were placed. The rest of the group formed a boat shape, sitting so that they touched each other, sang and 'paddled' with their rattles to aid the journey to the other world. The course organiser would receive the power-animal and blow it into the ill person. After the healing the group rattled while the person danced her power-animal. Finally she told about her experience to the group. The woman for whom the group travelled had multiple sclerosis. The course organiser commented that it was a typical illness of the West caused by our society.

The importance of receiving the attention, the care of the whole group and the transformation that takes place in the person from this ritual is very striking. During several healing ceremonies, where the 'energies' of the group have been directed towards one person, I have observed people undergo a substantial transformation. It can be a very emotional experience. Modern medicine does not direct so much human attention towards an ill person. The person in the group is a known individual and has related to everybody in some way. The healing ceremony literally touches all involved. The one-to-one healing which follows this 'spirit boat' continues the healing in the atmosphere created by having seen the strong impact such a healing ceremony can have on another person. 'An area of your life that you would like to receive help with. It might be work, health, emotional problems, a pattern of your life, etc.' The course organiser then repeated the instructions:

(1) Rattle round the person to get help from the helping spirits.
(2) When you feel their presence use the rattle over the partner and feel for the ailment.
(3) Sing a song to your partner.
(4) When the drum starts, finish the rattling and get ready for journeying.
(5) Find help for your partner – a power-animal.
(6) Blow the animal into the chest and the top of the head of the partner.
(7) When the drum stops, rattle round your partner and close the area up with the rattle.
(8) Stay sitting next to your partner.

This healing procedure then ended the course. The procedure in itself has very strong links with healing performed by some South American shamans. As the course organiser is using the Michael Harner method this is not surprising as Harner had been trained by the Jívaro Indians. The head lifting diagnostic procedure in Greenland could be performed by people other than the *angakkut*. The role of the *angakkut* was communication with spirits and mastery of their behaviour, and they were called in when it was a serious illness that needed to be dealt with, i.e when soul stealing had taken place. Commenting on the risk of the healer becoming ill himself the course organiser explained this in the following way: 'Some use up their own energy. It is important to know your own limitation. The centre of shamanic work is the spirits. There can be more helpers but it is important to know the strength of each helper. The New Age has soft pastel colours, but it is not like that, it can also be tough.' The example given was the dismemberment of the apprentice.

During the course there had been some dancing and singing beside the above-mentioned journeys and healing rituals. The group had several times been in a circle in the meadow singing to the sun: 'Morning/Evening sun, come my way, take my pain, down below, cool water, down below.' The singing and dancing were sometimes used to induce a preparedness of mind for the journey. In the dancing the rattle and the personal power-song were used. The dancing had only one rule: move round the circle clockwise. Apart from that it was a free dance, where everybody followed their own patterns.

The course ended with holding hands in a circle where the course organiser emphasised that it was necessary to let the power flow through you and that it was always possible to come back to the circle. Because of the intensity of the course the experience of power being available on 'Monday morning', when everyday behaviour is re-established as well as adjustment to a daily routine in an environment that does not necessarily respect the spiritual experiences in the course, is of major importance to many participants.

Advanced Courses in Shamanism

The advanced courses use many of the techniques that have been mentioned in the section on 'The Basic Course in Shamanism'. The advanced courses are intended to expand the participants' knowledge of how shamanism can be used in different aspects of human life, be it a relationship to nature, to healing, or to death. These are areas that modern Western people often feel alienated from when living in an urban community. The relationship to Nature might have become one of leisure, a week-end experience, but it is not ingrained in the life of the person once back at work. The courses dealing directly with the relationship to Nature are therefore trying to re-establish this link on a spiritual level so that a person might feel close to Nature even sitting in a concrete building all week long. Contact with a tree spirit or the spirit of a plant still exists in non-ordinary reality and can be re-established at any time.

A detailed description of the advanced courses will be found in the appendix as the main principle of journeying and contacting helping spirits is similar to that of the basic course.

Approaches to the Role of Shamanism in Modern Society

The participants in the English and Danish courses in shamanism generally belong to the well-educated part of society. They are very articulate about their spiritual quest, especially on the advanced courses, and are well read in the literature concerning neo-shamanism. On the basic courses this is less apparent and according to the course organiser, it is approximately 10-20 per cent of participants in a basic course who are going to use shamanism in a more concentrated way.

The courses range from £90 for a non-residential basic course to £440 for a residential week of shamanic counselling training. It is therefore necessary to have a certain level of disposable income to participate in the advanced courses and that in itself influences who will be able to undertake such training. As mentioned earlier, although some participants sell their belongings and others take out bank loans I have not encountered any who complain about the price of the course – even when, as in one course I participated in, they received less time than had been stipulated in the initial programme. I see this as a reflection of the trust that the participants have in the integrity of the organiser.

My findings regarding those who participate in shamanic courses in England and Denmark seem to correspond with findings in the United States. Joan B. Townsend writes:

> This reawakening is occurring primarily among a small but important segment of the North American population, which is experiencing a new spirituality characterized by a turning to non-Western religious systems. It is especially significant because it includes well-educated, upper-middle-class people who are in positions where it is possible to influence the society's ideas and trends. Within this group, several distinct belief systems are being redefined and molded into a new mystical movement. Neo-shamanism is one major thrust of this movement. (1988: 73)

In this she agrees with Michael Harner, who describes the participants in counselling courses as follows:

Just as a matter of practical fact, however, the people who come to study these methods are typically well educated and intelligent individuals who are also curious and open-minded. Usually they are not 'followers' or advocates of blind faith in any particular teaching or dogma, but are inquiring individuals who would like to find some spiritual method that is workable and that they can trust in their own lives. Combined with these qualities they frequently also have a desire to recover their own authority and autonomy, and are often highly individualistic while at the same time wishing to find a deeper sense of community. (1988: 182)

The participants in courses clearly have common traits in these three Western societies, the United States, England and Denmark. The question is why is shamanism specifically interesting for this group and what role in society does a modern shaman take upon him/herself? The participants are mostly people who want to find a spiritual approach that is not making them dependent on a cult or on any organisation as such. They are, as Michael Harner remarks, 'inquiring individuals'. They do not need a leader but are questing for a 'renewed contact with the sacred' (Drury 1994: 113), that they can mould to their own spiritual needs.

The role of course organiser clearly reflects this attitude. He does not come across as a person who emanates a need to control on a personal level: rather he appears to be a very compassionate, caring person, who takes an interest in each participant's individual situation without being intrusive. When I asked him if he saw himself as a shaman, he answered that he used the same criteria on himself as he did on other people. He saw himself as a teacher and tried to do his best. He went with a lot of native, North American people, who did not go round saying 'I am a shaman', but rather let the people decide or the spirits decide. He saw the power as a loan and 'if one got too inflated then, when you went to the bank, the account was empty.'

The participants in courses are taught how to meet their own spirit-helpers, to learn techniques that will help them to get in contact with non-ordinary reality and thereby with their personal spirituality. There is no direct interference by the course organiser in this experience. Several of the people who are initiators of the neo-shamanic movement are very aware of their role. They do not want to be seen as exercising personal power but rather as guides opening up resources ever-present in each individual. 'Though a few individuals through their work and writing are clearly pioneers and initiators of this movement, I do not wish to imply that contemporary shamanism emerged simply as a consequence of their efforts, charismatic as some may be. Rather it is evident that people of integrity everywhere are turning to inner quest as a vehicle for transformation' (Larsen 1988: viii). The teacher or counsellor of shamanism is, in Michael Harner's words, 'a facilitator who puts clients in touch with the sources of guidance in non-ordinary reality, from which the answers received are typically wise, benevolent, compassionate, ethical, and harmonious' (1988: 184).

There is a clear attempt to create the concept that power is not personal but ought to be ascribed to the spirit world. The true characteristic of a shamanic experience is the capacity to enter into an altered state of consciousness and thereby establish contact with non-ordinary reality. If the intention is clear the spirits will co-operate, mostly in a benevolent fashion. Harner points in the above quotation to the harmonious and compassionate quality of the help offered by the spirit-helpers. This is one of the very obvious differences from traditional shamanism but speaks of a need in modern Western society of a spiritual realm of benevolence and homecoming. The course organiser expresses this experience about his workshops:

> A lot of people when they come on a basic workshop, they express this feeling of having come home. I think that for me shamanism is not a cultural thing, it is a natural ability. The ability to shamanize is something we are born with. People make these decisions, the ability to go into contact with the spirit world is something we all have. Some people find this thrilling and inviting; other people find it terrifying. So it is different with different people. One thing which has helped a little is the whole ecological awareness which is going on in the West and also Eastern Europe, an awareness of the aliveness of our planet and of nature in general. This is a feeling that a lot of people are very comfortable with and opens the door to shamanic awareness.[12]

The course organiser states that there is a natural ability to shamanise in each individual and his role is to waken that ability. It is not something for the selected few in the initial stages but might eventually lead to a small number being chosen by the spirits as true shamans: 'What I generally say is that it takes maybe thirty seconds to have a shamanic experience, but it takes a life-time to be a shaman.'

The participants do not therefore immediately become shamans after a week-end course, but they are given the instructions which might lead them on the road to become a shaman. They are taught the techniques of travelling and are introduced to an altered state of consciousness via the drumming but they do not become shamans through those two capacities alone. It is the relationship to the spirits and the use of their instructions for the benefit of the individual and the society as a whole which might ultimately lead to being a true shaman, a status that is not necessarily voiced but felt through the acceptance of the role by the surrounding society. The experience of a workshop nonetheless carries the seeds of the possible development of further involvement with non-ordinary reality. Nevill Drury comments on this experience:

> However, one thing never ceases to amaze me – that within an hour or so of drumming, ordinary city folk are able to tap extraordinary mythic realities that they have never dreamed of. It is as if they are discovering a lost fairyland of cosmic imagery from within the depth of the psyche. During the 'sharings' which is part of the workshops, all these marvellous revelations pour forth. So I am very much committed to the idea of urban shamanism, of encouraging modern urban dwellers to explore these realities.(1989: x)

The urban dwellers, the persons whose shamanic work is taking place within the lifestyle and confinement of the city, are the typical course participants. They are the ones that need a renewed spirituality in their lives, who are concerned about the ecological state of the Earth, who feel the daily estrangement from nature.

Manuals on Neo-shamanism

The extensive writings on neo-shamanism and the actual manuals describing how to go about learning the shamanic techniques offer promises of a different and more fulfilling life. The starting point is that the modern Western lifestyle is unfulfilling:

> After all, being an ordinary person – is no fun. You take everything so seriously and personally. You always search for something meaningful to guide yourself with, hoping for enlightening dreams or experiences. As an ordinary person you suffer, are afraid of and expect the worst, and

are oblivious to the power of the unknown. You are always defending your identity and your personal history. As a phantom, you constantly worry about how others judge you or what the future will bring. You neglect the impact of inexplicable forces, living life as if it were all up to you. (Mindell 1993: 8)

In this state of mind, still oblivious of the powers available to one, a person might go searching for the way to interact with these inexplicable forces. The way is to follow the manual and perform different exercises that might lead one into a frame of mind that makes one available for the insight to the shaman's body or the dreaming body, 'The shaman's body (or dreaming body) is a name for unusual experiences and altered states of consciousness that try to reach your everyday awareness through signals such as body symptoms and movement impulses, dreams and messages from environment' (Ibid.: 3), a concept Castaneda also mentions in *The Eagle's Gift.*

There are several manuals and just a few examples are taken to show the kind of persuasive description of what can be obtained through shamanic techniques:

> Shamanics is about experiencing the extraordinary whilst living an ordinary life. Shamanics is a word I have coined to describe a way to extend your awareness to new and exciting levels of perception and enhance your life in many ways. Its application will improve your vitality, balance your emotions, release your hidden potentials, and stimulate your creativity. It will develop your inner powers by bringing you into harmony with the beneficent energies of Nature and the Cosmic forces of the Universe. (Meadows 1995: xiv)

Or from another manual: 'In turn, *shamanic* mastery can help you achieve *personal* mastery. In other words, by mastering the techniques and methods of shamanism – the means to your desired goals, you can gain that end result which is sought – in this case, a mastery and control of the self – leading to personal excellence' (Scott 1991: xi).

The different manuals try to widen the concept of shamanism to fit the experiences of modern man or woman. They deal with the emotional stress that is involved in Western society and give examples and case-stories to underline the suitability of using shamanism in an urban environment. Other manuals include elements of other traditions than shamanism. In their preface A. Cook and G.A. Hawk write:

> Post-industrial society seems to be polarised between cultural nihilism for the intellectuals and self-delusion, credulity and superstition for the masses. For millions of intelligent and educated people, the ancient human urge towards transcendence can no longer be satisfied though [sic] faith in the dying religions of the father. In the age of science, belief and faith have become irrelevant; it is precisely this that makes neo-shamanism increasingly important. Shamanism discards belief or faith. It suggests that you trust your own visionary experience. It offers ancient techniques that produce immediate results. ... This book is written for non-credulous people who believe in facing up to the unpleasant aspects of reality... We show you how you can be a powerful occultist or ritual magician, and at the same time retain your intelligent scepticism and critical mind. (1992: Preface)

The book continues to blend the shamanic techniques with the esoteric traditions such as tarot and kabbalah and methods such as I Ching, Astrology and so forth. The approach of the shamanic manual is that there is a void in the life of modern man. In modern society people do not have their spiritual life fulfilled, they are uncertain about their identity, although well-educated and critical, they feel isolated and dissatisfied with their lives but at the same time are aware of the dangers of persuasive cult movements. To these people neo-shamanism offers a highly individualised method that does not force the participants into any behaviour for which they are not prepared but leaves the spiritual experiences to exist between the participants and their spirits. 'In shamanism everyone is his or her own prophet, getting spiritual revelation directly from the highest sources. Such people rock the boat; they are subversive' (Harner 1988: 10).

The relationship with the spirits is crucial to the understanding of neo-shamanism:

> He [the apprentice] must also become familiar with its spiritual inhabitants – their names, habitats, powers, likes and dislikes, how they can be called, and how they can be controlled. For it is these spirits whom he will battle or befriend, who will help or hinder him as he does his work. It is they who represent and embody the power at work in the cosmos, and it is his relationship with them that will determine his success. So the cosmology the would-be shaman learns is no dry

mapping of inanimate worlds but a guide to a living, conscious, willful universe. (Walsh 1990: 43).

How to get in contact with these spirits varies according to the different techniques. As seen in the descriptions of the courses the journeying is one way, another is the 'sitting out', yet another the collecting of healing plants. Gini Graham Scott describes how the participants experience the calling up of an ally:

> To begin the test, Paul walked across the road and stood in front of a small rise, with his back to us. Serge followed and stood about ten feet away from him on the opposite side of the road. Then lifting up his hands, Paul wordlessly called on his allie [spiritual-helper], Ethan, to appear and make himself known to Serge. As he appeared, Paul and Serge later reported, the hillside was bathed in radiant white light and they saw a large purplish form emerge from this glow. (1988: 99)

Later, the leader of the group, Michael, discloses what one of his familiars is like: '"One of my familiars," Michael reported, "looked like a six foot white gorilla with insect-like antennaes on his head. I initially called him up when I was doing some workings in L.A. and I wanted to see what was out there' (Ibid.: 186).

These two quotations serve as examples of the variation of helping spirits, or allies and familiars that a participant might experience. As mentioned earlier there are no common concepts of what a spirit is and the neo-shamanic books are rather thin on the subject. That, however, does not mean that the concepts are not used as the main understanding of what exists in non-ordinary reality. In the courses I researched the spirits often had animal forms, such as an eagle, horse, badger, or beaver, often the kinds of animals found on the medicine cards.[13] Eliade comments on this concept of relationship established with the animal world: 'While preparing for his ecstasy and during it, the shaman abolishes the present human condition and, for the time being, recovers the situation as it was in the beginning. Friendship with animals, knowledge of their language, transformation into an animal are so many signs that the shaman has re-established the "paradisal" situation lost at the dawn of time' (1989: 99).

In the courses, I observed, the relationship with animals narrated after the journeys often had a 'paradisal' note to them. The initial meeting with the power-animal might be frightening but the final result mostly confirmed a bond between the participants and the power-animal. When the spirits encountered take on a more amorphous form, light is often mentioned. There is frequently a connection between the appearance of spirit and light.

The concept of the soul or souls is mostly connected with an individual human being. The soul or souls are part of the person and the spirits are the non-human or dead-human entities that have an impact on the living individual or the society as a whole. Åke Hultkrantz describes the soul-dualism that he perceives as part of shamanism:

> Another feature connected with shamanism is, as I have tried to show elsewhere, soul dualism, or the belief in two alternating soul formations, one – consisting of one or several souls – representing the vitality of the body, breath, and mind, and the other being the person himself in his out-of-body appearance during dream and trance. It is usually the latter that makes the shaman's ecstatic soul flight. (1988: 36)

The above concepts of soul and spirits follow closely the perception of many traditional shamans. Writers like Kenneth Meadows, on the other hand, expand the concept and define spirit and soul as follows:

> The Soul is a body of *light*. It is an inner light that is within you and within us all. Light is a form of energy and your Soul is your body of Light-energy and a centre of Life-energy. Although your Soul is integral to you and exists in approximately the same spatial location as your body, and interpenetrates it, it is not in the same 'place'; it exists in another plane or level of being-ness– in what we might call the Dimension of the Soul. (1995: 6)[14]

The term 'energy' is often used in New Age literature to describe the spiritual elements of human existence. Energy is somehow not loaded with Christian understanding as are concepts like soul and spirit and is therefore a more neutral word, describing the forces that are at work in the spiritual realm. Meadows takes the concept of spirit a step further when he claims that:

> You are a spirit! Not a body with a Spirit, but the very opposite of what you may have been led to suppose – a Spirit with a physical body. A Spirit with a mind. A Spirit with a Soul. A composite being comprising body, mind, Soul and Spirit, yet 'disconnected' from this totality when the body

and mind have no conscious contact with the Soul and Spirit, and when one or more is out of synchronization with the others. (Ibid.: 6)

Kenneth Meadows continues, not surprisingly, to include the concepts of *chakras* into the shamanic technique and the book is a manual with exercises which help the reader to incorporate this concept of soul and spirit into their lives.

Although there is no clear concept of spirit and soul in neo-shamanism, there is no doubt of the importance of the role of the spirit and the importance of the soul to the well-being of the individual and the society. As shown in the description of the courses, soul-loss or spirit intrusion are the main reasons for physical and mental dis-ease in the shamanic universe.

Power is another important aspect of the role of the counsellor and teacher of shamanism. The course organiser points to the different forms of power in his basic courses. One illustrates the positive energy that is available to a person of good intent, the other the power that suppresses. Both elements of power are present and it is important that the teacher should be aware of it. Therefore it is again and again stated that the role of the teacher or counsellor is non-intrusive: 'Then, after the problem can be precisely formulated, the client uses shamanic methods to seek help in solving it. But, again, this help does not come from the counsellor in ordinary reality; rather, it comes from the client's own divinatory journey to non-ordinary reality, *where the real counsellors are*' (Harner 1988: 186).

The teachers of neo-shamanism do not claim to want followers but rather wish to create independence in the lives of their students. Even the authors of books are careful to point this out:

> I want this book to enable people to walk their own walk, wherever and whatever it may be. I do not want people to rush to the reservations to walk the Indians' walk. And I most definitely do not want them to pound on my door and insist upon walking my walk. I want each individual to seek his own or her own way and to discover a personal truth. (Hammerschlag 1989: 17)

When I asked the course organiser what expectations he had as to what happened to people when they left the course, what kind of influence he thought they would have in their society, he answered that he did not really know, but that he could tell me what he hoped would happen. That they took that experience on to themselves and used the experience for the rest of their lives, that they allowed the experience to be part of their life and thereby these experiences would have an impact on many people's lives whether it was their children, friends or somebody they met who was in trouble. He thought that it was a ripple effect.[15]

Most course participants obviously just use the techniques for their own benefit and perhaps, for a small circle of friends. However, some incorporate the techniques into their work –which often means people in the caring professions – but there are people who offer services such as:

> Shamanic Finance. Let the magic work for YOU. Shamanic Finance is: Integrating Money with Spirit. Financial EMPOWERING, HEALING, ENERGISING. Blasting Money Blockages. A Wealth of Guidance. Don't you want to have FUN with Money? Would you like to FEEL more Prosperous. For a complete Financial Service of the 21st. Century, contact: [the address and the title of the adviser]. Accountant, Holistic and Ethical Financial Adviser (PIA and LAUTRO Licensed) Business Consultant, Workshops, and Personal Counselling.[16]

This 'holistic' approach to money is not the normal usage of shamanic techniques. Interestingly, spirit and money are not often connected in our society whereas in Asian societies such as Korea the *mansin* often work for the prosperity of the client. This, however, is seen as a dubious aim of happiness in the wealthy West. Not one participant from all the courses I studied cited improving his/her financial situation as the aim of learning shamanic techniques.

The people incorporating shamanism as a method in their work often are psychologists, counsellors, social workers, doctors, and so on. They are often people in the caring professions. One of the most famous of these practitioners is Sandra Ingerman, a counselling psychologist and a member of the International Faculty of the Foundation for Shamanic Studies. In her book, *Soul Retrieval. Mending the Fragmented Self,* Michael Harner contributes the preface:

> In the eleven years I have known her, Sandra Ingerman has moved from being one of my students of shamanic practice to being an outstanding shaman, an esteemed colleague, and a treasured friend. Beyond that, she is an inspiring teacher, as can be attested by her many students. What you read here by her, you can trust, for she exemplifies the highest

standards of ethics and practical knowledge in contemporary
shamanism and shamanic healing. (1991: x)

The course organiser also refers to her work in his course on Soul
Retrieval. The book is a mixture of manual of instruction and case-
histories, so the reader constantly obtains an insight into how the
method of soul-retrieval works. In the epilogue Sandra Ingerman
describes how re-connecting with the spirit quietens the ego and
makes it possible to 'tap into the universal flow':

> Many of us feel as though we are cut off from the spiritual aspects of
> ourselves. We feel isolated from the source. When we embark on a
> spiritual path, however, we can reconnect with the light that shines
> within us. We no longer have to seek the light outside ourselves. When
> we reconnect with Spirit, the ego quiets; our boundaries and defenses let
> down; and we can experience what it feels like to be part of life and
> connected to the whole. We lose the sense of being separate from any
> living being but feel ourselves being the air, the water, the earth, the fire,
> the animals, the trees, the plants, the insects, the rocks. We experience
> oneness with our friends and enemies. We connect with the spirit that
> moves in all things. We can now tap into the universal flow and find we
> have the strength and power we need for healing. (Ibid.: 196)

To introduce a client to the idea of oneness with Nature and his
fellow human beings is probably going to be met with an open mind
and a wish to be part of this sense of belonging. As isolation and
estrangement is clearly part of modernity this concept deals with the
most fundamental needs. What might prove more difficult is to
introduce the word 'shamanism' into the treatment of a client, along
with drums, rattles, power-animals and helping spirits. In the
Foundation for Shamanic Studies Newsletter, summer 1991, Leilani
Lewis, who has a 'psychology practice', describes how she was
introduced to Michael Harner's core-shamanism and how she is
now using this in her practice. Teaching shamanic methods to the
client is described by her in the following way:

> Some clients are eager to make the switch once I introduce the idea;
> others are not so inclined. I respect their inclinations. With many clients
> I don't even mention it. In general, I rely on my teacher and power
> animals for help in deciding. If I weren't so shamanically inclined, I'd say
> I rely on my intuition. The spirits are so much a part of my life now that
> I define my intuition as my guardian spirits talking to me. (1991: 3)

Lewis believes that, compared with techniques of guided imagery, 'for those people open and able to do it, the shamanic journey is more powerful and effective in terms of dealing with a wide range of problems' (Ibid.: 5). She hid her knowledge from her colleagues initially 'for fear of being discredited' but now thinks that 'it would be unethical for me not to share with others that are interested' (Ibid.: 12). She attracts a high degree of interest among other practitioners. This sense of curiosity about and openmindedness to the concept of shamanism among educated people is also confirmed when one reads articles and books dealing with neo-shamanism or core-shamanism. There is a growing interest and at the present moment the contemporary writing on shamanism is substantial.

There is no doubt that the New Age version of shamanism: core-shamanism or neo-shamanism is spreading rapidly in the West. The courses have long waiting lists, Michael Harner's basic course in shamanism now has several hundred participants in the basic course, people are prepared to pay relatively high course fees, there is a rapidly growing market for books dealing with shamanic topics; all point to the conclusion that the shamanic world-view has found a sounding board in questing urban Westerners. Whether it is 'cramming ourselves with the ages, customs, arts, philosophies, religions, discoveries of others', in the words of Friedrich Nietzsche or a 'new revision' in the words of Jolande Jacobi, still remains to be seen. The interesting fact, however, is that it is the middle-aged, well-educated person who is involved and this might ultimately lead to a reformation of spiritual values eventually reaching outside the world of courses and New Age bookshops.

NOTES

1. The grammatical peculiarities are in the original.
2. In Oxford, *The Inner Bookshop* provides a well assorted stock of such literature. In Copenhagen the bookshop called *Det ukendte* [The unknown] shares an atmosphere and stock with *The Inner Bookshop*. There is a sense of internationalism or rather 'western world-ism' about these bookshops.
3. This represents a remarkable omission of some of the most important areas in which shamanism is to be found.

4. I have omitted the name of the organiser as he did not accept the comparison between his courses and traditional shamanism represented by the Greenlandic *angakkoq* and the concept of mastery of spirits when he saw the results of the research, although he had been informed before the start of the fieldwork of my intention. My interpretation of his reaction is that the very idea of mastery, display of destructive power and the recognition of evil forces is alien not only to his version of core-shamanism but to most of the New Age concept of spirituality.

5. When I asked Michael Harner about his attitude to the shaman as master of spirits he stated that he did not use the word mastery but preferred to think of the spirits as allies.

6. The professional background of the participants in Denmark included psychiatric nurses, an actress, social workers, a plant colour factory-owner, graphic designer, yoga-teacher, school-teachers, owner of a health food shop, several psychotherapists, a former dancer, playwright, architect and several educated unemployed persons. In England, the participants included a former factory worker and teacher of English, engineer, administrator for a retirement home, school teachers, university lecturers, acupuncturist, healers, office workers, social workers, psychotherapists, course organiser of training course for business people, Jungian analyst and unemployed people.

7. It was pointed out by the course organiser that the circle formed during the course would always be there when people need it. They can always go back and get strength from the circle.

8. The Wicca movement is basically a nature moment based on theories of witchcraft. It has a strong feminist orientation.

9. In Denmark a person is born into membership of the Lutheran Church and will as wage earner have to pay a percentage of his tax to the church. To avoid the tax it is necessary to terminate one's membership.

10. I did not take notes on the journeys of other participants as they are highly personal and I did not want to have an impact on the free flow of information. My own journey is, however, a typical one: I travelled from a hole in the garden under a birch tree in Tisvilde, Denmark. I glided quickly into the hole and was in water where a dolphin received me and we undertook some swimming while sea corals were almost threatening us. In the end of the tunnel a shining staircase appeared which ascended to a plain. I went to a tree and sat under it. There was an eagle in the top of the tree. It changed into a young man who climbed down. I asked: 'Where is home?' He replied: 'Here.' I said: 'In non-ordinary reality?' He gave me a fruit from the tree. Then we went over to a group of dancers. I danced with the eagle on my shoulder and became an eagle as it slowly devoured me. All changed into birds and glided over a beautiful landscape which then turned polluted and desolate. But the eagles screamed and their screams fertilised the Earth. The deserts became oases, the polar sea full of seals. The flying reminded me of the movements of the dolphin, there was a connectedness between the dolphin and the eagle. The drum sang and then called me back. A quick change back to human form occurred, swimming back with the dolphin and arriving on the lawn. The answer was, 'The home is the Earth, her health is my responsibility too.'

    The elements of the journey consist of 'typical' New Age animals such as dolphins and eagles. The concept of the anthropomorphic form of a power-animal and the devouring are well-known in classical shamanism. The need to improve the conditions of the Earth is inherent in the New Age concept of what individuals should be aiming at achieving through their enlightenment. The journeying in itself was for me like entering into a mythological landscape.

11. I travelled via a beech tree remembered from my childhood. A pigeon was waiting at the top. I sat on its back and could feel the warmth and the smell of feathers. I was taken to a new tree with an inner stairway and ended up in a landscape of white clouds on which white young women danced in a circle in transparent light garments. They danced in a chain towards the black-blue sky. A large woman sat on a 'throne' and she told me that the question that I posed would become reality. She was very serious. I then danced with the women in the circle and then in a chain back over the white clouds through the tree back on the pigeon's back and down the tree. During the journey the drum had been singing high tones.

12. Interview December 1995.

13. Medicine cards are based on the North American Indian concept of the animal world. Each card shows an animal which represents special characteristics that can be transferred to human beings.

14. This concept of light as a spiritual entity is similar to the light mentioned in connection with the *angakkoq*.

15. Interview December 1995.

16. From a leaflet shown to me by Rolf Gilberg.

Chapter 5

THE REVIVAL OF
SHAMANISM IN
OTHER CULTURES

As far as I have been able to discover there is no real attempt to revive the shamanic tradition in Greenland. The Christian Churches are very well attended and interest in the old traditions of the forefathers is expressed through art and literature. The Tukâk [harpoon point] theatre in Denmark, established in the 1970s on the west coast of Jutland with the intent of using native Greenlandic actors and establishing a modern mythology based on the old myths and the experiences of the young Greenlander, included shamanic elements but not séances with an audience composed of believers in the magic performed on the stage.

In some cultures attempts have been made by anthropologists to revive shamanism, to re-establish the old belief systems while there are still old people present to tell the tale. As the acts of the shaman are highly individualised it is questionable which version is the one worthy of revitalisation. There has always been a versatility in shamanism, an openness towards other belief systems that has enabled the exchange to take place between, for example, shamanism and Buddhism in Mongolia. It would today be difficult to determine whether the behaviour of a shaman described by Danish researchers in Mongolia in the 1930s is influenced by the Buddhism of five hundred years ago or whether the Buddhist elements are shamanic in their origin.

The last of the 'real' shamans in Greenland admitted that the shamans before them were the great shamans and this vision of the past seems to be a universal tendency. The shamans in the latter part of the twentieth century in Siberia or Japan seem to believe that they are only a pale version of what was going on in the past. The shaman has changed and so has his audience and their needs. In Korea today the *mansin* performing the *Kut* is mostly concerned with the fortune or misfortune of the family and thereby with its relationship to the ancestors. She has a financially satisfactory life but has a low social status. She is often ashamed of her work (Kendall 1985: 63ff). On the other hand, some of the Christian Churches in Korea have ● incorporated shamanic elements and are on the rise, perhaps for that very reason. In post-Reformation Northern Europe shamanism seems to flourish in its core- or neo-shamanic version for the very reason that the individual can establish an understanding of supernatural experiences which are not easy to come to terms with in the framework of the Anglican/Protestant church.

Chang Chu-kun writes that, according to the Organisation of Korean Shamans, there are about 50,000 registered shamans in Korea and about 100–200,000 followers (1988: 34). There is no doubt that the number of followers might be difficult to establish as people might use a shaman but not admit to it. According to the writings of Laura Kendall, shamanism appeals first and foremost to the housewife in Korea. Present day shamanism therefore has undergone changes which have adapted it to the needs of the users and concentrates on divination and the life of the family. The performers of shamanism might also have their own economic interests at heart when they work:

> The avarice of many *mudangs* has further aggravated the misfortunes of shamanism. Rather than providing competent service which would reinforce communal solidarity, reaffirm the joy of life, and promote the healing of psychogenic and psychosomatic illness, some *mudangs* intimidate people with their supposed superhuman powers for the purpose of exacting money. By luring people with promises of good fortune, many *mudangs* encouraged dissipation and idleness. (Hahm Pyong-choon 1988: 95)

The intimidation of people by some shamans is known in any shamanic culture. Hahm Pyong-choon points to this fact as shamanism is under threat for precisely the reasons that neo-shamanism flourishes in the West:

> Clearly, the modern challenges to shamanism are serious threats to its continued existence. Already, modernization, Westernization, urbaniza-

tion, industrialization, the development of science and technology (and especially of mass communication), the vigorous propagation of Christianity, the humiliation of colonial servitude under Japan, and the continuing struggle against North Korea, have all exacted a heavy toll. As the breakdown of familialism and increase of individualism continue, shamanism is sure to be affected further. (Ibid.: 95)

The difference between present-day Korean shamanism and neo-shamanism is that in the former the relationship to the dead family members and their influence on the well-being of the living is the central point. The family is the centre of concern. In neo-shamanism the individual makes whoever needs attention the centre of concern and it is therefore better adjusted to modern Western urban life, where the extended family is not necessarily of major concern to the individual living in a nuclear family of parents and children.

In South America there are several healers continuing part of the healing techniques of the traditional shamans but, according to Marlene Dobkin De Rios, it is a very different challenge that the shaman has to deal with in an urban setting:

Today, healers like don Hilde respond to amoral breakdown in the city, to problems of drug abuse, prostitution, family breakdowns, and child and wife abuse. The healer's rectitude, his protection by the spirits and his ability to transform the spirit world to serve his clients is congruent with the ancient Amazonian patterns. His healing certainly differs in kind and substance from the orthodox medical techniques available, for a price, in the city. (1992: 59)

Don Hilde had visions of Christian saints as an adolescent. Later he became a healer and used *ayahuasca*. He relies on the help from the spirit world when healing. 'Spiritual realms, too, are important to folk practitioners. Most healers have a metaphysical system available to them and protective supernatural entities (such as forces, spirits, ancestors or ghosts) – beliefs which they share to one degree or another with their clients' (Ibid.: 25). In that aspect they share the traditional belief of the tribal shaman. 'The degree of success and power of a tribal shaman was directly linked to the number and variety of omnipotent spirit beings with whom he was familiar. His lack of healing success was credited to his inability to control powerful spirit forces to do his bidding' (Ibid.: 56).

The urban shaman deals with the despair arising from poverty in the deprived areas of urban life. His clients might believe that don Hilde can deal with the evil they experience but they do not necessarily share his concept of the spirit world. 'Healers like don Hilde may have complex philosophical or mystical systems that they study and follow, but such doctrines are not widely held among their clients' (Ibid.: 57).

The mixture of Christianity and the traditional techniques of the shaman seem to be common among urban healers in South America. John Perkins is told how the Virgin of Quito and the Quechua Birdwoman have merged: '"She is not just the Virgin ... she is also a Quechua Birdwoman, a powerful shaman who can fly into the past to consult our ancestors about the future. She embodies Pachamama as well as Jesus Christ"' (1994a: 46) According to John Perkins this concept has been encouraged by the church:

> On the one hand, it is true that shamanism in Latin America suffered under the Inquisition: officially, any philosophies, rituals, or celebrations that were not sanctioned by Rome were forbidden, and heretics were severely punished. But from another standpoint, pantheism and shamanism are greatly indebted to many of the priests who were responsible for carrying out Church policy. Although their motives may have been far from altruistic, these priests nevertheless accomplished exactly the opposite of what their peers from England and France did in North America. Rather than encouraging the annihilation of indigenous cultures, the Spanish clergy formed subtle and covert alliances with shamanic leaders and incorporated aspects of shamanism into their own ceremonies and symbolism. (Ibid.: 47)

If this has been the case it has features in common with the exchanges taking place in other parts of the world as seen between shamanism and Buddhism in Mongolia or Christianity in Korea. The work of the *angakkut* was also influenced by Christianity and an incorporation took place although not on the part of the Church.

South American healers are also the focus of many articles in the magazine *Shaman's Drum*. These deal with shamans from different areas of South America such as Peru, Ecuador, Guatemala. Often the description of the shaman is based on anthropologists participating in the rituals of the shaman but also people like John Perkins, 'an ex-Peace Corps volunteer and successful businessman turned environmentalist and spiritual activist – started taking small groups of Americans on trips to learn from these shamans' (1994b: 55). The fascination of the Westerner with the healer in these cultures permeates those articles. The readiness to accept the world of the shaman is obvious: 'His power filled the room. I was certain that everyone in the group could feel it. Outside, the Andean night was cold. But inside this man's lodge was an energy that warmed us (Ibid.: 55). 'Juan set his bolsa (shoulder bag) down and knelt beside it. I did the same. The night was pitch dark, but there was a different quality – an overpowering depth- to the darkness we were about to enter' (Betts 1993: 51). 'Although our ceremony was simple, several members of our group experienced powerful alchemical visions' (Joan Parisi Wilcox and Elisabeth B. Jenkins, 1996: 39)

The appeal of the indigenous culture to Westerners obviously will have a major impact on the future shape of the shamans of that culture. Serge Kahili King, the author of a handbook based on the Hawaiian way of the adventurer, describes the development in Hawaiian shamanism as follows: 'Today, however, the great healing, metaphysical, and shamanic traditions of Hawaii are being kept alive primarily by the same race that almost destroyed them completely. Without the audiences of white mainlanders, even the few Hawaiian teaching *kahunas* would have virtually no one to teach' (1990: 33).

King claims that Hawaiian shamanism is easily adapted to modern times and has therefore created a handbook that makes it possible to incorporate this in an urban setting:

Urban shamans doing a shamanic vision quest today do not require a lot of special preparation or conditions, because we are part of a unique society that has already, though unknowingly, prepared us well. The wilderness is not an essential aspect of the vision quest, nor is a high degree of isolation. The vision quest is not dependent on outside conditions because it takes place in your mind and our minds have had a lot of training. (Ibid.: 143)

The North American Indian culture has for many years been under siege by searching Westerners, so much so that there now is some hostility between the two groups. The interest in sweat-lodges, healing ceremonies, paraphernalia and so on, concerning the North American Indian tradition is large and a book like *Birth of a Modern Shaman*, by Cynthia Bend and Tayja Wiger, describing a North American Indian woman changing from being an alcoholic to a life as a shaman, is typical. Tayja Wiger is not coming to terms with her own heritage directly but through the help of willing Westerners. For Tayja Wiger it happens in a church healing ceremony: 'The second I placed my hand on Tayja's head I felt a bolt of energy. There was a frequency in my body – a motion that came from elsewhere. I was aware of a holy presence engulfing my own body. It was, I knew, coming from God, the Holy Spirit, through the instrumentality of my spiritual guide and teacher, Swami Sivananda' (Bend and Wiger 1989: xix).

The fusion of Christianity, Indian philosophy and shamanism is typical of the modern open-minded approach to the possible mixture of belief systems. Some North American Indians do not, however, view the adaptation of their belief systems by Westerners as uncomplicated. In a letter in *Shaman's Drum*, by Sungila Peta Wicokahiyasamya entitled 'A Little Advice about Sacred Objects From an Experienced Native' (1995: 6ff) she questions the whole commercial side of the approach to sacred objects: 'While many of us Natives are pleased to see an interest in our culture, there is still a lot of bad feeling between Natives and non-Natives. Please do not be careless and assume the right to possess traditional sacred things without truly understanding what those things mean.'

In the same magazine Hal Zina Bennett wrote a letter entitled 'A Case for Neo-shamanism', in which he claims that he has had paranormal experiences that took him fifteen years to come to understand. He got help through a peyote shaman in the 1960s and 1970s and has since written about the subject. It is this writing that apparently has caused problems:

It has seemed odd to me that, since I began publishing books about my own experiences in the shamanic realm, I have been attacked by some Native Americans as a kind of interloper. In one case, I was even accused of 'spiritual genocide – being a 'White guy stealing Native spirituality.' The bottom line for me is that I did not pick this path out of the blue sky. I did not even invite it into my life. And certainly I have sacrificed much in my dedication to service that this path has dictated. Native peoples can, of course, lay legitimate claim to their specific cultural ceremonies, and such claims should be honoured and protected. For this reason, I purposefully don't try to perform specific Native ceremonies. However, the use of shamanic tools in spiritual practice is a universal heritage, and nobody in their right mind can claim an exclusive franchise on universal tools and practices. (1996: 6)

Native American Indians nonetheless also cooperate with interested Westerners but these two letters point to inherent problems in the exchange of belief systems. For the present day North American Indian, the traditional rituals and paraphernalia help to create an identity as a culture. If this is watered down by the spiritual quests of others or commercial interests the whole basis of the sustaining of their culture is undermined. This debate, however, underlines the reason for Westerners to create a shamanism of their own, the universal core-shamanism, which cannot be seen as offending cultural claims.

Magazines like *Shaman's Drum, Kindred Spirit,* and *Sacred Hoop,* all cover the different aspects of spirituality in the New Age. *Shaman's Drum* covers shamanism throughout the world although there seems to be more of a focus on North and South America. The magazine also advertises courses and paraphernalia in connection with shamanism and has detailed reviews on new books on the subject. It is produced in the USA and therefore mostly deals with the American market. *Kindred Spirit* is produced in England. This magazine deals with several forms of spirituality, of which shamanism is one. *Sacred Hoop,* which is also produced in England, is comparable to the American *Shaman's Drum* as there is more focus on specifically shamanic aspects of the New Age. In Denmark *Nyt Aspect* covers the same area as *Kindred Spirit.*

The shaman, either in a traditional setting or in the New Age context, has to work with the spirits in order to restore health to the individual or society as a whole. He or she might be highly educated or have a very basic education, as in connection with shamanic work this is not of major concern. Ruth-Inge Heinze describes the role of shamanism in the modern world as follows:

Shamans are actively and successfully working in the modern world. Shamanic practices are, therefore, not confined to 'backward' or underdeveloped areas but flourish in all cultures, even those that pride themselves on their sophistication...We can no longer maintain that shamanism is only practised by the uneducated powerless. Shamanism is also neither a prerogative of the educated nor those with high intelligence but originates in a different part of the being, i.e., the shaman's heart, soul, and spirit (1991: 117).

Similarly in other areas of healing such as those exemplified in someone like Betty Shine, the English clairvoyant and healer, practitioners might not have a high level of education but they realise the potential for helping other people. While their social status might not be high in the society at large, within New Age subculture the person with special gifts experiences a total change of role. There are many people in need and publishers and course organisers are waiting to satisfy that need.

CONCLUSION

The relationship between the feeling of impotence in the face of the forces of nature and the resort to magic is well documented in several studies of religion among indigenous peoples. Among the Greenlanders the task of the *angakkut* was no different from shamans in other parts of the world: to keep the interaction between human beings and the forces surrounding them under control. The most important skill of the *angakkut* was therefore to master spirits that could serve as helpers in a world in which an unpredictable onslaught by evil forces might occur, be it in connection with famine, disease or the destructive emotions of human beings. Knud Rasmussen writes: 'It is not just the spirits of nature that threaten human beings but most of all the evils of Life itself created by human beings. Worst are enemies born out of hatred and slander, intolerance and envy, especially when those enemies at the same time take the supernatural in their service' (1921b: 11).

Human emotions out of control are a major threat to society and have to be prevented or, if necessary, destroyed. The apparent role of taboo rules is to appease the ever-present spirits but ultimately to keep human behaviour within a fixed pattern. Dealing with the transgressions of this pattern was the role of the *angakkut*. If, however, the *angakkut* could not control their own sense of power or greed they might themselves be destroyed. In a society consisting of few members the survival of the group was dependent on the behaviour of the individual and deviant behaviour was, therefore, suppressed.

To sustain a thriving community the *angakkut* had to be prepared to undertake dangerous and fearsome journeys on behalf of all and serve as mediators between the sacred and the profane, risking their own lives in the interaction with the supernatural. In an ideal world this would prevent disasters in the community. But *angakkut* might fall prey to their own sense of power and use the respect and fear in which they were held against the interest of the very people whose trust they had. The *angakkut* were first and foremost dealing with the collective interest of society; they were, in the language of Shirokogoroff, the masters of spirits and they possessed great insight into the psycho-mental complex of their fellow human beings. The *angakkut* would only use their skills when life-threatening events took place, as minor magic was available to everybody. They were, in other words, specialists in spirits and in communication with the invisible world with all that entails in terms of both bringing out the best and the worst in the nature of the single *angakkok*.

This very sense of the power of the specialist is what neo-shamanism is attempting to eliminate. While trying to preserve the positive aspects of interaction with a spirit world, in which the spirits first and foremost are allies and for the most part of good intention, the knowledge of the shaman is no longer of an esoteric character but instead available to all. There is no sense of a life-threatening tangible disaster instigated by Nature, which is instead perceived as the victim of human greed. Human suffering originates from a fragmented society whose value system has collapsed into mere materialism and whose spiritual values are starved out of existence. The sense of impotence is therefore directed towards the structure of society, and the secularisation of the institutions that uphold it. Medical care, the treatment of mental diseases and the social system as such have all lost contact with the sacred and, therefore, misfortune, disease and death cannot be explained from a spiritual point of view.

Today when people experience supernatural events in their lives, they often hide them so as not to be regarded as abnormal or as mentally unbalanced. Where, in the words of I.M. Lewis, the apprentice shaman and the mentally ill had behaviour patterns in common in traditional societies, modern Western society deals with deviant behaviour within the category of illness. A course participant might not, however, have suffered any disease before embarking on a shamanic course but most people I interviewed revealed a sense of deprivation of values. The shamanic view of the inspired world in which human beings are active participants re-establishes a sense of belonging, the lack of which, the sense of estrangement, has been the price paid for modernity. It is no coincidence that neo-shamanism is sometimes called urban shamanism.

Although Shirokogoroff claimed that shamanism had collapsed as a European concept (1935: 269) it has found its own new form in core-shamanism. The courses aim at re-creating a shamanic concept of the world in which the individual will gain the power to deal with life in a modern world, aided by helping spirits. To apply the theories of Jung to such experiences is obvious. The participants in courses journey to their own collective unconscious where they encounter archetypes shaped as power-animals and fairies. Perhaps this is the kind of psychological explanation Ward Rutherford hints at in his critical description of Michael Harner's courses where he claims that the experiences of the course participants 'can be explained in ways that have nothing to do with shamanism' (1986: 104). I, however, am more inclined to qualify the degree of experience for the course participants: for some, especially on the basic course, there are no experiences at all which can be related to the concept of shamanism[1] but for most participants, and especially those on advanced courses, there is a commitment to the idea of incorporating the shamanic way into their lives and achieving encounters with non-ordinary reality, however individual, which activate strong emotions and open the way to a spiritual experience it would be difficult to achieve on their own account.

The participants do not necessarily become shamans and are not taught to master the spirits but to use them as advisers and teachers. It is crucial to understand the difference between the concept of spirits among the Greenlanders, where they are seen at best as neutral, at worst as malevolent, and where they have to be controlled in order to be helping spirits, and core-shamanism where the spirits are mostly benevolent and are easily attracted to the assistance of the questing course participant. The relationship between fear and the accumulation of spirits is played down in the courses and although the participants are aware of their own fears, the experience of the journey mostly confirms the harmonious relationship that the courses aim to establish with non-ordinary reality.

Would it then be acceptable to call the course participant an apprentice shaman? There is no attempt to achieve mastery of spirits, instead the spirits are in control. Michael Harner describes them as allies. The trance state that some participants experience is very light, and although there is a certain change of consciousness at will, the journeying takes place on a highly individualised basis with no common concept of spirits, even when assisting another person in either healing or soul retrieval. There is no general social recognition except for those groups of people who might meet for drumming sessions or at further courses.

Whether the participants see themselves as shamans is up to the individual and his or her surroundings. There is no doubt that several participants perceive themselves as specially gifted in a spiritual sense and they might go on to attempt to heal or teach others. The courses are presented primarily as a means of helping individuals to take control not of spirits but of their own lives. Emotions such as fear, loneliness and insecurity can all find their outlet and elimination (catharsis) in the interaction with non-ordinary reality. Even though the courses are attended by several people from the caring professions the aim is ultimately to eliminate the specialist and give power back to the individual, the principle of self-healing.

The Greenlanders felt fear towards the forces of nature and the emotions of their fellow human beings and searched for help from the *angakkoq* as mediator and master if their own magic was not sufficient. Western people feel fear towards the forces of a secular society that might render them unemployed, ill, dependent on the good will of the state and the emotions of others, and become their own healers commencing a quest for re-introducing transcendental values into their lives in the hope that through the New Age network they can ultimately transform the world. To achieve this they undertake what could be described as *shamanic behaviour*.

There might, however, be a social gain to be achieved from introducing such values. As mentioned earlier, the role of the modern healer is highly esteemed among people adhering to the New Age idea. There is possible social advantage in becoming a spiritually gifted person, and both the financial gain and the social status available might call forth both the best and the worst in human beings. As with the Greenlandic *angakkoq* the role is available to many and the reasons for adhering to a shamanic world view are manifold.

The perception of the healing capacity achieved overnight has its adversaries. Jeanne Achterberg writes:

> The current 'New Age' belief that healers can be aware of their healing tools just by plugging into their intuition and bypassing the world of amassed information poses a danger to a balanced healing system. These would-be healers may offer a quickly learned technique, coupled with compassion, unconditional love (a difficult concept at best), and a

nurturing attitude, but their training with real people is often minimal and their understanding of suffering and disease, poor. (1990: 180)

As several informants pointed out, the sense of love and caring among people on the course is very important to those who participate. The popularity of New Age courses in general no doubt stems from this sense of belonging to a community albeit for just a few days where each individual matters and where all take an interest in the healing of each person. With the generation of a sense of love comes a need for sharing and well-intentioned, although not skilled, attempts at healing might be one result. This is, however, the reason why it is pointed out in the courses that there is a place for medical doctors in the world of healing.

Interestingly, there is also space for Christianity. Don Handelman mentions (1967: 455) how the Washo shaman blends the power of shamanism with that of the Old Testament. Among the South American healers Christianity and shamanism also thrive side-by-side. Some course participants reported meeting Christ or Mary when journeying. As with the *angakkut* of the eighteenth century, the modern adherents of neo-shamanism are prepared to be open minded about other religions and incorporate their belief systems in the shamanic world view; a holistic approach to religion. Whether the Christian Church is equally open minded has still to be seen. Piers Vitebsky writes, 'There can be no shaman without a surrounding society and culture. Shamanism is not a single, unified religion but a cross-cultural form of religious sensibility and practice. In all societies known to us today shamanic ideas generally form only one strand among the doctrines and authority structures of other religions, ideologies and practices' (1995: 11).

The word shamanism is applied to many different practices in the New Age setting. For some there is less direct relationship to the shamanic practices of traditional societies while for others like the core-shamanism performed by Michael Harner there is more of a correspondence. The *angakkut* of the past were supported in their work by a surrounding society of believers to whose service they, sometimes reluctantly, were summoned by the spirits and by the legends and myths which underlined their skills in dealing with non-ordinary reality. The modern Western performer of shamanic behaviour, on the other hand, is without recognition in society at large but thrives within a New Age sub-culture where no one will raise an eyebrow to an early morning trip to the power-place or an enlightening conversation with a power-animal. The mastery of spirits and healing is here transformed into a mastery of communication with the spirits of Nature, the sense of spiritual crises closely interlinked with an environmental crisis. Although sometimes frightening, the séance of the *angakkut* and the courses in shamanism contain the excitement created by an encounter with the supernatural. In both societies to live in a world inhabited by spirits lends sense to otherwise inexplicable events and power to human beings over their own lives.

The course participants undertake their own individualised pilgrimages into the field of non-ordinary reality using shamanic behaviour as their tool. They do so in order to achieve help in establishing a personal psychomental balance which might lead to a general 'de-Reformation' of society as a whole, where an acceptance of the existence of spirits and a holistic spiritual approach to the condition of human beings might again prevail. Their relationship with Nature is that of an exploited helper who then becomes a respected friend and kind provider of sustenance through the caring behaviour of the participants in their daily lives. A few might work as 'shamans' and become mediators between ordinary and non-ordinary reality, others might incorporate the shamanic behaviour and knowledge into their work as psychotherapists, social-workers and nurses; most, however, will become their own helpers and thereby may eliminate the role of the specialist, be it from the very same professions mentioned above. There is no cult figure and the self-help aspect of core-shamanism reflects the whole ethos of the New Age. Often the psychologist or psychiatrist has been seen as the modern version of the shaman dealing with the psychomental balance in society. My research, however, shows that for the people I interviewed these professions often fell short because of a limited understanding by psychologists of their spiritual experiences. The shamanic courses are not substitutes for the psychiatrist's couch but rather a tool for the individual enabling him or her to deal with a spiritual void in a society where encounters with spirits are either seen as evidence of mental disease or as an attempt to intrude on gifts that were meant for the selected few.

The role of the teacher in the courses can be compared with the adviser of the apprentice *angakkok*. They are instructors, and ultimately each person, whether a Greenlander or urban Westerner, establishes personal contact with the spirits. As the course organiser, in whose courses I participated, takes small groups and offers a personal interest in the single individual, he comes across as a compassionate person who has a genuine interest in the well-being of the individual participant. Michael Harner on the other hand has larger groups, up to several hundreds in a basic course, and therefore is primarily an instructor.

For traditional shamanism, the concept of mastery of spirits as it has been set out by Shirokogoroff, and which has been my argument throughout, has shown itself applicable to the work of the Greenlandic *angakkut*. I wish, along with Shirokogoroff, to confine the concept of shamanism precisely to the definition presented in my first chapter. My conclusion is, therefore, that in traditional shamanism the shaman is a master of spirits who undertakes magical flight to visit these spirits in some level of trance when society is under stress. In core-shamanism the participants are taught to use shamanic behaviour when the individual is under stress due to a complex social structure that provides little understanding of spiritual experiences.

Holger Kalweit mentions the fear and isolation which these experiences cause in Western societies (1992: 53), and there is no doubt that several of my informants had felt precisely this before signing up for courses. Core-shamanism might have aspects in common with psychoanalysis, but shamanic behaviour is a tool for a spiritual quest, where the first stage is a recognition of a spiritual dimension, the second is contacting the spirits and the third is to include the spirits in one's life as advisers. With the focus on mastery of spirits instead of ecstasy as the most important part of the complex of which shamanism is comprised, it becomes possible to make a clear distinction between that of *possession* by spirits and *possessing* spirits. The courses might include journeying and some participants might enter into a light trance, but as the spirits are seen as allies there is an important deviation from the traditional role of the shaman. The Greenlandic *angakkoq* was a master of spirits while the course participants practise shamanic behaviour. The word 'shamanism' ought therefore to be applied to traditional shamanism and the concept of 'shamanic behaviour ' used to define the acts of the course participant.

NOTES

1   An example of such a participant would be the man who, on a basic course in 1992, explained that his presence was due to his divorced wife paying for him to partake. Then he proceeded to sleep and snore through most of the journeys.

Appendix
ADVANCED COURSES IN SHAMANISM

Nordic Shamanism and the Spirits of Nature

The course is described in a leaflet, stipulating the relationship between shamanism and Nature, the profound connection to the landscape, the change of season and the animal and plant spirits. The participants will follow in the footsteps of their ancestors and learn to work with the spirits of trees and herbs, and receive help from power-places. The course offers thereby a link to two important areas: the spirits of Nature and the roots of the participants, key issues in modern Western people's sense of alienation. To be connected with the methods of the ancestors is to achieve 'nativeness'. Instead of reading about the traditions of other cultures and participating in North American Indian sweat-lodges and dressing up in North American Indian clothing, this course creates a connection to the Nordic culture that existed before Christianity was introduced and the old wise woman or man was marginalised.

This kind of course naturally attracts participants from the Nordic countries but other nationalities also participate. The intention is to build up a shamanic identity not by becoming Bronze Age people but by being inspired by their traditions. The emphasis is on creating a link back to the traditions of the past but fitting that link into the reality of present-day Western society. To be a receiver and creator at the same time, to build on existing knowledge and to respect your own experience in your own society and thereby make new rituals inspired by the past is to continue the tradition of shamanism as such. Each shaman in a traditional society added his own methods as well as adhering to the traditions of the past. In the Greenlandic society the shamans were prepared to include Christianity as part of their cosmology when they were introduced to it. In Alaska this happened too and in South America the urban shamans might mix a whole set of religions into their work such as Christianity, Hinduism and Buddhism (Dobkin De Rios: 1992: passim). This constant exchange between the shaman and a changing environment has always been at work.

To connect with the roots of Nordic people, the *vølve*, the old wise woman of the Nordic tradition, and carrier of the tradition of the wise men and women is an important theme during the course. The incense used is all made from herbs that come from Denmark.

As performed at the start of every course, the circle was rattled together by the course organiser. His partner first went round with incense that she 'brushed' out with a brush made of feathers. During the course the participants were taken to the meadow or to the lake to perform songs and rituals. The relationship to the moon was emphasised and a breathing technique introduced whereby the breath sent messages to the moon and took in messages from the moon. This was performed by the lake at dusk.

Middle Journey into the Wood

In performing this, the participants were to pay attention to both realities, non-ordinary and ordinary, and walk in both at the same time. The intention was to find a power-place, a place where they felt at home and supported, a place that nurtures them. The assistant organiser added that it was important to be aware that there could also be places that could draw from you. The participants should not talk to others on this journey. The aim was to find a gate, maybe two trees, a threshold and go through there.

'Call your spirit-helpers after you have passed the gate, stay in contact with them and be led to your power-place. Try not to decide with your head, be led. Notice the signs: a tree waving at you, and then establish yourself there. Announce that you have arrived to the spirits of the wood. Open yourself and listen with your whole being. You have come to learn. Be aware of the feeling in your body. Walk with your hands out as if they were antennae. Feel the earth and allow yourself to be taken. It is a strange journey between concentrating and relaxing.'

After this journey[1] the participants shared their experiences, often very emotional ones. They met different non-ordinary reality beings connected with the place they had been visiting. Everybody seemed to have experienced such an encounter. Then a journey to the same place in non-ordinary reality took place. The most common power-place for the participants is a tree-power-place. The strong bonding between the participants and their power-place is then used to prepare for the next step.

The Sitting Out

The 'vision-quest', which had also been practised in pre-Christian Scandinavia, was introduced to the participants as one of the ways to gain power. Some might already have had instructions where to sit on the previous journey and should follow these. The participants should go to the place of 'sitting out' before it got dark and stay until it got very light. They were not to bring their watches as they had to remember they were in non-ordinary reality. They were not meant to have dinner as fasting made one see the hidden things. When sitting by water, by healing springs, in the full moon and mid-summer the non-ordinary reality became very alive and active. It was important to write down the intentions for sitting out and to have a helper in ordinary reality that would take the person to the place and pick him or her up the next morning.

The experiences of sitting out by the participants were recounted to the circle the morning afterwards, and during the rest of the course. One example has already been partly described in the chapter on the participants.

Participants narrated a host of intentions:

1. To gain courage – a person who had been afraid of the dark all her life, had a talk with a fox and an old woman.
2. What to do with her life – a woman received the message that she had to leave her husband or she would become ill. She also felt that she overcame her fear of darkness.
3. To gain energy and strength and give balance to feet and legs.
4. A person had held a tree for an hour singing all the time. It gave peace. There was some fear, but very little after a while.
5. Conquering fear; the person then felt no fear.

6. Relationship to family, the person had experienced incest in the past.
7. Relationship to oneself; fear came and went.
8. To escape from drug and alcohol addiction.
9. Relationship to the wood, the person had expected fear but felt none.
10. To overcome fear one must feel compassion and love. The participant was grateful for the insight.
11. How can I continue my shamanic work by myself?

What is clearly being dealt with are the unresolved emotional states of mind that burden the individual. The accounts of the experience of sitting out were often very emotional not only for the individual concerned but also for the rest of the circle. There is an obvious link between the work of a psychotherapist with a client to the experience of the person vis-à-vis the spirits. The difference is that the 'sitting out' moves the healing process into the hands of non-ordinary reality and thereby the spirits which ultimately are connected with the questing person and this keeps the healing power within that person.

The purpose of sitting out was to realise that the explanation of reality that we have learned through our upbringing does not hold together any more. 'You get to the point where you do not know what is up and down, some people get scared, go into isolation. Fear is one of the first doorways to get through when you start on this work. It is not the most important part of it.' It was pointed out that the shaman was a special person but still a member of a society. It was not about getting personal power. Sitting out was asking for a vision, a vision which was going to guide the participants for the rest of their lives. Sometimes these visions came very spontaneously.

Several people sitting out had communicated with animals. One person had seen the medicine wheel and flickering stars. Most had been afraid and overcame their fear regarding major issues in their own lives. In the attempt to overcome fear the participants were going through the same experience as the traditional shaman: fear as a hindrance to insight and the contact with spirits had to be overcome. Although fear was recognised it did not play the same role as in traditional society. In this respect the transformation of the apprentice into a fully-fledged *angakkoq* is of quite another character. Fear often has a physiological outlet such as nose-bleeding, cramps and trance-like states. It takes years to overcome the fear of the spirits themselves.

The Plant-Helper

The participants were also taught to ask for a plant-helper. When a plant had attracted the participants they were told:

1. Get to know its body – tell the plant why you have come. Use your senses, draw a picture. Establish a friendship. Ask to take four little pieces, eat two.
2. Identify the plant, but keep your innocence and ignorance before you start to look at other people's writings.

There is no such thing as a poisonous plant, claimed the assistant organiser, just a poisonous dose. After the collection of plants the next step was to perform a journey in non-ordinary reality to the plant-spirit. The participants were to go back to the place where they had found the plant and ask the spirit of the plant to show itself. The spirits might be in the form of an insect – or a reptile. The intention was to talk to the non-ordinary version of the plant and ask how they could work together. It could have to do with illness. They were instructed in eating two pieces of the non-ordinary reality plant to ask how to heal, ask for a recipe and for the name of the plant.[2]

The link between traditional shamanism and this procedure is clear. Nature possesses healing potentials for human beings. If a person searches for these potentials they are there ready to help the searcher and assist the searcher in helping other human beings. Nature is seen as a source of care and healing, a source that modern man is slowly destroying. The link back to an earlier lifestyle in closer contact with Nature and an understanding of a holistic universe is created through repetition of old methods of communication with Nature. The plant is a kind of amulet protecting the carrier from disease. Later the participants are told how to make leather-purses where the plant can be stored and carried on the chest of the owner. There is also a dance where the participants dance the plant: 'You have a part of the plant inside you.'

The assistant organiser talked about other plants and their ability to open doors to non-ordinary reality. She would not recommend Flying Ointment, henbane, thorn apple, belladonna, as the return journey was not certain. It could take from six to nine months to get it out of the body. There were flash-backs and involuntary trips. The toxic level could built up in the body and have a permanent effect on the nervous system. If anyone claimed to have knowledge about these it was important to make sure for oneself and to have a teacher who was a highly ethical person.

This clearly points to the same attitude that Michael Harner expresses in his work on core-shamanism. The use of hallucinogenics is not encouraged. The method of entering into an altered state of mind should be through the use of sounds: the drum and the rattle. In that way the neo-shaman is in control and master of the transition between the two realities. Another way of stimulating the change of consciousness is through the use of incense. The assistant organiser called incense 'the shamanic tent'. There was a detailed instruction for the making of incense from local plants such as juniper, woodruff, bed-straw and others.

The Sight-Song

Just as in traditional society the ability of songs to change consciousness was emphasised. The assistant organiser gave an etymological explanation to some Danish words leading to the understanding that the old word for singing out loud, 'gale', also covers the word 'mad' or 'crazy'. The shaman's singing is connected with the change of consciousness. The instruction was that the singing took place in pairs, the one person journeyed to heal a specific problem while the other asked to get a song that would help the person journeying. The importance of being open to the coming of the song was underlined. The rattle was used for this purpose. 'Try to give yourself into the song. You will notice the shift, it will become effortless to sing. Let yourself go with the song. Don't try to notice the shift.'

The rattling, song and the drumming sounded quite in tune. One participant went into a trance-like state and sang very loud in a tuneless version, more like cries and sobs and sighs – a very 'traditional' sound. The partnership, singing for another person, also points toward the shaman's healing skills. There is an opening of emotional outlets, the participants are both highly individual as their journey and song are their own inspiration but at the same time there is a sense of community. In traditional societies in

Greenland the participants often had the obligation of singing the
angakkoq into a trance. Children had to be very silent and no other
activity could take place. The transformation of consciousness
through singing and listening to a song is known from most
religions and is far from being specific to shamanism.

Divination

The *vølve* could read signs from objects, *tage varsel*, and this was
another skill that the participants were to be familiar with. The
method of divination was to find a stone the size of a grapefruit and
use the pattern of the stone for inspiration. It was important that
the intention was clear and that a 'snake-eyed' way of looking was
used. When working on the information that the stone had to give,
the following techniques should be applied:

1. Ask the question.
2. Find four images on the first side of the stone.
3. Find four images on the second side of the stone.
4. Repeat the first four images and see what they tell about the
    question.[3]
5. Repeat the second four images and see what they tell about
    the question.
6. Sum up the first and second side.

All this was done by the person him/herself with the partner as a
helper. It was pointed out that the crystal ball was the more
'civilised' version and that in other cultures the shoulder-blade of an
animal was used. A walking journey could replace the stone
divination. The runes and the Sami drum as divination methods
were mentioned. Following up on this skill a game of bones, 'seeing'
through the hands of the opponent and guessing the number
of bones hidden there, was performed in the evening with
great enthusiasm.

The Sejd

The shamanic tradition in the Nordic context, *sejd*, was in
Scandinavia done by the *vølve*. This woman was described as the
one who carried the magic staff. *Sejd* was a form of divination, a

gathering of power and directing it at somebody. It could have anything from healing power to destroying power. There was a warning against using this as love magic. The role of the Nordic gods and the *vølve*, who is an oracle, were explained. 'Don't ask her "yes" and "no" questions. Put clear questions to her, for example: "How do I turn my anger into power?"'

The gathering of power and using it either for destruction or for healing is part of the reason for the ambivalent emotions in traditional society towards the shaman. On the one hand he is caring for the community, whilst on the other, the Greenlandic *angakkoq* can destroy. The use of the *tupilak* is one way of dealing with unwanted people, soul-stealing another.

During the course five people volunteered to be *vølve* for the following two evening sessions. They were asked to go out and find a staff. The assistant organiser added that the *vølve* had to go underground in Christianity and the staff was transformed to a broom. The staff is a magic wand, a power-antenna. The first night there would be one *vølve* working for the group on a common topic. The second night there would be a three-faced *vølve* like the *Norns*, the Nordic goddesses of fate. This was not, however, limited to women.

> One can also ask help for a person or for plants and animals in need of support. The three divination people are journeying on the singing. The throwing of a plant can be the sign for the singing to stop. The *vølve* should then try to keep the stage she is in when the questions are put to her. Then everybody can come up with their personal questions. If the person being the *vølve* feels that the power is disappearing, leave! We don't want any 'ego' because you can mess up somebody's life. The people who are singing can also be in a state where they feel an answer.

The decision was made to ask what the wood needed, because many of the participants had a feeling that the wood surrounding the hut suffered from over-use. The diviner should keep the staff at all times and use her spirit-helpers. An 'altar' of chairs and blankets had been made by the group. There was a maple branch lying on it for the *vølve* to throw, when she was ready to divine. The circle forming round the *vølve* on the altar then sang and sent her on her journey. The assistant organiser pointed out that powerful does not equal loud. When the *vølve* was ready the personal questions were asked first.[4]

The divination of the *vølve*:

I have to say thank you for the song. Saturday evening you should all
sing the same song in the meadow. The area needs love. Human beings
should learn to love again, the trees are in need of caresses. We should
all go out and collect waste to try to heal the misshaped trees, cut away
wire etc. Give love to the children, everything alive. Love is not a wish
to possess. Love the wood, do not want to possess it.[5] The most
important of all is love and not to possess a living thing. Do not
condemn people for what they do, forgiveness is most important. I went
out with my staff followed by a falcon and an eagle, who showed me the
waste and the mistreated trees. I went to the Upper World with the eagle
and was shown a beautiful but scarred area. The trees have a need for
love and caresses. I went with a wolf to the Lower World and he could
only say that love is not to wish to own anything but to be able to let go.
The staff was my support.

The *vølve* was crying when delivering this message. Others also
reacted emotionally. The three *vølve* performed in the same way,
each divining what was important for the participants personally
through an answer to their questions or in general about the
condition of human beings or nature. The assistant organiser
advised about this method of divination:

> Do not teach it to anybody else, unless you have studied it. Things might
> come up you don't know how to deal with. If a few people are doing it,
> for example four, I would not call it a *sejd*. It is a pity if the technique
> gets watered down. Of course you can get inspiration from this. The
> power of the song can be a gathering of power. A song journey can be
> done instead of a *sejd* for fewer people. Remember that you can get a
> song on a journey. *Sejd* is the strongest method.

Divination in traditional societies was obviously of great
importance. Most human beings are concerned with their fate,
which the many present-day psychic fairs confirm.

The assistant organiser continued to say that the way she
understood ecstasy was the following: 'You can step aside and let the
universe flush through you.' It can happen through singing and
dancing. She then talked about the *sejd* branch or the rune branch.
It is esoteric knowledge and one should not work with it before
understanding the background. A participant commented that it was
good that one got curious so that things were open. The assistant
organiser added, 'but show respect'. She then gave a talk about the

witch after having spread different pictures of representations of the witch round the cloth in the middle of the room.

The need to protect these rituals from mis-use was clear. Their 'sacredness' was to be preserved. When one makes what was hidden available to all, the question is whether it loses its power or preserves its potency although used in different kinds of contexts. Does the sacred become profane? Are sacredness and secrecy interlinked? In most traditional societies the answer would have been 'yes'.

The Fetish Sacrificed to the Fire

The participants were encouraged to ask themselves: how can we make all the things we have learned work for us? What is standing in the way of a real connection? What do I need to let go of? A journey to answer these questions was then performed.[6] The participants were advised to get rid of this hindrance by using fire. They were going to make an amulet, a fetish, and look for objects that could serve that purpose, but were warned against using flint or letting others touch the charged objects.[7]

In the evening there was a bonfire near the house and a circle was formed round it, each participant with his or her fetish and a rattle. When a person was ready he or she would walk into the circle near the fire, move about in whichever way felt right and burn the fetish, then walk back to the circle and rattle. When everybody had finished, the group then told the others what they had thrown away: inhibitions, rationality, inferiority complexes, shyness, dependency on other people's opinions, a sense of being outside. People then spontaneously started to jump over the fire.

Again it is clear that it is unwanted emotions which are dealt with. In traditional societies those emotions could have been ascribed to the intrusion of unwanted spirits; in modern society those emotions are the responsibility of the individuals themselves.

Other Journeys

During the course there were 'free journeys' in between the journeys connected with rituals. In those the participants could deal with purely personal matters. There was also a tree-journey to connect with the wisdom of a specific tree, which was related to the old concept of a *kludetræ*, a rag-tree, a tree where illness can be cured. The last journey the participants undertook was asking the question: how shall I take this teaching with me into my ordinary reality life? The group danced and sang to call spirit-helpers and then lay down and went on a journey.[8] The following messages had come: forgiveness, not to find the easy solutions, trust, dance with other people in the circle, be here, here and now, learn from Nature.

The course organiser then summed up the whole of the course experience. He said it was very important for him and his work that so many special people had come. He especially thanked the person with addiction problems, because she gave so much. The course organiser gave her an eagle feather. The assistant organiser then continued to say that they were not doing this to say that this tradition was better.

> What I hope is that you have got a good feeling about your native place. There is a pitfall in believing that this is better than any other. There can be discussion about what is really important. We are all children of the Earth. For some of you this was very strong and you experienced woundedness and a conflict between giving and taking.[9] There is nothing wrong in being nourished. We are going out of our ignorance, but let us not forget our innocence.

A participant exclaimed, 'I'm alone and I'm not alone.' The assistant organiser said that it had been a good group. The course organiser added that people did not put things into boxes, but that all these things touched each other and in that way their lives became more circular. He said that nature tended to move in circles, that our civilisation tended to move in boxes. Classification was trying to stop the flow of life. The work life and the spiritual life should be connected. He ended by saying that it had been a very good circle of people and it was nice to see how they had been teachers and students for each other. The end was a dance – and cleaning the house.

Shamanic Healing and Spiritual Ecology

This course took place in England in a rural setting in Devon. A brochure about Hazelwood House described it as a 'place of extraordinary peace and beauty, set in the heart of the South Devonshire countryside. There are 67 acres of woodland, meadows, river-bank and orchards ideal for walking, painting, or simply relaxing. Hazelwood has it's [sic] own source of exceptionally good water from a deep underground spring. Hazelwood has a full programme of creative courses, events and concerts.'

At the end of a long narrow lane with high hedges, Hazelwood House appears in the bottom of a valley. Green slopes rise from the sides of the house which almost engulf it in greenery. The house itself has several rooms with views of the hills. Bathrooms are shared. The sitting rooms of the house are used for communal gatherings.

The course was described in the leaflet as dealing with the shaman's intimate relationship to Nature. The participants would learn how to 'sense, recognise, and safely remove the spiritual causes of illness and pain', they would be taught how to acquire help from plant spirits and power objects and the use of power places in healing work.

As mentioned earlier in the chapter on the New Age, the relationship to Nature is of crucial importance to many modern Western people seeking an alternative lifestyle. The concept of illness as being created by a community in which the individual is feeling powerless, and under stress and therefore prone to sickness, will result in a search for alternative healing methods that are closely intertwined with an alternative relationship to Nature. The damage to the spiritual side of a person's life is causing 'dis-ease' and the way to counteract this disease is to search for spiritual methods of healing. Illness is seen as a kind of vacuum in the body where wrong spirits then can enter.

The course in shamanism took place in an old converted chapel five minutes from Hazelwood House. The participants had been asked to bring warm comfortable clothes, bandanna or scarf, cushion, rattle and drum.

General Introduction to Healing

The starting procedure of each course and the paraphernalia used is more or less identical and I shall therefore proceed to the characteristics of the actual course. In a talk about Shamanic Healing the course organiser stated that he sometimes used the word 'technique' for lack of a better word. He stated that the essence of healing was to get in contact with the spirits and to ask for help. The concept of asking for help was again and again emphasised. The course organiser pointed to the fact that healing oneself is not a shamanic concept and can be dangerous. He gave an example of a woman who had to have her uterus removed after thinking that she could heal herself of cervical cancer. She ended up having a guilt feeling about her own inability to heal herself. The course organiser said that he sometimes called his doctor on the advice of the spirits.[10]

The participants had been told that all had good connections to the spirit world. At the same time it was necessary to draw attention to the limitations of that connection, to avoid dangerous situations whereby a misconception of the extent of the healing power could lead to former participants in courses putting themselves at risk. The fact that Western medicine has its own use, even for a shamanic healer, is in line with the views of many modern healers worldwide. The course organiser quoted the assistant organiser by saying that the cure should not be worse than the ailment. He then proceeded to talk about the power of prayer and the Bible and mentioned how some people believed that Jesus was a great shaman. The Dakota people also used prayer, the smoke of the pipe sent prayers into the spirit world.

The ethical aspects were then dealt with. 'When you are working with healing you have to ask yourself when the work you are doing ceases to be beneficial. Sometimes it is time for a person to die. Part of your work can therefore be to prepare them [the ailing persons] to go beyond this world. It can be a great honour to be asked for help.' The course organiser explained that healers who get ill themselves were using their own personal power and life energy. It was very important when doing shamanic work to be aware of losing the life power. When power was lost some inappropriate power might come in and the healer might get sick instead.

The word 'power' seemed to cover many aspects of the shamanic healing process. What was important to appreciate was that the power available was believed to come from the spiritworld. It was not a personal power that was at work. To a question from a participant who was taking care of a cancer patient the organiser replied: 'You have spirit helpers. You do not have to make yourself sick to make somebody well.' The course organiser then pointed out that one had to put all 'ego' up on a shelf when doing shamanic work and let go of expectations. The shaman was in the past working within a smaller group of people and leaving his own hopes and fears in ordinary reality. He was only working with the spirits.

The dependency of the interaction with spirits in all that the shaman does is obviously of great importance. It was underlined that what is achieved was only done by being a channel not a source. This concept is identical with traditional shamanism. The shaman is a mediator with the capacity of communicating with non-ordinary reality and who can make transitions between the two realities, but he is a human being not a spirit. Where the shaman does give way to personal ambitions, evil spirits may be at play.

The Journey to the Power-Place

The participants had been outside finding their own personal power-place and danced and sang to prepare themselves to meet the spirits of that place on a journey. It was a Middle World journey and the aim was to ask for help for shamanic healing and for a spirit-helper. It was important to go through a gate to the power-place. If on the journey a person began to observe herself she should try to let this 'body' merge with his/her own. 'It is an out-of-spirit experience if you see yourself at a distance.'

The need for true identification with the experience is here emphasised. To see oneself at a distance is to distance oneself from the experience. The participants wrote down their experiences and some presented them in the circle. One participant had travelled to an oak tree and met with a group of small people connected to it. The course organiser explained how the oak tree is very dependent on the growth underneath it and the small people could be seen in that light. Another participant had also travelled to an oak tree, climbed the tree but not had any communication. This person was advised to ask for help and to be accessible. Yet another had experienced a green man leaning up against her tree and had had very profound advice from this helper. Several participants had information from their helpers about death and dying. Profound conversations took place between the spirits and the participants, both directly related to their lives or to more general global matters. The session ended with the course organiser advising the group to check their power-places every morning before they met in the group. He suggested that they should dance to it, rattle to it, whichever way they wanted to communicate with it. The connection with the power-place was identical with that described in 'Nordic Shamanism' but the experience of the power-place was different because the focus was on healing.

Healing in Pairs

For the healing procedure the participants were divided up in pairs and the aim was to get a healing song from the teacher who had been encountered in the morning. One person was to rattle over the body of the other. There might be a feeling of electricity or heat or a finger might start to shake. During this process it was important to have one of the non-ordinary helpers present. The course organiser emphasised that the aim of this course was to learn shamanic techniques – not to heal people.

> Use your non-ordinary vision. Turn the person's body into glass and look for the spirit of the illness. Try to find the spirit cause of the illness. Use your sense of smell or hearing, in a non-ordinary way. See and feel and hear. Don't hold the song back, it will increase your attention and your sense of perception. Have the eyes closed or slightly open, maybe use a scarf. Go over the whole body also the bottom of the feet.

The partner lay down and the other rattled over him/her while getting a song. The rattling first called helpers and then there was a search with a hand between the rattle and the body of the partner. Beforehand, there had been an exchange of health problems between the partners and after the rattling the active person lay down beside the partner, touching him or her, and journeyed in the above-mentioned fashion to get help for the partner. The song was created while rattling over the body, not on the journey itself. The latter gave information about the person's situation.[11] In the sharing of experiences afterwards the course organiser underlined that it was the performer and the spirits that took care of the person. During the conversation about the diagnostic elements of healing the participants had different experiences during the rattling over them. Some had involuntary body reactions, some felt a breeze, some felt as if their heads had opened and energy had been poured in. The course organiser emphasised again that the aim of this course is to learn shamanic techniques to heal – not to heal people on the course.

The pairing up of the participants and the sharing of information about intimate details of one's life creates a certain bond with the person one is paired with. The choice of partner might be random but one ends up relying on the person's 'good intentions'. When I raised the issue of 'good intentions' with the course organiser later he did not want to expand on that matter, although I find it very important. In traditional societies one shares one's trust with a shaman of repute. One does not give one's innermost thoughts about one's health to a complete stranger whose personal abilities or intentions are not clear. The Greenlandic *angakkoq* was known by his society and the dubious *angakkut* feared. It is a matter of trust but trust can be misplaced. The idea might be that one's spirits will protect one against a wrong move, but one might meet a greater shaman than oneself, a concept that was prevalent among the *angakkut* in Greenland and induced a lot of fear in them about the power of other *angakkut*.

The next part of the healing instruction was to find a plant helper for a partner and then perform a journey to the spirit of the plant. Apart from the difference in finding the plant for somebody else, the procedure was identical with that of the 'Nordic Shamanism' course.[12]

Tunnel Cleaning

This was diagnostic work with the rattle. The participants were instructed to go into their own tunnel (the tunnel leading to the Lower World). They might take their spirit-helpers. They were going to look for any changes in the tunnel. On this journey any change had to do with the partner. They were not to enter into the person's body. Travelling in their own tunnel they were on safe ground. 'You might see either slime or gold. Don't fill your own pockets. You travel for someone else.'

The group had some difficulty understanding how something of another person would appear in their own tunnel but the course organiser explained that they were all sophisticated shamanically speaking and therefore knew what to clean out by using the helping spirits. The method of tunnel-cleaning was first to rattle round the body of the person to the beat of the drum, then to lie down and journey to one's own tunnel. They had to remember that they were travelling for their partners and, therefore, needed to ask their partners beforehand if there was something they did not want to have cleared out. A spider for one person might represent something positive and not for another. 'Stay in contact with your spirit-helpers. Remember to touch your partner.'

The experience of cleaning out another person's problems and in that way also stating what they actually are can be very personal and several of the accounts hit raw nerves with the partners. Some cried, some felt a great release. It was quite striking how much influence these experiences had on the participants. The benefit was that another person was taking a real interest in one's health, a benefit that makes all kinds of alternative healing flourish in a society where medical doctors look at one through a computer-screen. The danger is whether this process is according to the principle of letting the spirits work through one. Few persons in a traditional society would dare leave their well-being in the hands of an absolute stranger. Although the course organiser stressed that this is an educational situation the personal impact cannot be excluded.

Relating to the Four Elements

The first element that the participants were relating to was Water. On a trip to the seaside the participants were asked to wander round at the beach for about one and a half hours, not talking but rattling. After that time a circle was made and each person told the others the wisdom they had received from the sea in one sentence.[13] The air was consulted at the power-places. 'Ask the Air what is good for you. Ask the Air to give you a teaching. Ask about the healing properties of the Air.' The Earth was consulted and finally Fire should have been lit. Hazelwood House does not, however, accept open fire on the grounds and the Fire-ceremony had to be performed slightly differently. The course organiser had sought advice from his helping spirits and came back with a solution to the problem. The essence of the ceremony was to sacrifice something to the Earth. The course organiser explained that it was only in the last few years that he had combined ecology and healing. The intention of the Fire ceremony was to pledge something to the Earth, our mother; to pledge energy and power to the Earth. The course organiser was shown by his helpers that he was using energy on things that he should not: jealousy, envy, and so on. He should instead take the energy he used on these emotions and pledge that into the Earth. The way to do this was to make a fetish. 'Go out in nature and make a fetish. In this you put the qualities you want to get rid of. Burn it.' Some participants were worried about the fact that one gave negative emotions back to the Earth but was advised to go to their teacher and get information. 'It is the energy that you put back into the Earth.'

The participants journeyed to their teachers to get information about what they were meant to remove from their lives, which emotions they had to rid themselves of so that they could give the energy this left back to the Earth. The experiences were shared in the group and then all left to create a fetish which would represent the emotions each had been informed about on the journey. They should create it out of objects from nature and then bring it back to the chapel. While walking round in nature one should not talk to other people. Coming back to the circle the group was then told that as it was not possible to burn the fetish it should instead be offered to the power-place. Everybody then walked to their power-place to place the fetish there. As can be seen, this ritual is similar to that of burning the fetish in the 'Nordic Shamanism' course and there were similarities in the concepts that participants wanted to rid their lives of. The ritual cleansing of the person as a sort of purification is known in most great religions.

Extraction Work

The course organiser described the healing by extraction of the illness from the body. 'This is very advanced work and one should follow the advice of the helpers. No bright ideas, no intuition.' The hands on/hands in technique was described as follows:

1. Lay the person down and let them feel at ease and relaxed.
2. Explain to them what you are going to do.
3. Try to see the spirit cause of the illness.
4. Try to reach into the body.
5. Pull it out with a snap.
6. Throw away the illness.
7. Cool the hands. Use a bowl of spring water as the spirit of the illness is often hot or warm.

Another method was to sing and rattle the illness out of the body and close the wound up again with the rattle. The course organiser pointed out that one was working in both ordinary and non-ordinary reality at the same time. 'You never know what is going to happen until you start working. Bring the person some sort of a helper back. Don't leave an open space. If you work with a person who wants to die you can get a helper for them that will help them to die. If you are in doubt, don't do anything.' As it later turned out, the group never performed this work as the course organiser had been advised by his helping spirits not to commence it with this particular group. The reason for this might be that there was some personal tension among some of the participants.

Other Journeys and the Singing and Dancing

Singing and dancing are performed regularly during the course in support of the different rituals. The dance was mostly performed in an individualised form: each person dancing with his or her rattle while singing their power-song or any song arising during the dance. The drums were played by different volunteers. In connection with the drum as a support instrument for healing, the course organiser mentioned that it might be an idea to gather people for the healing who know the person well. The drumming can also be done by someone who knows the ill person well. As an example, he mentioned asking the mother of an ill child to drum. 'Bring friends and loved ones, someone that you trust very much.' This obviously furthers a sense of not being alone with the sick child, of being supported in a community of friends and family.

In a general round of questions the course organiser was asked whether one can have too much power. He said that it sometimes was possible to come back from the journey with that feeling. 'Dig your fingers into the Earth and give the power to the Earth.' When a participant asked how people bottled up energy, the organiser answered that he did not know but that the practice of sorcery was to bottle up power. 'To be a clean sorcerer[14] you must not want anything.' The emphasis on the clean sorcerer, on not being a participant for one's own sake but for the sake of others, is obviously of great importance when a healing ceremony is performed and therefore relevant to stress for people who are not normally in an altruistic environment. In a traditional society the ever-present spirits would, to a certain degree, keep the shaman from mistaking the gift of power as coming from a source of his own making. The 'black' shamans would on the other hand still misuse that same power to further their own interests and can, therefore, be dangerous.

The final two journeys that the participants performed were first to go to the power-place with the intention of getting an answer to the question: What is my involvement/my contribution to the ecological mess? Coming back, the participants shared their information. Some had very philosophical messages, some very practical ones dealing with cars, eating meat, and so on. Then the group went on a journey to ask: How shall I use the liberated energy for the Earth? How can I keep the flow going? This was then shared in the circle. The participants had met their teacher who told them how to deal with the ecological aspects of their lives.

The course organiser then talked about how the week had progressed. 'I've been very moved to see how you have worked together. It has been a very special group to work with. Someone came up and asked me whether all groups are so wonderful to work with.' The group, however, had according to earlier experiences during the week actually been quite a complicated group where the course organiser had to change his programme and leave out working in pairs with extraction of illness. The influence of the praise at the end of each course is of great significance. The participants leave with a sense of achievement on both a human and a spiritual level.

Again the organiser stressed his purpose in teaching these courses by saying 'I don't teach these courses as therapy courses, but to widen your own shamanic awareness.' He then underlined that commitment and said that responsibility was what it was about. 'So many of you have very wonderful experiences, so many different things going on than I had had in mind.' Explaining that he had had the instruction from his helpers to contain the group, the course organiser thus demonstrated that all he did was connected with the spirit world. He then gave a final piece of advice as to how to go about the healing procedure:

1. Wait until you are asked. This is very important as a shamanic healer.
2. Journey to the teacher. If you make essential changes in yourself it will have an effect on others.
3. Be aware of the biggest pitfall: doing healing work and then ending up taking people's power away. This is one of the major causes of soul-loss.
4. If people start leaning on you, show that you are just a mirror. We are all individuals. We are all self-contained. Let the power flow through you.

It is clear that the closeness of the shamanic courses to the methods of therapy has to be mentioned. The role of the spirits obviously is one of the major differences. In therapy the participants are dealing with their own psyches; in the shamanic course they are dealing with spirits. The belief in the existence of spirits must therefore prevail in the world-view of the participants.

The course ended by the participants forming a circle and singing two songs. The concept of the circle and the power of the circle is important. Each circle starts with the statement: 'Let power flow through you. You can always go back to the circle even if you have left it. When we leave we are still connected. We can dance our own dance, not anybody else's.' Each person has his/her own reality to return to but the power of the circle is everlasting and ever-present.

Soul Retrieval Training

The YHA that catered for the accommodation for this course offered the following: bunk-beds where several people did not sleep well, basic food and nowhere available where the group could gather on its own in the evenings or during meal times as many other people were using the dining-sitting room. The course itself took place in a village hall in Oxfordshire.

In the brochure on this course soul-loss was described as the major reason for much serious illness. 'Soul-loss keeps us from feeling connected to the Earth, and to the joy and power she has to offer us. Soul-loss can also make us feel separated from our bodies, our relationships, and from Life itself.' The participants would be taught to work with soul-loss from a shamanic perspective, but also to have the possibility of having lost soul parts returned. The course was intended for people who wanted to bring soul-retrieval into their work with others, not for people looking for personal healing. To participate it was necessary to have experience in shamanic journeying, have good connection to spirit-helpers and have completed the basic workshop.

What is significantly different in this course is that it is aimed at those who will use shamanism in their work with other people and therefore are expected to have been through the preliminary work so that they are prepared to deal with the problems of others. As mentioned earlier, many of the participants have a background in the caring professions and this course attracted several with an education in psychotherapy, counselling and psychoanalysis. The concept in shamanism of illness and disease (or 'dis-ease' as it is now commonly emphasised in New Age circles), both mentally and physically being connected with a loss of soul or soul pieces, is a worldwide phenomenon. It is the shaman's task to go searching for the lost soul and to reinstate it in the body of the diseased person. In East Greenland the *angakkoq* can even use part of an animal's soul if it is not possible to locate the person's own lost soul. Soul and life are closely connected and without the soul or part of the soul the body will be exposed to danger and even be open to the intrusion of unwanted spirits or be affected by the evil intentions of other human beings.

The course started with the circle being formed and the holding of hands, but the group was not rattled together as one participant had not yet arrived, and this happened later. A cloth of a green print of a reindeer was placed in the middle of the circle. On the cloth were incense, a candle, and a stone. Apart from this, the paraphernalia consisted of drums and rattles. The course organiser wore a waist-coat with different trinkets, some gifts from earlier clients, and a necklace of bone pieces when he was conducting a soul retrieval for a participant.

The course organiser introduced the course by talking about traditional shamanism and the role of soul-loss. In a person there can be two different states:

1. Something which should not be there.
2. Something which should be there but which is missing.

It is the shaman's role to deal with these states. The course organiser then referred to the Orpheus and Eurydice myth, where he pointed out that the important lesson is to trust what the spirits tell you. 'The aim is to find a piece/pieces of the person's soul and bring it/them back. The main rule therefore is always to work together with your spirit-helpers, make them do some of the work.' In traditional shamanism the help of the spirit world is of great importance to the result of the soul retrieval. If the relationship with the spirits is not satisfactory the shaman will not be able to achieve his goal and may even put his own life at risk. If the soul has disappeared to the world of the dead the shaman has to be able to travel into that realm with the help and protection of his spirit-helpers. Even finding the way is in itself impossible if the spirits are not there to guide. The shaman is the mediator; it is the spirits, however, that are at work.

The course organiser expected to perform a soul retrieval on a participant and therefore asked if anybody would like to be the one demonstrated on. 'Talk to me and let the spirits decide. You might not feel that you are ready to do this work yourself yet and you do not have to do one. If you have read Sandra Ingerman[15] you might have felt that this is what you need.'

He then proceeded to talk about how to deal with the person who comes for help. It was important not to be too fast and to examine the person first and do some diagnostic work. It was necessary to make a journey to ask for help from the spirit-helpers. The person might need a power-animal retrieval first. The person might be missing a part of his/her life essence by having lost a soul part, pieces of souls, or a whole soul. The course organiser then gave an account of a soul retrieval he had performed for a friend: 'I found him on the top of a burial mount, dancing. I could see that a house was burning and I told him. He responded that it was amazing; that when he was about six years old his mother set the house on fire. They had a burial mound on their land where he used to go.'

The course organiser proceeded to say that most people in the course of their lives experience soul-loss. He stated that everybody in the room had been born with a healthy amount of power. Giving a soul-piece away was the most common way to lose one's soul. The wish to please one's parents, and this is especially true in dysfunctional families. 'Soul retrieval is the shamanic way of looking at co-dependancy as it is called in psychology. One person might always give power away in a relationship.' He explained how very often one person would feel that it was time to give a relationship up and the other therefore gave more and more. 'The leaver goes away with too much of the ex-lover and this is not a desirable situation.'

The whole modern Western way of establishing relationships is here being focused on. In a society with a high rate of divorce or where marriage is not a necessity and people therefore do not have to confirm their relationships through official rituals, the breaking up or down of emotional attachments can be a recurring and often painful event in a person's life. The concept of soul-loss and the way of dealing with it must be attractive to the many who have had such experiences. 'The vampire pattern continues in families. If you lose power early on in your life you will take power away from somebody else.' This also covered areas such as physical and psychological child-abuse.

> Soul-loss can occur for a sensitive person by just falling down the stairs. Some people send their soul out of their body until the abusive situation stops. Some then cannot come back, others totally forget. The soul does not want to come back... If a person comes to you with lots of problems that person is not yet ready for a soul retrieval. The person has to have a life situation that makes it possible for him/her to cope with it. One or two retrievals per year is generally sufficient. Be sure you have all the help you need, if your spirit-helpers say no, don't go. Don't play the hero, there is no future in it.

Again it is emphasised that the spirits are to be consulted if any soul retrieval is going to take place. Without their consent, nothing which happens will benefit the person who is seeking help. The role of the performer of the soul retrieval is made clear: this is not a matter of being a hero, but a mediator.

The course organiser pointed out that surviving is not living and that spiritual black holes existed. Sometimes dead people were stuck in the middle world. If they had died in an accident, they may not know that they were dead. That was why some people experience their attempt at communication – for example things moving in the house. A participant asked where the parts of the soul went and the course organiser replied that they went to non-ordinary reality. This rather broad answer offers the opportunity of several possible experiences of the place where the soul-pieces or souls are found. There is no set place of lost souls as there is no set concept of spirits or of the different worlds of non-ordinary reality. All takes place within the concept of the non-ordinary reality specific to each individual participant.

A participant asked if somebody gave one a piece of himself whether that could cause an illness. The course organiser responded that breaking away from a marriage might lead to a feeling of a guilty conscience, which might stem from one person having a soul-piece which belongs to the other, and thereby again connected soul retrieval with the break-down of relationships. Another participant, a psychotherapist, had experienced a spontaneous soul retrieval. The course organiser replied by saying that he always discouraged people from doing this for themselves. The way the shaman worked was by asking for help. A participant then asked what happened if one was journeying for power for somebody who was terminally ill. The course organiser answered that the intention should be clear. It could help either to get better or to die. The shaman's job for somebody who had left this life was to carry it to the next stage. He here pointed to the role of the transporter of the souls of the dead that in some cultures is also the role of the shaman as also a psychopomp.

Journey to Ask for the Help of the Spirits

The group was then asked to journey to their spirit-helpers to say that they were working with soul-retrieval work and to ask whether the spirit-helpers would help. In plenary session three participants said that they had received the message that they should get on with it. One participant had experienced being in the land of the dead, seeing shadows of the souls. The course organiser replied that she should not go into the land of the dead just yet but wait till she was more clear. Another participant commented that this weekend felt very different from other courses and the course organiser replied that to do soul retrieval a person must be very clear. The participants on this course were at a point where they were to practise their knowledge of shamanism not for their own benefit alone but for the benefit of others.

The group was then instructed about the hide-and-seek exercise. They were to organise themselves in pairs. The idea was to find one's partner in non-ordinary reality although he was hiding. The drumming only lasted about five minutes. In the narration of the hide-and-seek there seemed to be several similarities between the hider and seeker in the group. The course organiser said that in soul retrieval it can sometimes be difficult to bring the person's soul/soul-pieces back because some do not want to come back. 'It is very difficult to make a promise on the person's behalf when you bring the soul back, to promise that everything will be all right.'

The course organiser pointed out that the technique of soul retrieval can easily resemble modern psychotherapy techniques, as this nowadays also works on a spiritual level. Shamanism on the other hand has its foundation in animism. Shamans often used tools: drums, rattles, power objects that could help them in their work. A lot of people liked to use crystals as containers for the soul, or other power objects such as bones or stones. 'A word of warning: it is a fine idea to have special objects for special tasks, but the danger is in getting dependent. The most important are the spirit-helpers, the clearness of intent and the trust.'

It is obvious, when participating in the courses on shamanism that there is a link with psychotherapy and other psychological methods of healing. The difference lies, as the organiser underlines, in the belief in the existence of spirits and their interaction with and interest in the well-being of human beings. The spirits connected with all the objects involved have to bring power to these objects so that the objects can fulfil their healing tasks. Trust and clarity of intent are again and again emphasised during the course and are part of the focusing of the mind of the participants which is necessary for any travel to non-ordinary reality.[16]

Journey to ask: Is there some special object that I should use in soul-retrieval work?

Beforehand the group had danced with their rattles and sung their own individual songs. These dances served as a way of creating a frame of mind that opened up the participant for the journey and set him/her in contact with the spirits. The journey was performed in the usual way.[17] During the journeying the participants received instruction in the use of different objects: cloaks, a mirror from a car, a bag of beautiful objects, a scarf, an orb, staffs. These objects clearly have ritual connotations already; although a car-mirror is an unusual type of mirror, it is connected with life and death in the modern world.

The course organiser then continued to talk about the spiritual vampire, somebody having somebody else's soul-piece. A violent person might take over a piece of soul by beating out of another individual a piece of his/her soul. A lot of people had experienced soul-loss as children. They might be getting power back by taking other people's souls away. Other people's soul-pieces were not doing that person any good. They might make it difficult for that person to retrieve his/her own power. Sometimes it was necessary to give the taker something else instead of the soul part which has to be taken back to its original owner.

It here becomes very clear how this concept of soul-loss is closely connected with psychotherapy and it is tempting to ask whether this is just another way of making people come to terms with the problems of childhood: a new name for an old concept. It may partly explain the high number of participants with an education in therapy. In a discussion with the group the course organiser explained that parents take soul parts from their children for compassionate reasons. Therapists may do the same for their clients.

Journey to ask: What is the best way to get a soul-piece back from a person who will not return it, including people who are dead?

Before the journey started a participant said that she had an ethical problem. 'Do you have to have permission to get it back?' The course organiser answered that she might want to investigate that. He then said that it was all right to come back without the soul-piece if you were not meant to do it. A participant asked what the reaction of the person involved would be to that situation of receiving nothing. The course organiser answered that the person will just ask somebody else.

In the plenary session concerning the journey, the participants received advice such as trickery, persuasion, shock, and appeal to get the soul-pieces away. Three ways that were the most common were then mentioned:

1. Trickery;
2. Exchange;
3. Persuading a release.

Journey to ask: How do I avoid taking on other people's soul parts/power?

The course organiser pointed out that when one starts to do this kind of work one realises that people give one authority – for better and for worse. 'A loving heart, an open heart is important. Then you are able to establish a very good rapport. Sometimes people might fall in love with you. The idea is that you do not detour their power. This is good to know even in everyday life.' He then pointed to the fact that in some traditional societies the shaman takes on the illness, but that he himself did not teach that. The mechanics of soul retrieval are basically the same as that of the power-animal retrieval. When he set out to do a soul retrieval he could never be sure that he would do that in the end. He advised asking a person carefully if one was phoned up by somebody for help. He would not do work for people that he had not met before. He asked them to go on a basic course and they might then learn that they could cope without help. Before doing a soul retrieval it was important to undertake a journey on the situation. It might be that the person was not ready for a soul retrieval. He/she might need it but not be ready for it.

The course organiser referred to Sandra Ingerman's book again and said that if people are totally cut off and have no contact with friends or family they are not ready. A power-animal will do them good. He advised not to overload a person and limit it to two soul parts at the time. 'You can bring back a power-animal at the side to help the soul parts to come back.'

The Soul Retrieval

The course organiser performed a soul retrieval on one of the participants. Before this took place he instructed the group in the technique. There was no call back with the drum. 'You come back and when you blow into the chest of the person then the drumming stops. Keep in close contact with your spirit-helpers. The first ten soul retrievals that you do, do a preparatory journey. Do diagnostic work too.' The idea of blowing into the body elements of the non-ordinary reality is known worldwide. I have seen that procedure performed among the Indians on the Napo River in Ecuador but the *angakkut* also used the method of blowing. The universal concept of the connection between breath, life and soul is used here to make the participants reinstate the lost soul or soul parts.

The course organiser then proceeded to talk about his choice of person for the soul retrieval among the number who had volunteered. He explained that he would start by calling in the spirits by rattling round the circle and around the person in question and finally around himself. When the rattling had finished he would then do diagnostic work and the group would help by rattling in time with the rhythm of his rattle. If a song started while he was doing the diagnostic work the group could sing along. Then he would lie down and the drumming would start.

All then stood up and sang and danced in their own rhythms and with their own song to lend power to the work. When the soul or soul-parts had been gathered he put his hands on the person's chest and blew there and afterwards on the top of the head. He had given instructions that it was important to warn people beforehand of what was about to happen. Sometimes the blowing could be to the mouth or the nose and it was necessary to take care that the person felt comfortable. 'Sit and listen to them before you get going.'

The participation of the group is an important aspect of this whole procedure. The sound arising from the monotonous rattling and the change over to the singing and the rattling in different tempi brings about the possibility of an altered state of consciousness. The insight by the participants into the important procedure going on for the person to be cured is also of significance. There is a prevailing sense of a unified and intensified wish for help for the person about to receive the soul retrieval. In traditional society the help of the audience's presence at a séance was of great importance to the success of the work of the *angakkoq*. The audience was under a strict code of behaviour and breaking it might cause harm to the *angakkoq* and thereby society as a whole. The audience might be instructed to sing to help the *angakkoq* on his travel to the Mother of the Sea or the Man in the Moon.

The course organiser proceeded to dress up for the retrieval. The man for whom the retrieval was to be performed was put comfortably near the middle of the circle. The course organiser explained about his outfit and about the origin of some of the trinkets. He also put bird feathers in the middle on the green cloth. His hands were shaking and he was clearly nervous. The soul-retrieval then took place as mentioned above. When the course organiser blew onto the chest, the man burst out in strong sobs which also affected many of the other participants. The organiser then explained how he had seen the person's soul part running like a small boy in the orbit of the earth. He had to grab him by the shirt and the legs still ran.

The group then proceeded to do soul retrieval on each other. Some did not participate and helped with the journey by rattling. In the plenary session after this experience the course organiser explained that there sometimes were parts that wanted to come back before those that the person wanted back. Some people had experienced having soul parts back that they had not thought of and that had made them upset. 'The main thing is that the spirits are doing the work, even if it was not what you hoped for, it can be a way of learning. In a month you should be communicating again', he advised the pairs who had that experience.

After the questions, the course organiser suggested a journey asking for advice for two questions.

1. How can I include this in my life?
2. What ritual shall I do to ground this in the person?

This was performed and after a short plenary session the organiser asked the people who had had soul retrieval to keep an eye on the full moon. He explained that soul retrieval was the most dramatic work to do. People who came for help would often have the knowledge of journeying. During a journey for yourself a spontaneous soul retrieval might happen. It was also possible to perform a long distance soul retrieval. It was important to get rid of soul-pieces that had been accumulated in oneself and therefore necessary to ask for a ritual to return them. 'Sharing is what happens in a healthy relationship, there is a natural flow. With a crisis you end up with a piece of somebody else and they of you. I want you to find out who you have soul-pieces of and perform a ritual to return them.' In a client situation the role was to help the client do likewise.

The concept of the health of the healer being important for the success of the treatment is also known in traditional shamanism. The initiatory shamanic illness which happens to some shamans makes the shaman knowledgeable about the experience of disease and the transformative aspects of a life-threatening condition. He therefore also is aware of the origin of illness and should be clear about his condition before dealing with others.

A participant asked about the Internet and the course organiser called it a high tech supermarket mentality: a healing supermarket. 'Some people are so desperate and sometimes people call just because they want a week-end occupied. Sometimes people who go on to practise shamanism can't get the people to come to the follow-up session.' He said that it was advisable to ask to be paid in advance because then they would come.

The question of payment for treatment is an interesting aspect of the whole healing side of the New Age. Should one not just give one's services away to people in need, especially if one is a 'part-time healer' with an ordinary job? The argument most frequently encountered is that people have to cherish what they receive from the healer and thereby from the spirits, the energies of the universe.

To create a balance between receiving and giving for healer and patient a contribution is necessary. It can be in an exchange of goods or services but it can also be money. Often the treatment is not cheap, but as one Reiki healer said 'it shows how much value you are prepared to put on your body. You don't question the service of your car, when it needs it. You can change your car not your body.' The exchange of money or goods is perceived as helping the receiver of healing to truly value his/her treatment. This is also known in traditional shamanism. The shaman performing the healing might have asked quite an important gift from the receiver of treatment, such as a deeply valued item. The whole healing ceremony might be a show of the wealth of the recipient as it is seen in the Korean Kut. The concept of what one pays as a deciding factor for how much something is valued ought to sound familiar to people in Western societies.

The course organiser pointed out that when one does a soul retrieval it is like a birthday present for the person and that the recipient should be given something like a piece of amber. A participant then asked about giving gifts to the spirits. The organiser explained that the spirits cannot use money but they can enjoy a gift that you receive from a client.

The group had a choice of two journeys:

1. Whose soul-piece do I have and how do I get it back to the right owner?
2. Please give me a ritual to return soul-pieces for other people.

The course organiser said that it was necessary to consult one's spirit-helpers. One might work through a power-animal. A participant commented that she had a piece of her brother and she did not like it to be there. The course organiser answered that when one is facing a problem then it is the time to do something about it. 'You ask your spirit-helpers and they will help you out. It is very moving stuff when things get re-arranged. The only thing that we as human beings cannot stop is change.'

Journey to ask: What practice or belief do I have which is holding me back from being the person I know I am?

This kind of question is again dealing with the health of the healer. The healer has to be aware of his own obstacles to reach the point of the right communication with the spirits. The course organiser addressed the problem of seeing something awful happening to the person whom one was helping and how one dealt with that. He advised that if one saw something horrible one did not have to say it to the person. The memory holes started to fill again for the person in therapy. People with severe soul-loss were often in therapy already. This last statement confirms the possibility of using shamanic techniques alongside other forms of therapy.[18] The course organiser progressed to talk about his attitude to teaching about soul retrieval. He said the he was a very cautious person and liked to train people in a cautious way.[19]

Journey to ask : What is especially important for me to remember when doing soul retrievals?

The advice was of a very similar nature. Single concepts were given to the participants to follow in their healing work. The course organiser said that the purpose had primarily been to get the participants educated. He advised trying to formulate a thread through the teaching. It was important to be able to articulate what went on in ordinary reality and what went on in non-ordinary reality when a person was practising shamanism.

In the last plenary session the course organiser talked about the people participating in the workshops: he said that people came looking for personal help on the basic course. Out of these, between 30 and 40 per cent came to other workshops. There they got a different experience: it is not enough with personal empowerment. When they first realised this they were fearful but that was a fear that he loved.

He then proceeded to talk about how the course had run; that he was very satisfied and felt very grateful and humble. 'I know it has been very difficult for many of you. I went out to greet the sun and was told that we are very fortunate, all of us, to get all these teachers. If you are doing your best you can't be hurt. I feel very confident that the experience you have had makes it possible for you to do a soul retrieval.' As always, the course ended on a positive note and the participants left with a feeling of a special personal achievement.

NOTES

1. I have used my own examples of travelling as they are typical of what many participants experienced and as I felt it necessary to respect the privacy of very personal accounts in the circle. The journey described below takes place in the wood, not during drumming:

     I went through an oak entrance into the wood near the lake. I walked in a straight line among the trees and found a stump which looked like a seat. Next to it was a trunk lying on the ground as if it was growing into and out of the ground. As I passed through the 'gate' the name I had been given in the night came to me. I sat down on the stump and felt my legs becoming like trunks themselves. I then stood up and felt I grew tree-high. There was a strong sense of life surrounding me. I sang my old power-song: 'Solen, solen, kraft og magt' (the sun, the sun, power and force). And the sun came out. I then proceeded to the meadow as I felt called to go there. I lay down and felt heat. I then went back through the wood to the power-place and thanked the place. There was a strong wind blowing in through the 'gate' as I was passing through it.

2. I picked Herb Robert. In the journey to the plant-spirit I again met my helper at the oak 'gate' and we went together to the plant. The face of a beaver protruded through the flowers. I asked about the healing power of the plant: the beaver replied that it helped in building up the immune system.

3. This happens in co-operation with the partner. The images are interpreted in relationship to the question.

4. What task is it that F. and I shall solve together? *I see a turtle that swims and carries the world on its back.*
    Why are the leaves of the trees on the meadow so misshaped? *Because of hate.*
    How can I in the best way get a good nature/personality? *Love.*
    Who will help me to get healed? *Only one – thyself.*
    Where is my strength concerning spirituality? *Listen to your heart.*

5. There was a dispute with the owner of the wood near the hut. He banned entrance because of hunting. But this wood, which was protected by the owner, was in much better condition as it was not being used by scouts.

6. I journeyed to the Upper World where I flew over *nunatakker* (mountain tops protruding from the inland ice) in Greenland. A big androgynous being was sitting in a long robe. I asked the question and received the answer: common sense. The being then pointed out in the polar night where a polar bear and a fox were wandering out of the blue-black darkness. They placed themselves in front of the teacher who pointed to the universe and the myriads of stars. Is this common sense? I sat down among the animals at the feet of my teacher.

7. My fetish was made out of a couple of twigs and dry canes from the lake, an old shirt sleeve found near the lake and a coin. It turned out to be quite an interesting feeling to burn even a small amount of money.

8. In the lower world the plain was first empty, then the eagles and my helper came. I asked how I should continue this work and my helper took me to a small stream where he fetched a crystal and put it into my hands. From the water the crystal melted in my hands. Then he said, 'You shall see clearly into the human beings with a sight as sharp as the eagle's. Then you shall heal them.' We returned to the plain where the helping spirits came out. The bear is calm

and strength, the wolf is wisdom and presence of mind, the beaver the power of the plant to build up the immune system, the hedgehog ability to protect yourself. We were dancing around and my helper and I changed into eagle shape and flew over the human beings, seeing their needs.

9. This referred to an earlier discussion where some participants had pointed out that it was also important to give back to Nature.

10. Michael Harner mentioned that he also used a medical doctor. 'I will use anything that works,' course in London, July 1996: 'The Way of the Shaman'. Harner generally had quite a humorous approach, and sometimes it came across as having taken him over and he asked the participants not to laugh at his jokes as that might set him off.

11. I found on my partner's body precisely the place she had problems with and which had just been x-rayed. I felt a clear sense of heat at that particular spot. This had nothing to do with the ailment she had told me about, which was high blood pressure. On the journey I saw a heart suspended from a tree, hanging and beating frantically and later being rested into the body of the partner. Her husband turned up and lay beside her under the tree. (This is a reduced version because of the privacy of the partner).

12. My own experience in telling my partner about the plant, and the spirit of the plant's advice to her brought tears into her eyes. It makes one appreciate the influence that the information you give has on one's partner. I apparently said something about her life that I had received on the journey which for her was very precise.

13. Some fishermen in the remote corner of the beach where I turned up with my rattle looked rather disturbed by the sight.

14 This is the only place where the concept of a sorcerer was used in place of that of a shaman. It is not clear how he defined a sorcerer as in an earlier course he used the concept in a purely negative way, to describe a person using power for his own end.

15. The course organiser was referring to the book by Sandra Ingerman, *Soul Retrieval*, in which she gives case stories of her work with patients. He had in the beginning of the course asked how many had read this book, which turned out to be the majority of the participants.

16. In an interview with the course organiser he commented on the danger of 'spiritual materialism' i.e. the fact that some people surround themselves with so many objects for their spiritual work that the objects in themselves take over and become the main focus.

17 I passed through the tunnel with the dolphin onto the plain where the bear was waiting. In its paws was a piece of amber representing the life force, the world tree. Out of the creek the bear fetched a diamond-like crystal and put it into my hands where it melted and became water dripping into a bowl. I should have a bowl of water while working: the nature of water is that it is flexible without losing its character.

18. This open-minded attitude was later expanded in an interview where the course organiser said that belonging to other religions such as Christianity did not exclude using shamanic techniques. There were some Christian people on the courses, it was not the religion as such but the Church. 'I think that there are a lot of priests and monasteries that are open to this. I know people on courses

that communicate with Mary, Christ, Francis of Assisi, they can be included as helping spirits.' I asked whether he saw his courses as in any way in conflict with Christianity? He replied, 'Not at all, and I think it helps people to have a deeper experience of their previous religious conviction. I think you will be a much more profound Christian. In Native American churches they say: the white man talks about Jesus, we talk to him.' This kind of flexibility has always been characteristic of shamanism as several *angakkut* in Greenland included aspects of the new teaching in their existing world-view. Christ and Mary as helping spirits is not a new concept.

19. The course organiser will advise people whom he does not find ready, with the assistance of his helpers, to wait for a specific course that they wished to participate in.

BIBLIOGRAPHY

The bibliography is composed of works referred to in the thesis. []
is used when there are more than five years between the
composition of the work and publishing. This is relevant when
older material appears in new journals and therefore is mostly
applied to the Greenlandic texts.

Acerbi, Joseph (1802), *Travels through Sweden, Finland, and Lapland, to
the North Cape in the years 1798 and 1799*, Joseph Mawman, in the
Poultry, London.

Achterberg, Jeanne (1990), *Woman as Healer*, Rider, London.

Andreassen, Karale (1935), *Nogle af mine oplevelser*, Det Grønlandske
Selskabs Aarsskrift i kommission hos G.E.C. Gads Forlag,
København.

Bäckman, Louise and Åke Hultkranz (1978), *Studies in Lapp Shamanism*,
Almquist and Wiksell International, Stockholm.

Bang, Kirsten (1944), *Aandemaneren Maratse og andre beretninger fra
Angmagssalik*, Ejnar Munksgaards Forlag, København.

Bell, John of Antermony (1788),*Travels from St. Petersburgh in Russia to
Diverse Parts of Asia*. Illustrated with maps, Geo. Robinson and Co.
Edinburgh, London.

Bend, Cynthia and Tayja Wiger (1989), *Birth of a Modern Shaman. A
Documented Journey and Guide to Personal Transformation*,
Llewellyn Publications, Minnesota.

Bennett, Hal Zina (1996), 'A Case for Neo-shamanism', *Shaman's Drum*
no. 40.

Berthelsen, A. (1914), *Neuropatologiske Meddelelser fra Grønland II.
Profeter og Djævlebestatte*, Quist & Komp., København.

———— (1915), *Folkemedicin i Grønland i ældre og nyere Tid*. Det
Grønlandske Selskabs Aarsskrift, i kommission hos G.E.C. Gads
Forlag, København.

Betts, Robert C. (1993), 'Speaking with Dios: A Costumbre in Highland
Guatamala', *Shaman's Drum* no. 33.

Birket-Smith, Kaj (1924), 'Ethnography of Egedesminde District with
    Aspects of the General Culture of West Greenland', *Meddelelser om
    Grønland*, Bd. 66.
——— (1927), *Eskimoerne*, Gyldendalske Boghandel, København.
——— (1946), *Tro og Trolddom. Kampen mod det onde*, Jespersens og
    Pios Forlag, København.
——— (1950), 'Åndemanere og medicinmænd' *Ciba-Tidsskriftet*, no. 22.
——— (1953), *The Chugach Eskimo*, Nationalmuseets Publikationsfond,
    København.
Bogoras, W. (1904-1909), *The Chuckchee*, Part II, The Jesup North
    Pacific Expedition, vol.7, E.J. Brill, Leiden.
Campbell, Eileen and J.H. Brennan, (1990), *The Aquarian Guide to the
    New Age*, The Aquarian Press, Northamptonshire, England.
Campbell, Joseph (1960), *The Masks of God: Primitive Mythology*,
    Secker & Warburg, London.
Campell, Joseph (1972), [1959], *Levende Myter*, Gyldendal, København.
Castaneda, Carlos (1992), [1981], *The Eagle's Gift*, Arkana, London.
Chang Chu-kun (1988), 'An Introduction to Korean Shamanism', in
    Shamanism. The Spirit World of Korea, eds Chai-shin Yu and R.
    Guisso, Asian Humanities Press, Berkeley, California.
Christian VI (1934), [1746]: 'Brev'. *Meddelelser om Grønland*, Bd. 55.
Christiansen, Reidar Th. (1953), *Ecstasy and Arctic Religion*. Liber
    saecularis in honorem J. Qvigstadii. Editus Pars 1., Studia
    Septentrionalia IV, Oslo.
Cook, Angelique S. and G.A. Hawk (1992), *Shamanism and the Esoteric
    Tradition*, Llewellyn Publications, Minnesota.
Crantz, David (1820), [1767], *The History of Greenland; including an
    account of the mission carried on by the United Brethren in that
    country*, 2 vols., Longman, Hurst, Rees, Orme, and Brown, London.
Czaplicka, M.A. (1914), *Aboriginal Siberia. A study in social
    anthropology*, Clarendon Press, Oxford.
Dalager, Lars (1752), *Grønlandske Relationer: Indeholdende
    Grønlændernes Liv og Levnet, Deres Skikke og Vedtægter, samt
    Temperament og Superstitioner. Tillige nogle korte Reflectioner over
    Missionen; sammenskrevet ved Fridirichshaabs Colonie i Grønland,
    anno 1752 af Lars Dalager, Købmand*, Trykt og findes hos Rudolph
    Henrich Lillies Enke, boende i store Fiolstræde i den forgyldte Oxe,
    København.
Dennett, John Frederick (1837), [1826], *The Voyages and Travels of
    Captain Ross, Parry, Franklin and Mr. Belzoni, forming an
    interesting History of the Manners, Customs and Characters of
    various Nations*, J. Jaques & W. Wright, London.
Devereux, G. (1961), 'Shamans as neurotics' *American Anthropologists*, 63.

Diószegi, Vilmos (1968),*Tracing Shamans in Siberia*, Anthropological Publications, Oosterhout.

Diózegi, Vilmos, and M. Hoppál (eds.) (1978), *Shamanism in Siberia* Akadémiai Kiadó, Budapest.

Dobkin de Rios, Marlene (1992), *Amazon Healer. The life and times of an urban shaman* Prism Unity, Dorset, England.

Doore, Gary (ed.) (1988), *The Shaman's Path. Healing, personal growth and empowerment* Shambala, London.

Doro, Karl Isaksen (1985), 'Vi tror ikke på noget, men vi frygter noget' *Atuagagdliutit*, no. 50.

Drury, Nevill (1994), [1979], *Inner Visions. Explorations in magical consciousness*, Arkana/Penguin, London.

(1989),*The Elements of Shamanism*, Element Books, Dorset, England.

Durkheim, Emile (1976), [1915], *The Elementary Forms of Religious Life*, George Allen and Unwin Ltd., London.

Egede, Hans (1741), *Det gamle Grønlands Perlustration eller Naturel-Historie*, Johan Christoph Groth boende paa Ulfelds platz, København.

—— (1818), [1741], *A Description of Greenland* A new edition with an Historical Introduction and Life of the Author, T. and J. Allman, London.

—— (1925) [1741], *Relationer fra Grønland 1721-36 og Det gamle Grønlands ny Perlustration 1741* Udgivne af Louis Bobe. *Meddelelser om Grønland*, Bd. 54.

Egede, Poul og Niels (1939), [1741], *Continuation af Hans Egedes Relationer fra Grønland* Ved Ostermann. *Meddelelser om Grønland*, Bd. 120. The references to Journals by Poul and Niels Egede are published in this volume.

Egede Saabye, Hans (1942), [1770-1778], *Brudstykker af en dagbog holden i Grønland i aarene 1770-1778* Ved Ostermann. *Meddelelser om Grønland*, Bd.129,2.

Eliade, Mircea (1989), [1951], *Shamanism. Archaic Techniqes of Ecstasy*, Arkana, London.

Evans-Pritchard, E. E. (1965), [1937], *Witchcraft, Oracles and Magic Among the Azande*, The Clarendon Press, Oxford.

—— (1965), *Theories of Primitive Religion*, Oxford University Press, Oxford.

Ferguson, Marilyn (1989), [1980], *The Aquarian Conspiracy. Personal and Social Transformation in the 1980s*, Paladin Grafton Books, London.

Findeisen, Hans (1957), *Schamanentum*, Urban Bücher, Kohlhammer.

Firth, Raymond (1967), *Tikopia Ritual and Belief*, George Allen and Unwin Ltd, London.

Flaherty, Gloria (1992), *Shamanism and the Eighteenth Century*, Princeton University Press, Princeton, New Jersey.

Freuchen, Peter (1963), [1955], *Erindringer,* Gyldendals Tranebøger, København.

Gennep, Arnold van (1977), [1960], *The Rites of Passage*, Routledge and Kegan Paul, London.

Georgi, Johan Gottlieb (1776), *Beschreibung aller Nationen des Russischen Reichs, ihrer Lebenssart, Religion, Gebräuche, Wohnungen, Kleidungen und übrigen Merkwürdigkeiten*, St. Peterburg Verlegts Carl Wilhelm Muller.

Geertsen, Ib (1990), *Kârale Andreassen. En østgrønlandsk kunstner*, Atuakkiorfik, Nuuk.

Gilberg, Rolf (1978), *Ånder og mennesker,* Nationalmuseet, København.

Glahn, Henric Christopher (1921), [1763-68], *Missionær i Grønland Henric Christopher Glahns Dagbøger for Aarene 1763-64, 1766-67, 1766-68* H. Osterman. *Det Grønlandske Selskabs Skrifter*, vol. IV.

Hahm Pyong-choon (1988), 'Shamanism and the Korean Worldview, Family Life-cycle, Society and Social life', in *Shamanism. The Spirit World of Korea*, eds Chai-shin Yu and R. Guisso, Asian Humanities Press, Berkeley, California.

Halifax, Joan (1982), *Shaman: The Wounded Healer*, Crossroad, New York.

Hammerschlag, Carl A. (1989), *The Dancing Healers. A Doctor's Journey of Healing with Native Americans,* HarperSanFrancisco.

Handelman, Don (1967), 'The Development of a Washo Shaman', *Ethnology 6.*

Hansen Resen, Peder (1987), [1688], *Groenlandia* Udgivet af Det Grønlandske Selskab ved J. Kisbye Møller i 300 aret for manuskriptets færdiggørelse. *Det Grønlandske Selskabs Skrifter*, vol. 28.

Hanseraks Dagbog (1933), Grønlandsk Kateket [1885], *Om den danske konebådsexpedition til Ammasalik i Østgrønland 1884-85.* Udgivet af W. Thalbitzer. Oversat af pastor O.K. Skårup i Grønland 1886. *Det Grønlandske Selskabs Skrifter*, vol. Vlll.

Harner, Michael (1973), *Hallucinogens and Shamanism*, Oxford University Press, Oxford.

────── (1988), 'What Is A Shaman?', in *Shaman's Path*, ed. Garry Doore, Shambala, London.

────── (1988), 'Shamanic Counseling', in *Shaman's Path*, ed. Garry Doore, Shambala, London.

────── (1990), [1980], *The Way of the Shaman*, HarperSanFrancisco.

Heinze, Ruth-Inge (1991), *Shamans of the 20th Century*, Irvington Publishers, Inc., New York.

Helms, Henrik (1868), *Grönland och grönländarne. En skildring ur isverlden,* P.G. Berg, Stockholm.

Hertz, Robert (1960), [1907], *Death and the Right Hand,* Cohen and West.

Hess, David J. (1993), *Science in the New Age. The Paranormal, Its Defenders and Debunkers, and American Culture,* The University of Wisconsin Press, Wisconsin.

Hodgen, M.(1964), *Early Anthropology in the Sixteenth and Seventeenth Centuries,* University of Pennsylvania, Philadelphia.

Holm, Gustav (1888), *Ethologisk Skizze af Angmagsalikerne Meddelelser om Grønland* Bd. 10.

—— (1914), [1887], *Legends and Tales from Angmagsalik.* Collected by G. Holm. *Meddelelser om Grønland* Bd. 39.

Holtved, Erik (1963), 'Tornarssuk, an Eskimo Deity', *Folk, Dansk Etnografisk Tidsskrift,* vol. 5, Dansk Etnografisk Forening.

Hoppál, M., and Otto von Sadovsky (1989), *Shamanism. Past and Present,* Istor Books, Los Angeles/Fullerton, California.

Horwitz, Jonathan (1991), 'Shamanic Rites seen from a Shamanic Perspective' Presented to The Donner Institute for Research in Religious and Cultural History at the Symposium on Religious Rites, Åbo, Finland, on August 16, 1991.

Hultkranz, Åke (1973), 'A Definition of Shamanism', *Temenos,* vol 9.

—— (1978), 'Ecological and Phenomenological Aspects of Shamanism' in *Shamanism in Siberia,* eds Vilmos Diózegi and M. Hoppál, Akadémiai Kiadó, Budapest.

—— (1988), 'Shamanism: A Religious Phenomenon', in *Shaman's Path,* ed Gary Doore, Shambala, London.

—— (1989), 'The Place of Shamanism in the History of Religions', *Shamanism. Past and Present,* part 1, eds M Hoppál and Otto von Sadovsky, Istor Books, Los Angeles/Fullerton, California.

Ingerman, Sandra (1991), *Soul Retrieval. Mending the Fragmented Self,* HarperSanFrancisco.

Jacobi, Jolande (1953), preface [1945] to C. G. Jung, *Psychological Reflections,* Routledge and Kegan Paul, London.

Jacobsen, Werner (1965), *Asiatiske akkorder,* Forlaget Rhodos, København.

Jørgensen, O. (1980), *Sjæl gør dig smuk,* Lobo Agency, Århus.

Kalweit, Roger (1992), *Shamans, Healers and Medicine Men,* Shambhala, Boston & London.

Kendall, Laurel (1985): *Shamans, Housewives, and Other Restless Spirits. Women in Korean Ritual Life,* University of Hawaii Press Honolulu.

King, Serge Kahili (1990), *Urban Shaman,* Simon & Schuster, New York, 1990.

Kleivan, Inge (1983), 'Herrnhuterne eller brødremenigheden i Grønland 1733-1900' Temahæfte: *Brødremissionen 1733-1900. Tidsskriftet Grønland* nos.8-9-10, Det Grønlandske Selskab.

Kleivan, I. and B. Sonne (1985), 'Eskimos Greenland and Canada', *Iconography of Religions, section VIII: Arctic Peoples.* Institute of Religious Iconography State University Groningen, E.J. Brill, Leiden.

Kruuse, Chr. (1912), 'Rejser og Botaniske Undersøgelser i Østgrønland mellem 65 30' og 67-20' i Aarene 1898-1902 samt Angmagsalik-egnens Vegetation', *Meddelelser om Grønland* Bd.49.

Larsen, Stephen (1988), [1976], *The Shaman's Doorway. Opening Imagination to Power and Myth*, Station Hill Press, New York.

Leden, Christian (1952), 'Über die Musik der Smith Sund Eskimos und ihre Verwandtschaft mit der Musik der Amerikanischen Indianer', *Meddelelser om Grønland*, Bd.152,3.

Lévi-Strauss, C. (1963), *Structural Anthropology*, Basic Books, New York, London.

Lewis, I.M. (1981), 'What is a Shaman?', *Folk, Dansk Etnografisk Tidsskrift*, 23, Dansk Etnografisk Forening.

—— (1986), *Religion in Context. Cults and Charisma*, Cambridge University Press, Cambridge.

—— (1989), [1971], *Ecstatic Religion. A Study of Shamanism and Spirit Possession* Routledge, London and New York, 2nd edition.

Lewis, Leilani (1991), 'Coming Out of the Closet As a Shamanic Practitioner', *The Foundation for Shamanic Studies Newsletter*, vol. 4 no. 1.

Lidegaard, Mads (1986), *Hans—en eskimo. En grønlandsk livsskæbne*, Nyt Nordisk Forlag Arnold Busck, København.

Mathiassen, Therkel (1933), 'Prehistory of the Angmagssalik Eskimos', *Meddelelser om Grønland*, Bd 92,4.

(1934), [1929], 'Contributions to the Archeology of Disko Bay' *Meddelelser om Grønland*, Bd. 93.

Meadows, Kenneth (1995),*Where Eagles Fly. A Shamanic Way to Inner Wisdom*, Element, Shaftesbury, Dorset.

Merkur, Daniel (1985), *Becoming Half Hidden: Shamanism and Initiation Among the Inuit*, Acta Universitatis Stockholmiensis. Stockholm Studies in Comparative Religion. Almquist & Wiksell International, Stockholm.

Mikkelsen, Ejnar (1934), De Østgrønlandske Eskimoers historie, Gyldendalske Boghandel, Nordisk Forlag, København.

—— (1960), *Svundne Tider i Østgrønland. Fra Stenalder til Atomtid*, Gyldendals Forlag, København.

Mindell, Arnold (1993), *The Shaman's Body. A New Shamanism for Transforming Health, Relationships, and the community* Harper, San Francisco.

Mylius-Erichsen, L. (1905), 'Grønland og grønlænderne i vore dage' Grundrids ved folkelig Universitetsundervisning nr. 99. Udgivet af Universitetsforlaget i kommission hos Jacob Erslev.

Nansen, Fridtjof (1893), *Eskimo Life*, Longmans, Green, and Co., London.

Nietzsche, F. (1983), [1893], 'On the Uses and Disadvantages of History for Life', *Untimely Meditations*, Cambridge University Press, Cambridge.

Parbøl, Inge (1955), 'Qivitut, grønlandske fjeldgangsmænd', *Grønland*, nr. 12. Det Grønlandske Selskab.

Perkins, John (1994a), 'Earth, Shamanism and the Catholic Church', *Gnosis* no. 33.

———— (1994b), 'The Dream Changer of Otavala', *Shaman's Drum* no. 35.

Peters, Larry G., Douglas Price-Williams (1980), 'Towards an experiental analysis of shamanism' *American Ethnologist*, 7.

Petersen, Johan (1957), [1894-1935], 'Ujuâts Dagbøger.' *Det Grønlandske Selskabs Skrifter* XIX.

Petersen, Robert (1964), 'The Greenland Tupilak' *Folk* Vol. 6,2, Dansk Etnografisk Tidsskrift, Dansk Etnografisk Forening, Forlaget Rhodos, København.

Phillips, Glen (ed.) (1993), *The New Age Primer. Spiritual Tools For Awakening*, Light Technology Publishing, Sedona.

Qúpersimân, Georg (1982), [1972], *Min eskimoske fortid — en østgrønlandsk åndemaners erindringer*, Det Grønlandske Forlag.

Rasmussen, Knud (1908), *The People of the Polar North*, A record compiled from the Danish originals and edited by G. Herring, Kegan Paul, Trench, Trubner & Co. Ltd., London.

———— (1915a), *Min Rejsedagbog*, Gyldendalske Boghandel, København.

———— (1915b), *Foran Dagens Øje. Liv i Grønland*, Gyldendalske Boghandel, Nordisk Forlag, København.

———— (1918), *Fra Verdens Ende. Mænd og kvinder i Kap York Missionen*, C.C. Petersen Bogtrykkeri, København.

———— (1921a), *Greenland by the Polar Sea. The story of the Thule Expedition from Melville Bay to Cape Morris Jesup*, William Heinemann, London.

———— (1921b-24), *Myter og Sagn fra Grønland I-III*, Gyldendalske Boghandel, Kjøbenhavn.

———— (1927), *Across Arctic America. Narrative of the Fifth Thule Expedition*, G.P. Putnam's Sons, NewYork, London.

———— (1928), *Den II Thule Expedition til Grønlands Nordkyst 1916-18. Nr. 14. Report of the II Thule-Expedition for the Exploration of Greenland from Melville Bay to De Long Fjord, 1916-1918 Meddelelser om Grønland*, Bd.65.

────── (1929), [1921-24], *Intellectual Culture of the Iglulik Eskimos*, Report of the Fifth Thule Expedition, Gyldendalske Boghandel, Nordisk Forlag, Copenhagen.

────── (1930), [1921-24], *Observations on the Intellectual Culture of the Caribou Eskimos*, Report of the Fifth Thule Expedition, Gyldendalske Boghandel, Nordisk Forlag, Copenhagen.

────── (1931a), *Den store slæderejse*, Gyldendalske Boghandel, Nordisk Forlag, København.

────── (1931b), *The Netsilik Eskimos. Social life and spiritual culture.* Report of the fifth Thule expedition 1921-24 Gyldendalske Boghandel, Nordisk Forlag, Copenhagen.

────── (1932), [1921-24], *Intellectual Culture of the Copper Eskimos*, Report of the Fifth Thule Expedition, Gyldendalske Boghandel, Copenhagen.

────── (1938), *Knud Rasmussen's Posthumous Notes on the Life and Doings of the East Greenlanders in Olden Times*, ed. by H. Ostermann. 6. and 7. Thule-Expedition til Sydøstgrønland 1931-33, *Meddelelser om Grønland* Bd.109.

────── (1981), *Inuit fortæller. Grønlandske sagn og myter I-III* Ved Regitze Margrethe Søby, Bogan Forlag, Lynge.

Rink, H. (1982), [1866-71], *Eskimoiske Eventyr og Sagn 1-2.* Rosenkilde og Bagger, København.

────── (1868), *Om Grønlændernes gamle Tro og hvad der af samme er bevaret under Kristendommen*, Thieles Bogtrykkeri, København.

────── (1877), *Danish Greenland, its People and its Products*, edited by Robert Brown, Henry S. King & Co., London.

ᵖ Rosing, Christian (1946), [1906], *Østgrønlænderne Tunuamiut. Grønlands sidste Hedninger. Det Grønlandske Selskabs Skrifter XV.*

Rosing, Jens (1963), *Sagn og Saga fra Angmagssalik*, udgivet af Nationalmuseet og Det Grønlandske Selskab i samarbejde med Forlaget Rhodos, København.

Rutherford, Ward (1986), *Shamanism The Foundation of Magic*, The Aquarian Press, Wellingborough, Northamptonshire.

Rüttel, F.C.P. (1917), [1884-1903], *Ti aar blandt Østgrønlandske Hedninger. Dagbog fra Angmagssalik*, Gyldendalske Boghandel, København og Kristiania.

→ Sandgreen, Otto (1987), *Øje for øje og tand for tand*, Otto Sandgreens Forlag, Stenby Tryk, Bagsværd.

Sargant, William (1973), *The Mind Possessed*, Heinemann: London.

Sauer, Martin (1802), *An Account of a Geographical and Astronomical Expedition to the Northern Parts of Russia, Performed by Command of Her Imperial Majesty Catherine the Second, Empress of all Russias, by Commodore Joseph Billings, in the Years 1785, &c. to 1794*, T. Cadell, jun. and W. Davies, in the Strand, London.

Schultz-Lorentsen, C.W. (1951), *Det Grønlandske Folk og Folkesind*, Statsministeriet, København.

Scott, Gini Graham (1988), *The Shaman Warrior,* Falcon Press, Las Vegas Nevada.

—— (1991), *Shamanism and Personal Mastery. Using symbols, rituals and talismans to activate the power within you,* Athena Books, N.Y.

Shirokogoroff, S. M. (1982), [1935], *Psychomental Complex of the Tungus*, Kegan Paul, Trench, Trubner & Co., Ltd., London.

Sonne, Birgitte (1986), 'Angakkut puullit i Grønland og Alaska', *Vort sprog – vor kultur*, foredrag fra symposium i Nuuk oktober 1981 arrangeret af Ilisimatusarfik og Kalaallit Nunaata Katersugaasivia, Pilersuiffik.

—— (1986), 'Toornaarsuk, an Historical Proteus', *Arctic Anthropology*, vol. 23, nos. 1&2.

—— (1988) 'In Love With Eskimo Imagination and Intelligence', *Études Inuit Studies*, vol. 12, Nos 1-2.

—— (1990), 'The Acculturative Role of Sea Woman. Early contact relations between Inuit and Whites as revealed in the Origin Myth of Sea Woman', *Man & Society,* 13, *Medelelser om Grønland.*

Steensby, H.P. (1910), 'Contributions to the Ethnology and Anthropogeography of the Polar Eskimos', *Meddelelser om Grønland*, Bd. 34.

Steenstrup, K. J. V. (1893), [1878-80], 'Beretning om Undersøgelsesrejserne i Nord-Grønland i Aarene 1878-80' *Meddelelser om Grønland*, Bd.5.

Streiker, Lowell, D. (1990), *New Age comes to Main Street. What worried Christians must know,* Abingdon Press, Nashville.

Søby, Regitze Margrethe (1970), 'The Eskimo Animal Cult', Folk, *Dansk Etnografisk Tidsskrift*, Vol. 11-12, Dansk Etnografisk Forening.

Thalbitzer, William (1910), 'The Heathen Priests of East Greenland (Angakut)' Verhandlungen des XVI Internationalen Amerikanisten-Kongresses. Wien, 9. bis 14. September 1908, A. Hartleben's Verlag, Wien und Leipzig.

—— (1914), 'Ethnographical Collections from East Greenland (Angmagssalik and Nualik) made by G. Holm, G. Amdrup and J. Petersen and described by W. Thalbitzer, *Meddelelser om Grønland*, Bd.39.

—— (1915), *Grønland og Eskimoerne* Grundrids ved folkelig Universitetsundervisning, nr. 236, Universitetsudvalget, København.

—— (1923), 'The Ammasalik Eskimo. Contribution to the Ethnology of the East Greenland Natives', Second part *Meddelelser om Grønland* Bd.40.

—— (1926), 'Eskimoernes kultiske guddomme' *Studier fra Sprog- og Oldtidsforskning*. Det filologisk-historiske samfund, nr. 143, Pios Boghandel, København.

Townsend, Joan B (1988), 'Neo-shamanism and the Modern Mystical Movement,' in *Shaman's Path*, ed. Gary Doore, Shambala, London.
Trevelyan, George (1977), *A Vision of the Aquarian Age,* Conventure, London.
Walsh, Roger N. (1990), *The Spirit of Shamanism*, Jeremy P. Tarcher, Inc. Los Angeles.
Wavell, Stewart, Audrey Butt and Nina Epton, (1966), *Trances*, George Allen & Unwin Ltd., London.
Wicokahiyasamya, Sungila Peta (1995), 'A Little Advice about Sacred Objects From an Experienced Native', *Shaman's Drum* no. 39.
Wilcox, Joan Parisi and Elisabeth B. Jenkins (1996), 'Journey to Q'ollorit'i: Initiation into Andean Mysticism, *Shaman's Drum* no. 40.
Vitebsky, Piers (1995), *The Shaman*, Macmillan, London.
Wolf, Fred Alan, (1991), *The Eagle's Quest. A Physicist's Search for Truth in the Heart of the Shamanic World,* Mandala, London.

Magazines:

Gnosis, published by the Lumen Foundation, San Francisco.
Kindred Spirit, published by Kindred Spirit, Foxhole, Dartington, Totnes, Devon.
Nyt Aspekt, Nannasgade 18, København.
Sacred Hoop, Cowl Street, Evesham, Worcestershire.
Shaman's Drum, published by Cross-Cultural Shamanism Network, Ashland, Oregon.

Newsletter:

The Foundation for Shamanic Studies Newsletter, vol. 4, no. 1, 1991.

SUBJECT INDEX

altered state of consciousness,
8–10, 160, 165, 183, 196,
252
amulet, 47, 74–5, 138n57n58,
228
angakkoq, x, , 216–17
as perceived by missionaries,
26–37
~ female, 55–7, 122, 128,
130–31, 135n28
murderers, 12, 49, 112
secret language, 59–60, 79
see also shaman
apprenticeship/initiation, 52–65,
98, 113, 117, 126–28,
136n42, 162–4, 185

belief systems, xii, 24, 45–6, 129,
194, 208
Buddhism, x–xi, 23, 208, 211
burial rituals, 100–3

Canada, 65
Celtic shamanism, 148–9, 155,
166
Christianity, x, 19, 25, 47–8,
94–5, 111, 115, 129–30,
132n1, 146n105, 150, 154,
178–9, 208–9, 2115, 220,
257n18
see also missionaries

Chuckchee, 7, 11, 46, 190
Conibo Indians (Peru), 160
core-shamanism, ix, xi–xiv, 8–9,
158–65, 217
and caring professions, 167–9,
203–4, 221
courses, ix, xii–xiv, 165–7, 179,
181–94, 202, 218–9, 224–55
participants in, 167–82, 194–7,
203, 206n6
costumes, 13–14, 17n7, 73,
137n53, 191

dance, 12–13, 15, 189, 193, 242,
249
death/rebirth, 55, 62–4, 181
Denmark, 158, 165, 182, 194,
206n9
divination, 230–2
dreaming body, 157, 198
drugs, 12, 157, 161, 176, 229
drum/drumming, 12–13, 22, 73,
76–9, 81–4, 123–4, 179,
189–90, 192, 229, 242,
245

England, 158, 165, 194, 234

feuds, 106–7, 125
Foundation for Shamanic Studies, 8,
159

Greenland,
  colonisation of, x–xi, 47, 116,
    125
  decline of shamanism, 85, 180,
    208
  explorers in, 18–22
  myths and legends of, 103–14,
    145n98

Hawaii, 212
healing, 33, x, 89–94, 122–3,
    143n84n85, 144n89, 156–7,
    190–93, 210, 219–20, 235–9,
    241–43, 254

ilisiitsoq, 60, 80, 93–100, 109–10
inua, 46, 127, 132n3

Jívaro Indians (Ecuador), 160–1,
    192
journeying, x, 4–5, 7, 85–89,
    120–21, 185–90, 206n10n11,
    225–6, 228, 233–4, 237,
    248–51, 256n1n6n8, 257n11

Korea, 13–14, 73, 203, 209–10

Land of the Dead, 85, 88–9, 103
Lapland, 19–20
Lower World, 178, 189, 239

masks, 74
mental illness, xii, 7, 10–11,
    50–51, 119, 184
Middle World, 237
missionaries, xiii, 18–21, 24–5,
    47–8, 63, 69, 112
Moon Man/Spirit, 66, 71, 85, 88,
    135n33, 137n50, 143n79
Mother of the Sea, 66, 68, 70–71,
    85–9, 104, 137n47n49,
    141n76n77, 142n78

Nature, 20, 169–70, 178–9, 195,
    217, 228, 235
  and environmental crisis, 151,
    221
neo-shamanism, *see* core-
    shamanism
New Age, ix, xi–xii, 148–58, 166,
    205n2, 214–15
  see also core-shamanism
non-ordinary reality, 178, 184–5,
    195–6, 200, 226
Nordic shamanism, 224–33
North American Indian
    shamanism, 148–9, 157, 180,
    212–4

oral tradition, 103, 114–32

power-animal, xii, 161, 189–91,
    200–1
psychotherapy, 167–8, 171, 227,
    248–9, 255

rattling, 187–8, 191–2, 229, 238,
    245, 251–2
revenge, 50, 121–2

sacrifices, 47, 132n4
séance, 8, 13–14, 23, 34–5, 75–85,
    123–4, 127–8, 138n56,
    139n71, 140n72, 141n74
sejd, 230–3
shaman,
  female, 10, 12–14, 22, 179
  role in society, 1–2, 4–5, 7, 48–9,
    81, 102, 105–6, 109, 111,
    113–4, 165, 183, 194–7, 214
  see also angakkoq
Siberia, 3, 22
social humiliation, 61, 108, 114,
    128
social isolation, 169, 199

social marginalisation, 150, 155
song, 47, 132n5, 188–9, 193,
    229–30
soul, 7, 17n2, 36, 68, 80, 103,
    121, 139n65n66, 189, 201–2
  loss, 27, 115, 117–9, 202,
    244–7, 249
  retrieval, 81, 168, 244–55
  stealing, 52, 79–80, 89, 92, 94,
    115, 117, 126, 128–9
South America, 210–1
spirit possession, 7, 10, 14–15
spirits, 65–72, 79–80, 137n51
  helping, 6, 8, 53–5, 58, 61–2,
    85–9, 116–7, 120–22,
    134n20, 168, 198
  mastery of, x, xiii, 4–8, 72, 125
  relationship with, 8–9, 17n6,
    79, 108–9, 137n52, 161, 183,
    186–7, 199–200, 218
spirituality,
  and New Age, xi–xii, 147,
    150–1, 152, 156, 158–65,
    168, 177, 204
stone, 52–3, 62–3, 73, 134n22,
    138n55

taboo rules, 1, 46–7, 100–1, 103,
    104, 216
tobacco, 12–13, 130
toornaarsuk, 23, 54, 58, 63, 66–9,
    77, 88, 134n24, 136n45
trance, x, 9–17, 84, 123, 139n63,
    162, 218
Tukâk theatre, viii–ix, 208
Tungus (Siberia), 1, 3–4, 10, 17n7,
    23, 73
tupilak, 32, 55, 68, 75, 94, 98,
    105, 109, 135n27, 138n59

United States, 162–3, 194
Upper World, 190
urban shamanism, 210–12, 217
  see also core-shamanism

vølve, 225, 230–2

Wicca movement, 175, 206n8
witchcraft, 18–19, 27, 94–100,
    109–10, 136n37, 145nn93–5,
    176

Name Index

Acerbi, Joseph, 19, 24
Achterberg, Jeanne, 219
Andreassen, Karl (Kârale), 116, 118–19

Bell, John, 22
Bend, Cynthia, 212
Bennett, Hal Zina, 213
Berthelsen, A., 50, 119
Birket-Smith, Kaj, 95
Bogoras, W., 11, 46
Bourdieu, Pierre, xii
Butt, Audrey, 12

Campbell, Joseph, 105
Castaneda, Carlos, 157–9, 161, 165, 179, 198
Catherine the Great, 24
Chang Chu-kun, 209
Christensen, Haslund, 179
Cook, A., 199
Crantz, David, 35–6, 67–8, 97

Dalager, Lars, 91
Dennett, John Frederick, 102
Devereux, G., 11
Diózegi, Vilmos, 3
Dobkin de Rios, Marlene, 210
Drury, Nevill, 197
Durkheim, Émile, 16

Egede family, xiii, 20–21, 23–37, 63–4, 66–7, 70, 75–7, 85, 89–92, 102, 111–2
Eliade, Mircea, 2, 4, 6, 11, 200
Evans-Pritchard, E.E., 2

Ferguson, Marilyn, 151, 156
Firth, Raymond, 7
Flaherty, Gloria, 18
Freuchen, Peter, 75

Georgi, Johan Gottlieb, 21
Gilberg, Rolf, 6

Hahm Pyong-choon, 209
Halifax, Joan, 11
Hanserâk, 80
Harner, Michael, ix, xiv, 8, 158–61, 164–5, 177, 179, 192, 194–6, 204–5, 206n5, 220, 222, 229
Hawk, G.A., 199
Heinze, Ruth-Inge, 214
Helms, Henrik, 37, 68
Holm, Gustav, xiii–xiv, 52–3, 60, 68, 80–81, 83, 92–3, 98, 100, 116–7, 125
Holtved, Erik, 69
Horwitz, Jonathan, 8
Hultkranz, Åke, 5–7, 201

Ingerman, Sandra, 203–4, 246, 251, 257n15

Jacobi, Jolande, xi, 205
Jacobsen, Werner, 15
Jung, C.G., xi, 218

Kalweit, Holger, 222
Kendall, Laurel, 14, 179, 229
King Christian VI, 48
King Frederick IV of Denmark, 20
King, Serge Kahili, 163, 212
Kristiansen, Enok, 48
Kruse, Chr., 49–50, 68–9

Larsen, Helge, 103
Lévi-Strauss, Claude, 11
Lewis, I.M., 3, 6–7, 10–11, 16, 119, 219
Lewis, Leilani, 204–5

Mathews, John and Caitlin, 155
Mathiassen, Therkel, 85
Meadows, Kenneth, 201
Mikkelsen, Ejnar, 50, 115

Nietzsche, Frederich, 147, 205

Perkins, John, 211
Peters, Larry G., 11
Phillips, Glen, 154–5
Price-Williams, Douglas, 11

Rasmussen, Knud, xiii–xiv, 1–2, 45–6, 48–9, 61–2, 65, 68, 70–74, 77–8, 113–14, 216

Rink, Heinrich, xiii, 48, 71, 103–107, 111
Rosing, Jens, 116, 129–31
Rosing, Otto, 116
Rutherford, Ward, 218
Rüttel, F.C.P., 49

Sandgreen, Otto, 119, 125, 127, 129–31
Sargant, William, 14–15
Sauer, Martin, 20, 24
Scott, Gini Graham, 200
Shine, Betty, 214
Shirokogoroff, S.M., xiii, 2–3, 5–6, 8, 10, 13, 23, 179, 217–18, 222
Sonne, Birgitte, 69, 125
Streiker, Lowell D., 149–50, 153

Thalbitzer, William, xiii, xivn3, 74–5, 102
Townsend, Joan B., 194
Trevelyn, Sir George, 155

Vitebsky, Piers, 220

Walløe, Peder Olsen, 116
Wavell, Stewart, 12
Wicokahiyasamya, Sungila Peta, 213
Wiger, Tayja, 212–13
Wolf, Fred Alan, 159